NEWSPAPER
CRUSADERS

NEWSPAPER CRUSADERS

A NEGLECTED STORY

BY SILAS BENT

Whittlesey House
NEW YORK · McGRAW-HILL BOOK COMPANY, INC. · LONDON

Copyright, 1939, *by* SILAS BENT

All rights reserved. This book, or parts thereof, may not be reproduced in any form without permission of the author.

PUBLISHED BY WHITTLESEY HOUSE
A division of the McGraw-Hill Book Company, Inc.

Printed in the United States of America by the Maple Press Co., York, Pa.

To

HORACE MEYER KALLEN

*Who Encouraged and Counseled Me
in Writing "Ballyhoo: The
Voice of the Press"*

Preface

SUCH was the quantity and diversity of the material available for this book that its organization has been difficult. My first intention was to treat it chronologically, the simplest and easiest method; I found I must abandon this because it would entail tiresome repetition and would preclude the possibility of unity in dealing with outstanding figures and with campaigns in related fields.

How, for instance, to marshal the material about governmental reform? It ranged from the Colonial period to the present and manifested a singular sameness, for the political animal has not changed a lot since the day of Plato. It seemed clear that I must deal with a part of this in connection with the chief moving power, such as Pulitzer or Scripps, that I must assemble the story about Tammany in one section and group other political targets elsewhere.

Thus chronology in the strict sense went into limbo. In order to illustrate tactics and techniques, motives and characteristics, it seemed advisable to describe briefly in the beginning a few notable crusaders and their methods without regard to dates, and then, after glancing at some early journalistic examples, to let the matter of

Preface

sequence take care of itself. This was not meant to be a history anyhow.

History as an art has kept some bad company, and historians have been foremost among its faultfinders. Yet the instrument has its uses, and at certain times becomes indispensable. The foreground, the atmosphere, the context, and the consequences of some crusades had to be indicated lest the campaigns remain well-nigh meaningless. The struggling beginnings of a press which has waxed into our most powerful single agency of information, opinion, and reform needed some attention; the conditions which made for revolution against England and those which encouraged loyalty could not be ignored; the very character of the convention which framed our Constitution assumed significance in view of the newspaper fight for and against the document. And in dealing with the newspaper advocacy of human slavery and opposition to it, neither self-righteousness on one side nor emotional evangelism on the other could tell the story. To attempt an explanation of the whole complex of motives and argument in such cases was quite out of the question, but at least some light might be let in on them.

When a disaster such as the sinking of the *Vestris*, the loss of the *Titanic*, or the Iroquois Theater fire has stirred the daily press to crusade for greater precautions, the action was obvious and almost inevitable. The exposure of Dr. Frederick A. Cook as a humbug required more initiative but did not merit so much credit. A little digging convinced me that one or two of our newspaper "martyrs" would not bear close scrutiny. Thus the matter of elimination became more delicate if not more difficult than the method of organization.

Preface

As a channel of undesirable propaganda the newspaper has been thoroughly berated. Less account has been taken of its function as a medium of political ideas. It has served in this capacity since its beginning in this country, notably in the publication of the Federalist papers and during every political campaign. At times its work in this area has assumed the aspect of a crusade. In exploding financial fallacies and in the propagation of ethical concepts, its work, however valuable, as a rule has escaped that aspect. Between a good bludgeoning fight for a cause and a calm campaign for constructive purposes there is a vast difference in the ink spilled and the hullabaloo, yet both may deserve equally to be classified as crusades.

My purpose here has been to illuminate the character of the newspaper as a crusader and the results accomplished by its crusaders, not to catalogue all the campaigns that have merited attention. Too little attention seems to me to have been paid by everybody to a normal and immensely important function of the daily press, and I have set about as best I could to make amends.

SILAS BENT.

Contents

Preface		vii
Acknowledgments		xiii
I	A Neglected Story	3
II	Pulitzer: Past-master	20
III	Hearst: Playboy and Prodigy	43
IV	Scripps: Bare-knuckle Fighter	60
V	Colonial Crusaders	81
VI	Constitution and Amendments	99
VII	Suppression and Warfare	115
VIII	For and Against Slavery	124
IX	The Ku Klux Klan	138
X	Trying to Tame Tammany	155
XI	Other Augean Stables	165
XII	For Safer Traffic	185

Contents

XIII	Civic and Social Betterment	193
XIV	Janus in Chicago	211
XV	Phoenix in Toledo	223
XVI	Sins of Omission	234
XVII	Cerberus of the Cash Box	254
XVIII	Castor and Pollux	266
XIX	On Varied Salients	281
Bibliography		297
Index		299

Acknowledgments

NEWSPAPER men have been helpful almost without exception when I have asked them for material for this book. I am under obligation to so many of them that to set down all their names is impracticable. The files of *Editor and Publisher*, of the Graduate School of Journalism at Columbia University, and of the American Antiquarian Society at Worcester, Massachusetts, have been of great value. Professor R. E. Wolseley of the Medill School of Journalism at Northwestern University and George Seldes have supplied useful data. To my wife, Elizabeth Sims Bent, I am indebted for compiling this bibliography, for assistance in gathering material, and for unfailing helpful advice.

NEWSPAPER CRUSADERS

I

A Neglected Story

T IS singular that newspapers, seldom bashful about their virtues, have made so little to-do about their achievements in crusading. As champions of reforms, as defenders of individuals, as protagonists of their communities, they have exercised influences, I venture to believe, quite as important as the transmission of information and the expression of opinion.

Yet this has been written only in fragmentary form. Historians of daily journals, biographers of newspaper publishers and editors, and occasionally an instructor in a school of journalism, have dealt with it in particular, sometimes in its larger aspects, but not sweepingly. A treatment at once minute and comprehensive, indeed, is impossible within the scope of a single volume, such is the wealth of material available. What is presented here must attempt a representative selection.

More than once a newspaper, at the conclusion of a successful campaign, has preened itself or has paid tribute to a fellow; by and large our most articulate institution, sometimes almost as vainglorious as politics (God save the mark!) has been surprisingly reticent about one of its primary responsibilities. Yet it has recognized crusading as a natural function and as a responsibility, and has discharged it for the most part admirably, sometimes at severe sacrifice. That there has been default in certain areas none can deny, but the account balances heavily to the credit of the press and to the benefit of its public.

Here lies the best argument for newspaper freedom not only from governmental interference but from the coercion of a capitalist economy. The history of our press since Colonial days is shot through with the struggle for unrestricted critical activity and the right to crusade. Every crusade implies, to be sure, the expression of opinion or of an attitude, but it involves more than that. It means also a willingness to fight if need be. It means, according to my dictionary, "to contend zealously against any evil, or on behalf of any reform."

To contend zealously must mean surely to struggle with ardent devotion. The zeal which fires a crusading editor may bring him to the boiling point of fanaticism, and has done it time and again. None who has undertaken a campaign in the certainty that it would entail loss of circulation and advertising, perhaps permanently, but was a fanatic, just on the sunny side of lunacy. Skeptics who deny that campaigns are ever undertaken for other than sordid motives may disabuse their minds by examining the record. If newspapers have faced actual losses in the discharge of their duties as public servants, then they have an unmistakable claim to the guaranty of the First Amendment.

Yet the daily press almost never advances crusading as proof that it should be free of restrictions. We may accept as a fair expression of its attitude the report adopted unanimously by the American Society of Newspaper Editors, at its 1938 session, declaring that the public lacked appreciation of "the true value and true functions of a free press." What is this value, and what are the functions?

> Unfortunately all citizens do not think through the meaning of a free press [said the report]. Too many regard it merely as the profitable privilege of publishers, instead of the right of all the people and the chief institution of representative government. A free press is that privilege of citizenship which makes governmental dictatorship impossible. When editors fight for the liberty to speak and write, they fight for the greatest of all human rights under government. He is not thoughtful who cannot see that democracy cannot exist except through the maintenance of a channel through which information can flow freely from the center of government to all the people and through which praise and criticism can flow freely from the people to the center.

Our editors, it seems to me, overstated the case when they said too many regarded journalistic freedom merely as a profitable privilege. Newspapers can fatten as well financially under a dictatorship as in this country; and since the daily press here is published for private profit, there can be but few who regard the cash register as the basis of free opinion, or suppose that dividends should guarantee a privileged vantage point. There are millions, to the contrary, who echo (as our editors did, with an air of saying something not usually known) the Jeffersonian dicta that "our liberty depends on the freedom of the press, and that cannot be limited without being lost"; or that "no government ought to be without censors, and where the press is free, no one ever will be." These arguments, and the importance to democratic processes of a free flow of information and criticism, have been familiar to the American public for nearly three centuries.

Not one word in that report, be it noted, about the power of newspapers to correct abuses when they leave the field of obvious comment and sally forth from routine news to rebuild and regenerate through volunteer criticism and the creation of news.

William Allen White, elected president of the society at that session, spoke his mind candidly, according to his wont, a few days thereafter. He was talking to students of the Wharton School of Merchandising about "Merchandising News in a Machine Age," and touched trenchantly both upon crusading and freedom of the press.

"The problem of the American newspaper today," Mr. White said, "is to open its channels of cordial reception to new social ideals and to insure fair treatment for any reform or any reformer who is obviously honest, reasonably intelligent, and backed by any considerable minority of the public." He suggested that to become open-minded the newspapers "might try intelligence"; and, as a corollary: "They might try to hire as doorkeepers in the house of the Lord on copy desks and in editorial chairs men who are free to make decisions about newspaper copy."

By indirection Mr. White reverted presently to the old what-the-public-wants theme. "The newspapers," he said, "will broaden their sphere of influence and will come out of the present shadow only when liberal, open-minded opinion in the middle class demands a really free press." He thought that class consciousness was discrediting the press, especially in the English-speaking democracies. "It is not the department store but the country club that has discredited the American newspaper in so far as it has lost caste with the American people." But he said also that in newspaper offices "the sense of property goes thrilling down the line," and that to a wide circle "we are 'the capitalist press'."

A Neglected Story

An uneasiness about "lost caste" runs through newspaper men. More than one of them had used that precise phase in talking with me long before Mr. White delivered his homily. Prof. Harold L. Cross has listed five major causes of this, in his work at the Graduate School of Journalism at Columbia University; the causes range from partisanship to the invasion of privacy. James G. Stahlman of the Nashville *Banner* has declared that the public "is fed up with week-kneed, namby-pamby editorial policies. They are tired of sloppy editing, canned bunk, and pornographic filth." *Editor and Publisher* has sounded a warning to its audience that "their every move is being watched." S. E. Thomason of the Chicago *Times* has conceded that the public was "to put it conservatively, unimpressed with all the battle cries for a free press." Karl von Wiegand, foreign correspondent, visiting these shores, said he was "distressed to find that the newspapers of our country are steadily and increasingly losing their influence and prestige in the public mind." So it ran, through all ranks.

If, instead of writing a new book of lamentations, newspaper men had scrutinized the record of their fraternity in crusading, they might have thrown out their chests in a better opinion of themselves. To a man who mistrusted his own powers Goethe said: "Ach! You need only blow on your hands!" Forgetting caste and prestige, newspaper men might well blow on their hands and attend to a vitally important job; then the caste and prestige would take care of themselves.

A little blowing on the hands instead of blowing about a free press would help. Does the First Amendment guarantee freedom from taxation? One might suppose

Newspaper Crusaders

so. A Hackensack daily which spent a deal of money investigating township expenses, in a campaign to have them reduced, sought to have that sum deducted from its taxes (thus denying by implication that such an investigation was obligatory), and Washington properly refused. The publishers of the Arizona *Republic* and the Phoenix *Gazette* protested the right of the State to impose a license fee of $1 and a tax of one per cent upon gross income. Their attorney declared in the Federal Courts that this would give the legislature power to control the press of the State and even to destroy it. *Editor and Publisher* echoed with the discredited old maxim of Chief Justice Marshall that "the power to tax is the power to destroy." Taxes, a modern Justice of the Supreme Court said, "are the price of civilization." The Arizona papers carried their fight to the Supreme Court, which heartlessly upheld the tax.

Does freedom of the press include the right to publish in advance material that might obstruct justice? This question arose when L. G. Turrou resigned from the Federal secret service during its investigation of spy activities in this country, and made a contract with J. David Stern, publisher of the New York *Post*, to sell him articles about the confessions of four suspects who were awaiting trial.

Washington, contending that publication in advance would hamper the investigation still under way and make prosecution of the suspects difficult, sought to enjoin the projected series. Turrou vowed that he was animated by the highest patriotic motives; Mr. Stern said that the Government's move was "an unprecedented attempt to erase freedom of the press from the Constitution." *Newsdom*, a periodical of the trade, commented that although Mr. Stern was willing to accept financial responsibility, "the injury that publication of these articles might do the Government would hardly be compensated for by fines, jail sentences for contempt, or the like." *Editor and Publisher* observed that twenty years earlier it would have been "unthinkable for a newspaper to have entertained the notion of publishing the evidence which underlay an indictment not yet brought to trial." The St. Louis *Post-Dispatch*, to my way of thinking the greatest newspaper now functioning in this country, said:

> We regret to see Mr. Stern raising the cry of freedom of the press in this case. Too often it has been a false alarm—an alibi, not a genuine grievance. As we have said before, the cry of "wolf" can be used so often by publishers that it will meet only disbelief if and when the real wolf appears.

Reluctantly and with bad grace Mr. Stern abandoned his championship of freedom for the press, and agreed to postpone the articles.

When three-fourths of the revenue of the daily press was derived from the sale of space for advertising, I described freedom of the press as "an adored fiction," because, although I denied the power of the individual advertiser to influence or suppress news save in rare instances, I believed that the general pressure for the maintenance of the status quo was too strong for free expression. As this is written the revenue from advertising in proportion to that from circulation is about sixty-forty, so that the pressure has relaxed somewhat. But even when it was severest, the advertiser seldom held a whip over the crusading editor.

At the very outset, most crusades are likely to offend the advertising fraternity on the general ground that they tend to stir up the menagerie and disturb the placid purchaser. Sometimes objection is raised on the particular ground that a campaign invades the entrenchments of a favored group. It may be that in some instances newspapers have closed their eyes to situations which cried out for exposure on account of these objections; but Richard Lloyd Jones, while editor of the Tulsa *Tribune*, described the paper which would not search out facts and publish them boldly as "an enemy of society." He suspected that some of them exercised a form of self-censorship by dodging troublesome issues. We are accustomed to speak of criminals as enemies of society, and doubtless Mr. Jones thought that his fellows who neglected to crusade were tainted with felony. Certainly it is true that merely to print a great quantity of colorless news, however well arranged and ably presented, is not enough to acquit any newspaper of its duty. Until it has let the light into dark places, served as a cleansing agency, and manifested a valiant spirit, it has neither fulfilled its obligation to society not earned its privilege of freedom.

Richard Lloyd Jones was not alone in his doubt about the militancy of his fellows. There is a widespread impression that newspapers are no longer good crusaders, and I myself entertained it, regarding most of them, when I began gathering material for this book. I soon found out better; and so I felt impelled to write to the *New Republic* of June 1, 1938, a letter setting it right on this point, which may be worth repeating in part:

> Sir: In your editorial paragraph of May 11, dealing with the Pulitzer award to Raymond Sprigle, you say: "American journalism is not in a crusading mood these days; few campaigns of any sort are undertaken, a fact which may help explain the award to Mr. Sprigle."

A Neglected Story

When Whittlesey House assigned me to prepare a book about newspaper crusades, some six weeks ago, I said much the same thing; but when I began nosing around I found, first, that scores of recent campaigns were fully documented at the Pulitzer School of Journalism, so that your explanation of the award to Mr. Sprigle is cockeyed; second, that there had been at least two score noteworthy crusades this year and last. Even the sobersided Chicago *Daily News* had put its foot down on extortionate receivership fees, and other papers elsewhere had followed suit. One daily, espousing an unpopular cause, had lost nearly half its circulation but had stuck to its guns and carried the day. The wide range of voluntary service for the protection of the public was astonishing . . .

The magazine insisted that its statement was true, and that I would find it justified by a comparison of "the total number of important campaigns now as compared with the number some years ago." Quite aside from the fact that every newspaper campaign tends to reduce the opportunities for campaigning in its field, this impressed me as saying that if a man, having eaten a fuller lunch than usual, was rather sparing at dinner, then he must have lost his appetite. Moreover, the total number of campaigns now does compare favorably with the number "some years ago," whatever the *New Republic* may mean by that.

Bruce Bliven, a former newspaper man, was editor in chief of the *New Republic* when that paragraph appeared, and one might have expected him to know better. Ferdinand Lundberg, a former newspaper man, wrote "America's Sixty Families," and we find him saying:

The class inhibitions which haunt the contemporary press under its millionaire ownership are responsible in large measure for the neurotic character of American newspapers. Because so many fields of editorial investigation and exposition are taboo, the press as a whole must confine itself to a relatively restricted "safe" area . . . The pecuniary inhibitions that rule the press like a Freudian complex have brought such discredit upon newspapers that they are no longer trusted by informed persons or even by business interests.

Newspaper Crusaders

Mr. Lundberg was making the point that his sixty families controlled the daily press in this country, and that on their account the press must play safe. His group did not include the Pulitzers, and he could give no account or explanation of the fact that the elder Joseph Pulitzer, after he had become a multimillionaire outranking in wealth some of Mr. Lundberg's families, continued unabated his fight for the underdog. Probably the greatest crusader the world has seen, he continued to direct the fight even after his health was broken and his eyesight had failed. E. W. Scripps was another—not listed among the sixty—who fought as a newspaper owner for the underprivileged even after he had become a multimillionaire.

One is taken somewhat aback to find R. E. Wolseley, lecturer in journalism at the Medill School of Northwestern University, joining the chorus. Mr. Wolseley contributed to the *Commonweal* of July 29, 1938, an article, "Newspaper Editors are Sissies," in which he said:

> Today a thousand causes go unpublicized in the majority of American newspapers . . . How about a few really big drives against munitions makers who profit from the deaths of Japanese, Chinese, and several kinds of Spaniards? Or a campaign against lynch law? Against waste of natural resources by private business as well as by government? Against Frank Hague's fascism? Against municipal corruption in dozens of cities?

These questions will be answered, for the most part, a little later. As for the campaign against lynch law, it is one of the finest pages in the history of American newspapers. As for Frank Hague's fascism, newspapers were barred from sale in Jersey City because they were exposing Mayor Hague's violation of civil rights. It would have been more to the point if Mr. Wolseley had asked why newspapers had not fought for the child labor

A Neglected Story

amendment, why they had not demanded that the United States free the Philippines according to its promise, why they had closed their eyes to the meretricious Pullman Company, our last unchallenged monopoly, why they continued to print patent medicine advertisements and refused to support bills for better foods and drugs.

It must be admitted that there is a gap between the ideals and the performances of newspapers, just as there was a hiatus between the theory and the practices of medieval Crusaders. In that older day there was a Christian ideal and there was the ideal of a warrior aristocracy; the knight stood for the use of force, but his faith put the use of force on the side of humanity and justice. Yet only Sir Galahad was noble and pure, and he was a figment of the imagination. The knights who sought to wrest the Holy Sepulcher from the Saracens were not above reproach; of the seven Crusades, the first only, which resulted in the capture for a time of Jerusalem, was idealistic and truly religious. The others were tainted with commercialism and imperialism. But at any rate the returning Crusaders brought to Europe the bathtub.

Bearing in mind this lapse between the professions and the practices of crusaders, medieval and modern, let us see whether newspaper campaigners are quite as bad as sometimes they are painted. Here I find H. L. Mencken saying, in the pages of the *Atlantic Monthly*, that the primary purpose of a newspaper crusade is to "give a good show to the crowd," and that the way to do this is "by first selecting a deserving victim and then putting him magnificently to the torture." Even the campaign for good government, he vows, is conducted "in exactly the same way," "dramatizing and vulgarizing it." The editor, he explains, is a "mobmaster."

Never, Mr. Mencken declares, is the crusading appeal to "the educated and reflective minority of citizens, but frankly to the ignorant and unreflective majority." Hear now his confession of faith: "For morality, at bottom, is not at all an instinctive matter, but a purely intellectual matter." I am reminded of a conversation with Theodore Dreiser in which this question came up, and in which he threw a lightning flash upon it. "Read Villon's poetry," he told me; "marvellous! And yet France hanged that bastard for a good reason." There is some doubt, I believe, as to whether Villon was hanged, but there is no doubt that he merited it, nor is there any doubt as to his intellectual grasp.

Newspaper crusading, according to Mr. Mencken, is "a popular sport" for the ignorant masses, "always far more orgiastic than reflective." The crusade against William M. Tweed, corrupt boss of Tammany Hall, "shook the whole nation, for he was a man of tremendous power, he was a brave and enterprising antagonist." Thus is one of the most celebrated newspaper campaigns dismissed airily with praise for the "deserving victim" who was put "magnificently to the torture."

There is good reason to doubt whether any magazine less gullible than the *Atlantic Monthly* would have sponsored an outgiving so false. Mr. Mencken at that time, to be sure, was editor of the Baltimore *Evening Sun*, and the editors of the magazine may have supposed in their innocence that he voiced the views of newspaper men everywhere, instead of the policy of a journal, once liberal, which had turned reactionary. I cannot be sure of this, for the same editors ran a series of "articles" about corporations, written by Arthur Pound, which in fact were paid advertisements. But at any rate the *Atlantic Monthly* made amends to the extent of giving space to a reply to Mr. Mencken by Ralph Pulitzer, then president of the New York *World*.

Commenting on Mr. Mencken's "very unfortunate class arrogance," Mr. Pulitzer said: "A great many persons of guaranteed education are sadly destitute of any reflectiveness whatsoever, while an appalling number of 'the ignorant' have the effrontery to be able to reflect very efficiently. This is apart from the fact that the general intelligence among many of the ignorant is matched only by the abysmal stupidity of many of the educated."

But what about Mr. Mencken's charge that newspapers fight even their "constructive campaigns for good government in exactly the same gothic, melodramatic way"? Said Mr. Pulitzer:

> Now "muck-raking" rather than incense-burning is not a deliberate aim so much as a spontaneous instinct of the average newspaper. Nor is there anything either mysterious or reprehensible about this. The public, of all degrees, is more interested in hitting Wrong than in praising Right, because fortunately we are still in an optimistic state of society, where Right is taken for granted and Wrong contains the element of the unusual and the abnormal. If the day shall ever come when papers are able to 'expose' Right and regard Wrong as a foregone conclusion, they will doubtless quickly reverse their treatment of the two. In an Ali Baba's cave it might be natural for a paper to discover some man's honesty; in a *yoshiwara* it might be reasonable for it to expatiate on some woman's virtue . . .

Space does not permit me to quote much further, but I must select part of another paragraph:

> If Mr. Mencken's ideal is a nation of philosophers calmly agreeing on the abstract desirability of honesty while serenely ignoring the specific picking

of their own pockets, we have no ground for argument. But until we reach such a semi-imbecile Utopia, it would seem to be no reflection on ":the people's" intellectual or moral concepts that they should refuse to excite themselves over any theoretical wrong . . .

Mr. Pulitzer, in short, exposed Mr. Mencken's fallacies and misstatements mercilessly, punctured his supercilious pretensions, and left him on the field completely deflated. The chastening effect of this salutary drubbing was apparent in a subsequent statement Mr. Mencken gave to *Editor and Publisher:*

> The newspapers, fortunately, are still more or less free, and can thus speak plainly. They constitute the last defense of common honesty, common decency, and common sense. It is their highest function to scrutinize the acts of all public officials, high or low, with the utmost diligence, and to denounce instantly every sign of stupidity or false pretenses.

From terming the crusading editor a "mobmaster," and asserting that campaigns for good government were conducted by "dramatizing and vulgarizing" them, Mr. Mencken has been converted to regarding such campaigns as the editor's "highest function" and urges him to utter instant denunciation. Long ago it was apparent to everybody else that American newspapers could not qualify, even at their worst, for all the nasty adjectives he found in his thesaurus; maybe it has become apparent to him, too.

Let me set down here a sketch of what seems to me a perfect crusade, worthy of a very Galahad. It was not the work of a newspaper but of an individual, and its value therefore is solely illustrative. Behind it was no motive of publicity or of financial gain or of personal aggrandizement. By this even if for no other reason John Jay Chapman deserves to live as one of our immortals.

In Coatesville, Pennsylvania, on August 13, 1911, a Negro was hideously burned to death. He had been

A Neglected Story

drinking, and in his exhiliration had fired three shots according to his own account, near the plant of the Worth Brothers Steel Company. Arrested by a special policeman, he tried to pull away and then, in self-defense, so he said, killed the man. As he fled he was wounded and lodged under police guard in the Coatesville Hospital. A mob, apparently without resistance by the police, dragged him out bound to his cot, and set it on a pile of rubbish.

"Don't give me a crooked death because I'm not white," the Negro pleaded.

Fire was set to the rubbish, and the victim was done jubilantly to death.

On the following day New York newspapers carried stories of the horror. M. A. DeWolfe Howe tells us, in "John Jay Chapman and His Letters," that these "were indeed enough to stir a man of Chapman's sensitive fibre to the deepest feeling." As the anniversary of the event approached he said that "my inner idea forced me to do something." He considered organizing a committee and inviting protestants from far and wide to go with him to Coatesville, but he decided to go with but one friend, a woman, to hold a memorial prayer meeting, "not for condemnation but for intercession." He felt that if this outrage were permitted to lie fallow it would do an irreparable injury to his country's people, but that a single protest might serve somewhat as an expiation.

One may fancy how a community in the Deep South would have received an outsider who came to protest a lynching; Yankee Coatesville did no better. No public hall could be rented, but an empty shop was procured. The Coatesville *Record*, after a good deal of hesitation and questioning, permitted the insertion of a paid notice of the meeting. Beside Mr. Chapman's friend, only two auditors were present: an aged Negress from Boston and a man who served apparently as an outpost or spy. Nevertheless Mr. Chapman held his meeting, with Bible readings, a brief talk, a prayer, and silent prayer.

Elsewhere I shall wish to quote from the talk Mr. Chapman made. Mr. Howe is justified in speaking of its "austere restraint and tragic beauty." Here it is enough to say that something of the noble and fearless spirit which animated that obscure pilgrimage has flamed more than once in newspaper editors during their crusades. Mr. Chapman's move was stripped bare of any desire for applause, or any feeling that ultimately it might pay dividends in respect and good will. His was a voice crying in the wilderness. Mrs. Chapman feared, with good reason, that he was taking his life in his hands, but he derided the notion. It is certain that more than once crusading editors and reporters have risked their lives and in some instances have lost them.

Oftenest the risk has come through the exposure of political corruption. Let me say at once that this form of campaigning, with which most of us associate newspaper crusades, is not my sole topic. No, the crusades with which I shall deal cover a surprising territory, ranging through the fight against racial and religious intolerance, the integration of communities, the liberation of persons unjustly imprisoned, the rehabilitation of a city's reputation and fortune, the reduction of taxes and the rates charged by public utilities, the improvement of working conditions, to the reformation of State prisons and institutions for the insane. Governmental

A Neglected Story

housecleaning has been more spectacular than some of these, but not always of greater reach in social betterment.

After sketching the achievements of a few of our most famous crusaders, in order to look at their methods and their motives, I hope to chronicle briefly the part Colonial newspapers played in preparing for the revolution against George III. That rebellion could not have been fomented solely by pamphleteering and from the soapbox; it would have been impossible without the spur of the press. I would like to tell about the attitude of these newspapers toward the Constitution, toward the abolition of human slavery, and toward various matters of national import after the Civil War. It is a record, by and large, of which all of us may be proud; for it vindicates the privileges we have accorded in this republic to one of our greatest institutions.

II

Pulitzer: Past-master

REMIER among the journalistic crusaders of this country was the elder Joseph Pulitzer. He was convinced that a newspaper should "never be satisfied with merely printing news." He stood for political independence, fearless attacks upon demagoguery, injustice, corruption, and "predatory plutocracy." If told fully, his achievements in that field alone might well fill a volume; I shall attempt no more here than to indicate their scope and the methods he employed, disregarding chronological sequence.

Two of the earlier campaigns of the New York *World*, which serve to illustrate its methods, its courage, and its power, were completed within less than a month, one upon the heels of the other. The first concerned the disputed line between Venezuela and British Guiana. Drawn by a surveyor in the employ of the British government, this boundary had never been accepted by Venezuela, and when an attempt was made to map it the President of Venezuela appealed to the United States for help. His Minister in Washington cited the Monroe Doctrine, and newspapers opposed to Grover Cleveland were aroused to ridicule his delay in acting.

A Neglected Story

Then, on December 18, 1895, President Cleveland gave out a special message, declaring that the attitude of Britain menaced our "peace and safety," and saying that if Britain did not renounce her claims an American commission would be appointed "to determine the true divisional line."

Now, the *World* had virtually forced the nomination of Cleveland and had been the chief instrument in electing him. Yet its owner at once prepared an editorial in which he said:

> Are our peace and safety as a nation, the integrity of our free institutions, and the tranquil maintenance of our distinctive form of government threatened by an extension, however unwarranted and arbitrary, of the British possessions in Venezuela? The assumption is absurd. And with it falls the structure of ponderously patriotic rhetoric reared upon it by the President.

In spite of a succession of editorials in that vein, showing for one thing that the Monroe Doctrine was in no way affected, there was an outburst of jingoism, and under its pressure both Houses of Congress adopted resolutions providing for a commission to fix the boundary and appropriating money for the task. The President's message was read in schoolrooms, former soldiers volunteered their services, and many newspapers joined the outcry. The New York *Sun*, as John L. Heaton tells us in "The Story of a Page," denounced as "an alien or a traitor" any American citizen who did not uphold the President. It demanded that the State Department reach an understanding at once with France and Russia, in order that their navies might assist by making war in the English Channel and the Irish Sea. Commenting on efforts in behalf of peace downtown, the New York *Times* said:

Newspaper Crusaders

Under the teachings of these bloodless Philistines, these patriots of the ticker, if they were heeded, American civilization would degenerate to the level of the Digger Indians, who eat dirt all their lives and appear to like it. We should become a nation of hucksters, flabby in spirit, flabby in muscle, flabby in principle, and devoid of honor, for it is always a characteristic of the weak and cowardly to make up by craft and trickery for their defect of noble qualities.

Said the *Tribune:*

The message will not be welcome to the peace-at-any-price cuckoos who have been clamoring that the Monroe Doctrine is a myth, and that we have no business to meddle with affairs between Great Britain and Venezuela.

The *World* appealed by cable and telegraph to the reigning house in England and to church dignitaries there, as well as to leaders in this country. The Prince of Wales, later Edward VII; the Duke of York, who was to be George V; William E. Gladstone, Lord Rosebery, Archbishops and Cardinals replied with earnest expressions of their horror at the thought of a war with this country. Clergymen and other leaders in the United States lent their aid. The upshot was that war was averted, this country acted for Venezuela in negotiations, and an international commission laid down a modified boundary satisfactory to both sides.

High tribute was paid to the *World* and its owner. Peace societies of Great Britain arranged a meeting at which they presented a memorial of thanks, and Ralph Pulitzer read for his father an address, "The Reign of Reason *vs.* the Reign of Force," which concluded:

However we may differ on many questions, we have common sympathies for liberty and humanity, just as we have a common language.

We speak, we read, we think, we feel, we hope, we love, we pray—aye, we dream—in the same language. The twentieth century is dawning. Let us dream that it will realize our ideals and the higher destiny of mankind.

Let us dream not of hideous war and butchery, of barbarism and darkness, but of enlightenment, progress, and peace.

A Neglected Story

Sir Robert Head Cook, then editor of the London *Daily News*, emphasized the service the *World* had rendered to journalism as a profession.

In provoking that crusade, Richard Olney, Secretary of State, wrote the blundering Venezuela message; in the second of these concurrent campaigns John G. Carlisle, Secretary of the Treasury, was primarily to blame. In each the *World* rebuked President Cleveland, who was responsible, obviously, for the acts of his Cabinet members.

In February of 1895 the Treasury, to replenish its gold stock, issued $64,000,000 bonds at 104½ to J. P. Morgan and Company as head of a syndicate. In a short while the bonds were selling at 120. In the following August the chief of the *World's* Washington bureau said that another and larger issue was impending, under the same terms. At once the newspaper gave sharp warning that the Treasury must not permit itself to be "cornered" again. Nevertheless, word arrived that a contract had been signed with the Morgan firm.

George Cary Eggleston tells us, in "Recollections of a Varied Life," how Pulitzer took hold of such a situation and outlined explicitly to his department heads a course of action. His instructions are set down:

> We have made our case in this matter of the bond issue. We have presented the facts clearly, convincingly, conclusively, but the Administration refuses to heed them. We are now going to compel it to heed them on pain of facing a scandal that no administration could survive.
>
> What we demand is that these bonds shall be sold to the public at something like their actual value and not to a Wall Street Syndicate for many millions less. You understand all that. You are to write a double-leaded article to occupy the whole editorial space tomorrow morning. You are not to print a line of editorial on any other subject. You are to set forth . . . the patent falsehood that the United States Treasury's credit needs "financing."

You are to declare, with all possible emphasis, that the banks, bankers, and people of the United States stand ready and eager to lend their government all the money it wants at three per cent interest, and to buy its four per cent bonds at a premium that will amount to that . . .

Then as a guarantee of the sincerity of our conviction you are to say that the *World* offers in advance to take one million dollars of the new bonds at the highest market price, if they are offered to the public in the open market.

In the meanwhile, [E. O.] Chamberlin has a staff of men sending out dispatches to every bank and banker in the land, setting forth our demand for a public loan instead of a syndicate dicker, and asking each for what amount of the new bonds it or he will subscribe on a three per cent basis. Tomorrow morning's papers will carry with your editorial its complete confirmation in their replies, and the proposed loan will be oversubscribed . . . Even Mr. Cleveland's phenomenal self-confidence and Mr. Carlisle's purblind belief in Wall Street methods will not be able to withstand such a demonstration as that . . . If it is true that the contract with the syndicate has already been made, they must cancel it.

In reply to the *World's* queries, a mass of telegrams pledging capital for the purchase of the bonds was received. Then an editorial was printed telling specifically of Wall Street bankers and the amounts of gold they had accumulated to "invest in the speculation." It was not in fact so much a speculation as a sure-thing gambler's chicanery; but the newspaper's protest was against the "waste of ten or fifteen millions" in the transaction, and it made an appeal to the President "to save the country from the mischief, the wrong, and the scandal of the pending bond deal."

Two New York banks, in the face of these revelations, withdrew from the bond syndicate. The President yielded, and his Secretary of the Treasury, with bad grace, offered the issue to the public, although the Morgans offered six millions more than their original bid. The $100,000,000 bonds were oversubscribed more than six times. The Morgan syndicate had the small

A Neglected Story

consolation of getting five millions at a fraction less than 111 while another bidder was offering 114, but that was under a special ruling by Secretary Carlisle.

No such distinguished success attended every campaign undertaken by the *World*. Its effort, for example, to break the financial and political power of E. H. Harriman was a failure. The campaign was an outcome of its long fight against Theodore Roosevelt and its exposure of contributions to his campaign fund by J. P. Morgan and Company, the Standard Oil, George W. Perkins, George J. Gould, C. S. Mellen, C. H. Mackay, E. T. Stotesbury, Chauncey M. Depew, Harriman, and others, embracing representatives of the Steel Trust, the insurance companies, International Harvester, the Coal Trust, bankers, and so on.

A letter from Harriman to Sydney Webster, a New York lawyer who was active in politics, was published in the *World* of April 2, 1907, which showed that Harriman had raised $260,000 for Roosevelt's 1904 campaign. He told Webster that this was with the understanding that Depew was to be made an ambassador, that Frank Black was to succeed him as senator, and that Harriman was to be consulted by Roosevelt about railroad recommendations in the President's message to Congress. None of these things had been done, and Harriman wanted to know where he stood.

No proof was forthcoming that Roosevelt had asked Harriman to raise the fund. The *World* said that the President had asked the financier to the White House for a talk, and Roosevelt denied it, whereupon the *World* printed the invitation to Harriman; it printed also the President's letter to him, saying "you and I are practical

25

men." It exposed Harriman's manipulations of railroad stock. Finally Pulitzer instructed his staff:

> Put utmost vigor without violence into "Harriman must go" series—say one editorial addressed to each director, stating his character, career, moral, social, religious position, pretensions, responsibilities, etc., every second or third day. Directors alone responsible. Whole country's reputation involved. Harriman vindicates Hearst and almost justifies Bryan's State ownership; certainly helps both and even worse socialist attacks, as practical, horrible example to be pointed at railroad corruption generally. Harriman should go as railroad's worst enemy.

Later, he instructed C. M. Van Hamm, managing editor, to get biographical material on each director of the Union Pacific, one of the Harriman roads, "how he rose, what he did in a public-spirited way . . . and yet how they allow this man to be their representative, their Grand Elector, their Chosen. They are responsible, *not* Harriman." Yet Harriman remained. Perhaps his associates thought the more highly of him for the drubbing he got. At any rate, he was too well established to be ousted, although the crusade was waged with full Pulitzer persistence and vigor.

Although the crusade to oust Harriman failed of its ultimate objective, doubtless it impaired his power to dicker with Presidents and dictate to lesser political luminaries. It arose from Pulitzer's conviction that great wealth must not be permitted to impair democratic processes. From that conviction came the *World's* exposure of insurance corruption, in which also Harriman figured. Like the other crusades I have described, this was a single-handed fight.

A quarrel between James Waddell Alexander, president of the Equitable Life Assurance Society, and James

A Neglected Story

Hazen Hyde, heir to the majority stock (which under his father's will Alexander controlled), revealed conditions so questionable that the *World* began a series of two hundred editorials, "Equitable Corruption." In the first of these it said that the "most astounding, far-reaching financial scandal known to the history of the United States" was approaching a climax, told of stock jobbing by Jacob H. Schiff and Harriman with the insurance company, in which they were directors, and demanded a legislative investigation.

Against an investigation were arrayed powerful business interests in the City of New York, the legislature, Governor Francis W. Higgins, and the State superintendents of insurance and banking. In response to public feeling, a committee of directors was appointed and made certain recommendations, which the board rejected. The *World* continued its hammering and brought out more damaging facts. Reluctantly Governor Higgins directed the superintendent of insurance to look into the matter, and he made a report the most of which was suppressed for a time. Day after day the newspaper trained its guns on Albany until finally the Governor capitulated and advised the appointment of a legislative committee. As counsel, at the suggestion of Don C. Seitz, the committee chose Charles Evans Hughes, who became, by reason of his patience, perseverance, and skill in this investigation, a national figure.

It was shown that the big insurance companies in New York maintained what the *World* properly named corruption funds, and contributed generously to campaign chests. This resulted soon in a charge of larceny against George W. Perkins of the New York Life Insurance Company, in contributing $48,702.50 to Theodore

Roosevelt's campaign and then receiving that sum from the funds of the corporation. The Court of Appeals, to which the case was carried, absolved Perkins on the ground of motive, but the Chief Justice, dissenting, said that when Perkins reimbursed himself he was as guilty of larceny as though he had taken insurance money to buy a necklace for a woman. The crusade divulged a mass of malodorous facts.

The investigating committee drew two bills to reform insurance company practices. The day after the Governor had signed the second, the *World* said:

> The law now calls it a crime for any corporation, excepting such as are organized for political purposes, to contribute to any campaign fund. No railroad, bank, trust company or manufacturing or mining corporation may hereafter lawfully give one cent to politics. Neither may any corporation maintain in Albany a secret lobby . . .
>
> But the greatest of all in its service to the community is the blow the Armstrong laws strike at the system of high finance which uses the savings of the people to convert public franchises into instruments of oppression. The prohibition of any participation by any life insurance company in syndicates, flotations, or stock speculations cuts off the great source which Wall Street promoters draw upon for speculative funds.

Conditions had been improved but not perfected. James Hazen Hyde, for example, sold his Equitable stock, which had a par value of $51,000, to Thomas Fortune Ryan, a notorious figure of the day, for $2,500,000. The elder J. P. Morgan "persuaded" Ryan, so subsequently he told a Congressional committee, to transfer the stock to him, and paid him some three millions for it. Since that day insurance companies generally have been under suspicion, and dubious practices among them have come to light. But the *World* and its owner had confidence that these conditions would be set right in time.

A Neglected Story

The public conscience is sound [it said] . . . The force of moral ideas in the community is omnipotent. What it has done to insurance corruption it can do wherever and whenever the public safety is menaced.

Pulitzer was ill in Paris when strikers locked out of the steel mills of the Carnegie company at Homestead, Pennsylvania, were being killed by Pinkerton thugs and the Coal and Iron Police, a private force hired by the employers, and he was deeply agitated when the news began to reach him. Without his guidance, the *World* said editorially on July 1, 1892:

> Under the McKinley [tariff] Act the people are paying taxes of nearly $20,000,000 and a much larger sum in bounties to Carnegie, Phipps & Co., and their fellows, for the alleged purpose of benefiting the wage-earners. And yet there is war at the Homestead works, and the employers have enlisted Pinkerton Hessians and fortified their property that they may pour scalding water on their discharged workmen if an attack is made upon them.

Strong in his sympathy with the underdog, Pulitzer was thrown into one of the serious crises of his illness by the news and the editorials. A member of the *World* staff who was with him tried to reassure him by saying that the accounts might be exaggerated. "There have been as many men killed in this labor war," his chief retorted, "as in many a South American revolution." In that day the rights of labor were obscure, and the feudal conditions which prevailed in American industry had received little attention. The *World* continued its editorial campaign by demanding:

> Is it right that a private detective agency shall maintain a standing army, a thing forbidden even to the several States of the Union? Is it well that a body of armed mercenaries shall be held thus at the service of whomsoever has money with which to hire them?

Other newspapers, shocked at this impertinence to a big corporation, sharply criticized the news editors of the *World* for the sensationalism of the stories they were printing from the war zone, and these comments were sent to the owner in Paris. Meanwhile the editorials continued:

> If force must be used to sustain the beneficiaries of protection in reducing wages and breaking down labor organizations it is better that it should be the citizen soldiery of the State, for the workmen will not resist them.

On the next day, in response to cables from Paris, the newspaper spoke in a different tone:

> There is but one thing for the locked-out men to do. They must submit to the law. They must keep the peace. Their quarrel is with their employers. They must not make it a quarrel with organized society. It is a protest against wage reduction. It must not be made a revolt against law and order. They must not resist the authority of the State. They must not make war upon the community.

That moderation of the editorial note was due to direction of the owner, but he so much preferred an editor who would take a courageous course to one who was irresolute and weak that he bore no resentment. As a fact, and as subsequent developments bore out, the editorials told nothing but the truth and actually were not incendiary. The *World* continued, indeed, to denounce Henry Clay Frick and his associates for their "appeal to Pinkerton rather than to the lawful officers of the State."

After Martin Tabert was fatally lashed by a "whipping boss" in a Florida convict camp, a score of newspapers to which telegrams were sent asking that they give publicity to the facts, ignored the request. Tabert was an underdog, he had died nearly a year earlier, and he hailed from North Dakota, which had been unable to get action.

A Neglected Story

The *World*, however, immediately sent a staff man to Florida, and presently thirty-eight other newspapers were buying his syndicated articles, so that the news associations were compelled to take up the story. As a result, Florida abolished the prevailing penal system within six weeks, and forbade the use of the lash on convicts. The judge and the sheriff in the Tabert case were removed from office and the man who had beaten him was charged with murder. Once aroused by the *World* and the newspapers which followed the trail it blazed, public opinion forced action with exceptional speed, notwithstanding the influence of corporations which had profited from the leasing system and which had induced politicians to maintain it.

Corrupt business, national politics, and foreign affairs, however, were by no means the sole interest of the *World* in crusading. It forced an investigation of the gas monopoly in New York City and brought about lower rates. It was an untiring enemy of Tammany Hall, although a Democratic newspaper. Its reporters investigated hundreds of bakeshops in the city, found that many were violating the sanitary code, and forced municipal inspectors to clean them up. It exposed both the milk trust and the poultry trust, and caused scores of indictments. It revealed that rotten eggs were being sold widely for the manufacture of foodstuffs, and that the refrigerator system was utilized to control or affect prices. If it did not cure these conditions permanently, it put the public on its guard and made city officials more scrupulous and more wary. That a great deal remains to be done, with little newspaper inclination in the metropolis to take a hand, has become apparent repeatedly. It is not always true that a crusade, at least temporarily successful, creates a vacuum at that point. The *World* is dead, and it left no New York heir.

Not until 1883 did Joseph Pulitzer buy the New York *World*. He had come to this country near the middle of the century, friendless and penniless, had slept in a public park, had done the most menial work to fend off starvation, had served as a volunteer in the Civil War, and then had moved on to St. Louis, where he worked for a time for the *Westliche Post*, then edited by Carl Schurz. He was elected a member of the Missouri Legislature, and afterward helped organize the Liberal Republican Party in 1872, which nominated Horace Greeley for the presidency. Schurz refused to support the ticket, and Pulitzer, who had bought an interest in the *Westliche Post*, sold it back; then he stumped the midwest for Greeley, who was defeated. After working for a time as a Washington correspondent, he returned to St. Louis in 1878, and bought for a song successively the *Post* and the *Evening Dispatch*, which he merged. Semiliterate as an immigrant, he had spent all his spare time in reading and had educated himself; and although his accent lingered, he was a good speaker.

For a week or so the new paper was called the *Post and Dispatch*, then the *Post-Dispatch;* at the outset it stated a creed:

> The *Post and Dispatch* will serve no party but the people; it will be no organ of Republicanism, but the organ of truth; it will follow no causes but its conclusions; will not support the "Administration," but criticize it; will oppose all frauds and shams wherever and whatever they are; will advocate principles and ideas rather than prejudices and partisanship. These ideas and principles are precisely the same as those upon which our Government was originally founded, and to which we owe our country's marvellous growth and development. They are the same that made a Republic possible,

A Neglected Story

and without which a real Republic is impossible. They are the ideas of a true, genuine, real Democracy.

That pronouncement struck a new note in the journalism of the midwest. Moreover, the newspaper undertook to live up to it. Never a hidebound partisan organ, it undertook to expose frauds and shams regardless of political consequences, and made powerful enemies thereby, but established itself powerfully in the affection of its public. One of its first campaigns was against rich tax dodgers. The files of the assessor's office showed understatement of property values and false inventories on the part of the wealthy, while those not so blessed in worldly goods were blessed at least with more honesty. The *Post-Dispatch* printed side by side the returns filed by the well-to-do and the poor. By this simple device it subjected civic slackers to reproach more severe than editorial comment, and the practice was corrected.

When less than a year old the *Post-Dispatch* began a crusade against protected gambling. The chief of the industry was Alanson B. Wakefield, a political luminary; the Board of Police Commissioners was politically appointed. Wakefield was indicted for perjury and sent to the penitentiary, fifty of his employees were fined, and a lottery was put out of commission. The paper fought for two years, however, before gambling was made a felony in Missouri. Meanwhile it did not neglect less sensational matters; through its influence the municipality began the purchase of lands for a beautiful park system, cleaned and repaired its streets, and erected a permanent exposition building. Twice the owner of the paper was physically attacked, but his courage was undiminished.

Newspaper Crusaders

In 1880, while T. J. Pendergast's elder brother began building in Kansas City a political machine which was to achieve an unenviable fame (to which I shall refer presently), the owner of the *Post-Dispatch* heard that the Republicans were planning to buy Indiana in the presidential campaign. In Indianapolis we hear him, on October 9, speaking in a strain which the Pulitzer newspapers were to make familiar to the nation. Protesting against the "power of the millionaires" in elections, he reviewed the influence in Indiana of the banks, railroads, and protected industries, and added:

> We want prosperity, but not at the expense of liberty. Poverty is not as great a danger to liberty as wealth, with its corrupting, demoralizing influences. Suppose all the influences I have just reviewed were to take their hands off instead of supporting the Republican Party, would it have a ghost of a chance of success?
>
> Let us have prosperity, but never at the expense of liberty, never at the expense of real self-government, and let us never have a government at Washington owing its retention to the power of the millionaires rather than to the will of the millions.

Indiana had been a Democratic State, but the "power of the millionaires" lifted it over into the Republican column that year. At a banquet in New York in honor of S. W. Dorsey, who had charge of the Indiana campaign, it was said that Dorsey had been "able to save not merely Indiana, and through it the State of New York, but the nation." He admitted subsequently that some five thousand persons aided him in buying Indiana. "Each of these men," he explained, "reported what they could do . . . and how much it would take to influence people to a change of thought. We paid $20 to some, as high as $75 to others, but we took care that the three men from every township should know just what each got. There was no chance of 'nigging'."

A Neglected Story

Whenever that idealist who had spoken unsuccessfully at Indianapolis encountered the "power of the millionaires" in corrupt operation, he set himself to combat it; whenever he suspected that the ballot was being undermined, he sought to put it on an honest basis, and he handed down a tradition in the office of the *Post-Dispatch* which resulted long after his death in a political house cleaning, and in a challenge, across the State, to the power of Boss "Tom" Pendergast. The long-drawn crusade whereby St. Louis was taken out of political red ink and put on the credit side of the electoral ledger merits examination at some length because it illustrates, as the other campaigns I have discussed do not, untiring pursuit of a purpose and unwearied attention to minute detail. For the facts of this crusade I am indebted to Carlos F. Hurd, an especially gifted member of the *Post-Dispatch* staff; for the consequences in Kansas City I have drawn upon other sources of information.

Although Kansas City was but half the size of St. Louis, Pendergast bossed the State democracy as well as his local machine, and almost always named the candidate for Governor. In St. Louis, as in Kansas City, there was ballot-stuffing with a complaisant election board; and when a ward boss, making war on his overlord, added more than three thousand votes to his ward list, while the other added nearly five thousand, the unexampled inflation offered an opportunity to the *Post-Dispatch* to rivet the attention of its readers on the frauds. On July 22, 1936, it began a series of first-page broadsides which ultimately cleaned out the voting lists, gave the city honest elections, and compelled the Governor to oust the election board.

Work began with two overswollen wards. Reporters found empty brick shells with scores of ghostly voters, hotels with half a dozen names on the register and dozens on the registration lists, saloons with more votable names than there were bottles behind the bar. Their photographers pictured the walls on which were chalked the numbers of phantom citizens. The first story was enough to convince the average citizen of St. Louis; it was not enough to convince James A. Waechter, the back-slapping chairman of the election board, who, when he saw a copy of the first edition containing the exposé, nodded that he had heard that sort of thing before. If anything was wrong with the registration he would take it up, of course, but just then he was busy with a case in court.

The newspaper did not wait until the chairman of the election board got through with his case in court. A special staff worked daily, in sweltering heat, studying voting lists, ringing doorbells, taking affidavits—for beside each reporter was a notary public—and turning out copy by the column. The sworn statements of election judges and clerks corroborated their findings in many instances. The investigators moved on from the river wards, where corruption was taken rather as a matter of course by the public, into staid residential districts. In a north-side area of homes, where a street had been widened, rows of dwellings had been wrecked, and the tenants had registered from the new homes to which they had moved, but their names remained on the lists at the old addresses. South and west the reporters moved relentlessly. The solid element of the city was thoroughly aroused when it found that from ten to thirty per cent of the voters in their own neighborhoods were

A Neglected Story

duplicates or phantoms. There were mass meetings. Telegrams and letters poured in on the Governor.

When Chairman Waechter tried to evade a thorough examination of the rolls the *Post-Dispatch* demanded a recanvass of each of more than seven hundred precincts in the city. The election board capitulated and reported that some 46,000 registrants were "not found." But there was no time, so Waechter said, to strike those names off before an impending primary, and in most precincts judges and clerks voted them.

More broadsides in the news columns followed. A canvass was made by *Post-Dispatch* reporters of the vote on a bond issue a short time before, and the figures ran laboriously into pages of copy. Even the politicians who profited from the corruption began to perceive that the election board must go; and three days before a general election the Governor, under their pressure, announced that it had been removed "for the betterment of the public service" and because there had not been enough "diligence in supervision." In place of the members removed he appointed a new board satisfactory to the paper, and a purge of office clerks, precinct judges, and clerks, began. In their places new man power was recruited from banks, factory offices, and commerce.

It was a day-and-night job, both for members of the board and their underlings and for members of the *Post-Dispatch* staff. The outcome was the largest registration St. Louis had ever witnessed, but nobody made charges that the lists were padded. A grand jury, which indicted eleven six-man groups of election officials, and admonished the courts not to dismiss the charges on "immaterial technicalities," said in its report:

Newspaper Crusaders

> We think it worthy of comment that, acting under exactly the same laws as previous election boards, with a minimum of time at their disposal to prepare for the election, the present board carried through successfully an election at which the greatest number in the history of the city voted, and this without any evidence of fraud. The reason for this was simply that these gentlemen were possessed of what might be termed honesty of purpose, and handled a most difficult situation with no other thought than the carrying out to the fullest extent of their sworn duty. These gentlemen deserve the commendation of all honest citizens.

One may fancy that Tom Pendergast observed from afar with some perturbation the pertinacity, patience, and skill of that horde of *Post-Dispatch* reporters and photographers, with their notary-public accompanyists. His local machine had proved invulnerable to similar exposures, but had never been subjected to a test so thoroughgoing. Now the Kansas City *Star* adopted on a smaller scale the methods of its greater neighbor. Two reporters began an inspection of the registration lists, and found 270,000 names, in a city with some 400,000 population; they found a funeral "parlor" with one occupant and seventeen voters; they found other registrations from vacant lots and untenanted warehouses, others who had been dead for years. They found, in brief, as far as they went, what the *Post-Dispatch* reporters had found in St. Louis. A Citizens' League was formed, to demand a grand-jury investigation.

This investigation brought 199 indictments; in the first eighty cases tried, there were fifty-six convictions, one plea of guilty, and twenty defendants threw themselves on the mercy of the court. As time went on, the sentences to the penitentiary, ranging from a month to five years, multiplied. It looked gloomy for Tom Pendergast; but it did not defeat his slate in the 1938 election. Orators for the coalition opposition charged that the town's

A Neglected Story

good name was being besmirched because of stories about wide-open gambling, unregulated prostitution, and vote frauds. The outcome was merely a reduction by about one-third in the Pendergast plurality. The machine was still running, but was not in good working order.

After the election, Governor Lloyd C. Stark of Missouri declared that his administration was pledged to "eradicate the blight of crime and corruption from Kansas City," and instructed his Attorney General to oust officials who refused to assist court and grand jury proceedings. "Information from reliable sources," said the Governor, "shows that the gambling racket is carried on openly and in defiance of law and without protest from any official heads of the city's government; that houses of prostitution flourish within the very shadows of the Court House and the City Hall and the inmates solicit openly, unashamed and unafraid of official authority; that gangsters and racketeers, unmolested by official authority, ply their trade and prey, through violence and intimidation, upon citizens and business men alike."

That was but another repercussion of the *Post-Dispatch* crusade, in which the practices of the Pendergast machine had been held up as a vicious example of electoral corruption.

In long-term consequences the restoration of honest elections to St. Louis may prove to have been the most valuable of the numerous *Post-Dispatch* crusades; it was an evidence that the newspaper was still carrying on in the Pulitzer tradition, after the owner's death.

It was no easy tradition to live up to. One of the noteworthy exploits of the paper, for example, had been the exposure in 1898 of the Central Traction (street railway) bribery of municipal representatives. No action could be forced in that case, however, until 1902, when Joseph Jolk was Governor. Then the key man of the House of Delegates "combine" slipped away to Mexico. The *Post-Dispatch* sent a staff man to find him and persuade him to return. He gave State's evidence, and nine boodlers were sent to prison.

Instances of that sort had helped make the newspaper an immensely profitable enterprise. Within a few years after it was started it was netting its owner $200,000 a year. Pulitzer's success was won, I believe, through a certain art of getting close to the heart of a vast audience and through his fight for the underdog; his crusade against wealthy corruptionists was the brushwork of that art. Not long before his death, which occurred October 29, 1911, he wrote for the *Review of Reviews* an article in which he said:

> What is everybody's business is nobody's business—except the journalist's. It is his by adoption. But for his care almost every reform would be stillborn. He holds officials to their duty. He exposes secret schemes of plunder. He promotes every hopeful plan of progress. Without him public opinion would be shapeless and dumb. Our Republic and its press will rise or fall together. An able, disinterested, public-spirited press, with trained intelligence to know the right and courage to do it, can preserve that public virtue without which popular government is a sham and a mockery.

To but one of his sons did the elder transmit the strong sense of social justice and civic responsibility, the courage, and the high order of intelligence essential to a crusader of the first water. This was Joseph Pulitzer, Jr., to whom fell the management of the *Post-Dispatch*. It was under his hand that honest elections were restored finally to the city. In this and other reforms, until the middle of 1938, he had the assistance of Oliver K. Bovard, a superb executive and a crusader who had won his spurs under the elder Pulitzer. Together they made the Teapot Dome scandal so apparent that a Senate committee was compelled to investigate it, forced a corrupt Federal judge in the East St. Louis district off the bench, and brought kidnapers to justice. But it was Joseph Pulitzer's son and namesake who had the final say-so when the *Post-Dispatch* assailed the American Newspaper Publishers Association (ANPA), of which he was a member, for undermining public confidence by its mercenary attitude. This was just before the 1937 annual meeting of the association. Editorially the newspaper said:

> The ANPA is to be likened to the National Association of Manufacturers or the American Petroleum Institute or any other coalition of business men for the purpose of advancing the fortunes of themselves and their companies. This comparison is borne out by the by-laws of ANPA, showing it was created to foster the business interests of members, to procure uniformity of usage, to settle differences, to protect members from irresponsible customers, and so on.
>
> This is the language of business; it is not the language of the newspaper profession. It is the language of men engaged in manufacturing a product; it is not the language of men engaged in the high and responsible calling of writing, editing, and interpreting the news.

The editorial continued by saying that the association had gone far afield to engage in pronouncements giving the impression that it was "grinding its own ax at public expense," and set forth a formidable list, including its condemnation of the Wagner Act setting up a national labor board and its opposal of the Copeland pure food and drugs bill. In the latter case the position "represents pressure of advertisers." It added:

> How can the public be expected to separate these activities of the men who own and manage newspapers from the responsibility to the public interest borne by writers and editors? The fact is they are inextricably joined

in the public mind. Such activities cast a reflection on the whole press. They impair public trust in the disinterestedness of newspapers.

In that case the younger Pulitzer turned his batteries upon an organization of which he was a member, and held aloft the torch his father had raised more than once, that newspapers must not permit selfish interest to impair their public service. His services to the press have been marked, as well as his services to his city and his State. Among the officials of St. Louis and to a great extent throughout Missouri there has prevailed a sense that malfeasance in posts of public trust was not to be risked, with so powerful and vigilant a watchdog on guard. The newspaper has been a benison on occasion, when civic causes called, a builder as well as a scourge and a discipline. It remains a monument to the self-taught genius who made it his proving ground and the agency of his earliest triumphs over wrongs.

III

Hearst: Playboy and Prodigy

WILLIAM RANDOLPH HEARST has been more copiously vilified than any other American editor and publisher. Often fellow newspapermen, guilty of offenses as grave as ever he committed, have denounced him; sometimes others as eminent and as disparate as Elihu Root and Charles A. Beard. The blame has been uttered as a rule without acknowledgment of praiseworthy achievements, although there are pages on the credit side of the book. Thus Dr. Beard, addressing a progressive group of teachers in 1935 in Atlantic City, said:

> In the course of the past fifty years I have talked with Presidents of the United States, Senators, Justices of the Supreme Court, members of the House of Representatives, Governors, Mayors, bankers, editors, college presidents . . . leading men of science, Nobel Prize winners in science and letters, and I have never found one single person who for talents and character commands the respect of the American people, who has not agreed with me that William Randolph Hearst has pandered to depraved tastes and has been an enemy of everything that is noblest and best in our American tradition.

A superb historian, Dr. Beard was indifferently informed about the daily press, and appears to have permitted a gust of high moral indignation to run away with him. Under the sobering influence of Mrs. Beard, who collaborated with him in "The Rise of American Civilization," we find:

> No small part of the success achieved by the yellow press was due to its fierce denunciation of flagrant abuses passed over in silence by timid editors who fancied themselves more respectable. The severest critic could hardly deny that the sensational editors of the eighties and nineties, by resorting to merciless attacks and repeated exposures, contributed powerfully to the improvement of the methods pursued by American capitalists and politicians. They also aroused the interest of unknown millions never before reached by the daily newspaper, thereby making a contribution to the democratic process.

Dr. Beard noted Hearst's "new methods" in journalism, and John K. Winkler, one of his several biographers, speaks of his "revolutionizing completely its methods and its morals." Others have fallen into the same fallacy. Hearst was in lineal descent from the elder James Gordon Bennett and introduced no basic departure into the practices of the press. He did no more to revolutionize journalism than Theodore Roosevelt did to revolutionize progressivism.

No one has fathomed the vagaries of Hearst, his irresponsibility, his callous indifference to censure or praise, his reckless prodigality in the public service contrasted with his mercenary venality in other instances, his cosmopolitanism and his provincial loyalty to California, his solid enterprise and his didoes. One of his high executives told me: "He's an Oriental, that's all; he doesn't think as we do, about women or politics or anything else." This was as close as anybody seems to have got to an explanation of the man, and had been adopted more than once; but it was the substitution of a label for an analysis.

Boasting that "the present light and amusing character" of Washington dispatches was due to him, the elder

A Neglected Story

Bennett expressed his theory that vaudeville had its place in the newspaper; Hearst has elaborated that technique more fully than any other. The elder Bennett, by his championship for revenue only of the slavery cause, helped precipitate the Civil War; Hearst and Joseph Pulitzer are held partly responsible for the Spanish-American War, but did no more to precipitate that bit of braggadocio and international bullying than Henry Cabot Lodge and Theodore Roosevelt. The elder Bennett fashioned the news stereotypes of sex, scandal, suspense, and violence which his successors profitably employed, Hearst the most skillfully and profitably.

To quiet executives during widespread criticism, Hearst telegraphed in 1939 a sort of "general order" as follows:

> Much prefer that nobody did anything for me about boycotts. I don't mind them. I have been boycotted for being a pacifist and for being an imperialist. I have been boycotted by the Irish for being too friendly to the English and boycotted by the English for being too friendly to the Irish. I have been denounced for being too friendly to the Jews and denounced for not being friendly enough. I have been denounced for being too friendly to Hitler and have had my correspondents thrown out of Germany for being hostile to Hitler. I am now being denounced by the Socialists and boycotted by the Communists. The Republicans don't like me because I didn't support Hoover and the Democrats don't like me because I don't approve of Roosevelt. I guess I am pretty bad, but the circulation is going up, so we must be popular with somebody. Maybe with liberty-loving Americans. There are a lot of them left.

That was at once a confession and an averment of Hearst's agility in the *volte-face*. It was a philosophical acceptance also of the stream of abuse, much of it unmerited, directed toward him and his newspapers. Half a century in the journalistic cockpit had taught Hearst to accept complacently attacks, whether or not unfounded.

Newspaper Crusaders

As a Crusader Hearst would have taken higher rank if he had been endowed with greater stability of purpose. Each of his newspapers has conducted noteworthy campaigns against political corruption, "the plunderbund" of millionaires and the utilities. When the utilities were bribing the press of this country they could not reach the Hearst nor Pulitzer dailies; and these were the only papers to give prompt and adequate coverage of the Federal Trade Commission inquiry which uncovered the rottenness.

Not long thereafter, in 1929, Hearst sent a note to all his editors instructing them that brightness and brevity were to be their watchwords. (Terseness and accuracy were the Pulitzer watchwords.) "Condensation is the life of trade," said he.

Comparing the flapper of that day with the newspaper, Hearst said in his note that "the modern paper must be different from the sedate and sedative newspaper of former years," and like the feminine bobs and skirts "have got to be briefer and livelier and more attractive to look at." He lamented the competition in the amusement field of the radio, automobile, and motion picture. "The papers that are dying are the old-fashioned ones that run in a rut and cannot get out of it." Then came the collapse of the stock market and Hearst sent word: "Make the Hearst newspapers prosperity papers." Like Herbert Hoover, he wished to delude the public that prosperity was just around the corner. He suggested a first-page two-column box with the caption: "Good News of Good Times."

Although some Hearst executives, in response to the demand for brevity, ruled that no sentence should run past fifteen words, the newspapers of the chain continued

A Neglected Story

to crusade. In San Francisco a reporter posed as an automobile victim, and a physician faked an X-ray plate to show he had a spinal injury, so he could get damages. The outcome of that campaign was that two doctors and two orderlies were discharged and two other physicians suspended with eleven ambulance drivers and hospital stewards. At about the same time (this was in 1933) Hearst told his Chicago *American*, not then merged with the *Examiner*, to "go after rackets," and as a consequence twenty-four leaders and officials of labor unions and trade associations were indicted. Editorials and eight-column head-lines marked that crusade, urging that no one pay tribute, dues, or assessments for "protection." In the cleaning and dyeing industry alone, with 30,000 employees, the *American* crowed that it had stopped twelve millions in annual graft. Racketeering in Newburgh, New York, was the target as late as 1938 of the *Journal and American*, which charged that in this city of more than 30,000 people some public officials "literally welcomed underworld characters and big-time racket suspects," visited gambling houses, protected a vice ring, and a $15,000,000 illicit liquor ring. Fifty persons were indicted by a grand jury and the Governor appointed a special prosecutor for Orange County.

"It proves," said Paul Schoenstein, city editor of the *Journal and American*, "that the day of crusading newspapers is far from over."

Crusades like those, a commonplace among Hearst newspapers, were conducted along the conventional lines long familiar. As a political crusader Hearst was more nearly unique, for although he often ran for office and sat in Congress from 1903 to 1907, he was not animated by personal desire for office but was a candidate, I am confident, as a part of his newspaper adventures. His politics was as neutral as a pair of socks, suitable either for the Right or the Left. For years he was left wing and semisocialistic, but the time came when he was to root vigorously for Andrew Mellon's proposal, while Secretary of the Treasury, that a retail sales tax be imposed, a brazen attempt to saddle a greater burden on the poorer classes which Hearst had pretended to champion. He had supported William Jennings Bryan and had branded Mark Hanna in cartoons with the dollar mark, yet he set up a ballyhoo for Mellon for President. His agility in the about-face was acrobatic.

Former Senator George Hearst, multimillionaire owner of gold, silver, and copper mines, gave his twenty-four-year-old son in 1887 the seedy San Francisco *Examiner* as a plaything. William Randolph laid aside his banjo and made the town echo with his exploits. Doubtless he thought of himself as a Lochinvar when, having astonished the Coast with his thundering crusades against corporate privilege and political plunder, and having transformed his plaything into the biggest money-maker among Western newspapers, he ventured into the New York field in 1896 to buy the *Morning Journal*. Out of the ensuing warfare with Pulitzer came the phrase, "yellow journalism."

Early in 1905, Samuel Seabury wrote a booklet, "Public Ownership and Operation of Public Utilities in New York," to help along the Municipal Ownership League, one of Hearst's creatures. The *Journal* had been denouncing franchise steals, under Tammany control of the Board of Aldermen. One paragraph of Judge

A Neglected Story

Seabury's book about the utilities might well have been part of a Hearst editorial:

> Their record has been one of extortion. Their privileges were conceived in fraud and political corruption and throughout their existence they have been a constant source of temptation to corrupt officials. Both of these corporations [gas and electric] exist in violation of the law and both enjoy absolute monopolies in the necessaries of life. Both have violated the law of the State, both have made false reports to avoid the payment of their just taxes, and both have entered into a close and friendly alliance with public officers whose duty required that they should protect the public from extortion.

Hearst invited Judge Seabury to see him, and the two formed an alliance under which the jurist put him in nomination in 1905 for Mayor of New York. The *Journal* had leaped in ten months from 30,000 circulation when Hearst acquired it to more than 400,000, and was a power; Judge Seabury wished to use that power for idealistic ends, and had no notion that his new friend was a weathercock. At the Democratic convention in St. Louis the year before, Hearst's paid agents, who had been scouring the country on his behalf, had been able to muster 263 votes for him as Presidential candidate, so that he had begun to assume the proportions of a national figure. He had contributed freely to Bryan's campaign in 1900 and in return had been made president of the National Democratic Clubs. Moreover, Boss Charles F. Murphy of Tammany Hall had sent him to the House. He looked an ally well worth having.

George B. McClellan was mayor and a Tammany aide. Against him a fusion was formed, with Hearst's Municipal Ownership League as part of it, and it was proposed that Judge Seabury, who would have preferred to remain on the bench, be a candidate against McClellan. Reluctantly he agreed to make the race, provided he was nominated "with a full appreciation of the fact that if elected I am to be free from all partisan obligations . . . holding myself accountable only to the people." Walter Chambers tells us, in "Samuel Seabury: A Challenge," that Hearst and his fellow fusionists "were not so much interested in electing a Mayor who would be self-controlled and entirely independent in his administration of the office."

Unable to agree on a candidate, the fusionists split and the Municipal Ownership League ran Hearst for mayor in one of the bitterest campaigns the city had witnessed. The *Journal*, by now published both morning and afternoon, lampooned Boss Murphy in penitentiary stripes, with a caption: "Look out, Murphy! It's a short lockstep from Delmonico's to Sing Sing." The convict uniform angered Murphy deeply, and his orators retaliated by calling Hearst a "destructionist," a "radical," and "McKinley's assassin."

Hearst's followers were convinced he had won, but the ballot was not safeguarded in that day by voting machines, and it was impossible to prove, even on a recount, that Tammany had stolen the election. It was with some confidence, nevertheless, that his League announced in 1906 his candidacy for Governor. But Hearst, fearful that upstate voters would shy away from an organization dedicated to any cause so radical as municipal ownership of public utilities, changed the name of his organization to the Independence League. His henchmen rapidly organized throughout the State.

Singularly, this was as disquieting to President Roosevelt as to Boss Murphy, of Tammany. The former urged the Republicans to nominate Charles Evans Hughes, who had come out of the insurance investigation started

A Neglected Story

by the *World* with an enviable fame for courage and ability. Murphy began, despite the scars of that penitentiary cartoon, to make advances to the publisher; for if a Republican were elected and Hearst ran second on an independent ticket, or even the other way about, Tammany, under the old election laws, would have lost control of the election machinery. The motto of the Boss was: "If you can't beat 'em, join 'em." So he proposed that he and Hearst join forces.

That deal was made. By forcing on a reluctant convention the unit rule of voting in blocs by districts, and by other tactics described by a henchman as "the dirtiest day's work of my life," Murphy forced the nomination of Hearst. He did not, however, work feverishly for victory.

The opposition did work feverishly. Elihu Root was sent by President Roosevelt to speak on behalf of Hughes. At Utica he said:

> I say to you with the President's authority that he greatly desires the election of Mr. Hughes; I say to you with his authority that he regards Mr. Hearst as wholly unfit to be Governor; as an insincere, self-seeking demagogue who is trying to deceive the workingmen of New York by false statements and false promises.
> In President Roosevelt's first message to Congress, in speaking of the assassin of McKinley, he spoke of him "as inflamed by the reckless utterances of those who, on the stump and in the public press, appeal to the dark and evil spirits of malice and greed, envy and sullen hatred . . . " I say to you, by the President's authority, that in penning these words, with the horror of President McKinley's murder fresh in his mind, he had Mr. Hearst fresh in his mind; and I say, by his authority, that what he thought of Mr. Hearst then, he thinks of Mr. Hearst now.

Judge Seabury replied to this attack by the Secretary of State that it was unjustified and delivered by plan on the eve of the election. He said Root had made capital of a national tragedy, an assassination by a maniac. But he could not stem the tide. Hughes was elected.

In 1918 Murphy intended to place Hearst in nomination for the governorship again, but was balked. Judge Seabury had long since left the ranks of his followers, and as a delegate to the State convention denounced the publisher, on account of his opposition to our entering the World War, as a "truckler with our country's enemies." Hearst was seeking, so he said, "to capitalize by election to public office the latent treason whose total annihilation is the most pressing need of the hour."

No one need suppose that Hearst, who maintained estates more richly adorned and more regal than ever an emperor or the doges enjoyed and who had a dozen fascinating irons in the fire, yearned for the flatteries, the perquisites or the power of a mere mayoralty or governorship. His campaigns were publicity stunts for himself and his newspapers. They served to build circulation for his chain and to emphasize his editorial charges against the "plunderbund." They served also to give to a sub-circulation, which he had brought into being from the semiliterate classes, a sense that his dailies espoused great causes and protected the underprivileged.

If that was true in the New York campaigns, it was still more noteworthy in the national arena, which Hearst entered early in his career. When Alton B. Parker became the Democratic nominee for President in 1904 and repudiated Bryanism by declaring for the gold standard, the Hearst newspapers denounced the deal as having been promoted by Standard Oil, and the $450,000 contributed to the Democratic fund by Thomas Fortune Ryan as mostly Rockefeller money. Subsequently Thomas W. Lawson, stock market manipulator, testified before a Senate committee that H. H. Rogers and the Standard Oil "practically gave their agents at the convention carte blanche to nominate Mr. Parker."

In the 1908 campaign Hearst, who had up his sleeve a bomb equally damaging to the Rockefellers, the Democrats, and the Republicans, was forced to throw Bryanism overboard (which we may be sure he did without a qualm), and to put a third party in the field. His Independence League held a "national" convention in Chicago, with some two-thirds of the delegates on the Hearst payrolls as printers, clerks, and other employees, and nominated for the presidency Thomas L. Hisgen, a Massachusetts axle-grease manufacturer. For the vice-presidency John Temple Graves, a Hearst editorial writer, was named. William Howard Taft was the Republican candidate and the Democrats again put up Bryan. The Hearst ticket polled but 83,562 votes, and Georgia, Graves's State, gave it but seventy-seven. Nevertheless, the huge expense of this flash-in-the-pan was justified from the Hearst standpoint.

For Hearst, campaigning for his ticket, dropped his bomb in a speech at Columbus, Ohio. There he made news and scored a beat on his competitors by reading the first of a series of letters by John D. Archbold, vice-president of the Standard Oil Company, revealing that corporation's bribery of men high in the ranks of both major parties. The letters had been bought by Hearst underlings from clerks in the Archbold offices, who had stolen them from the files. The correspondence has been summarized as follows:

Archbold's correspondence . . . showed that in 1898 Standard Oil had given $2,000 to W. C. Stone, former Lieutenent Governor of Pennsylvania and later Congressman; that it had given sums of $5,000 to Representative John P. Elkins of Pennsylvania; that Representative Joseph C. Sibley, of Pennsylvania, president of the Rockefeller-controlled Galena Signal Oil Company, regularly took Standard Oil advice about pending legislation and committee appointments, and also frequently accepted money; that Joseph B. Foraker habitually accepted large sums of money for specified and unspecified purposes; that Senators Bailey of Texas, McLaurin of South Carolina, and Quay of Pennsylvania were on the Standard Oil payroll; and that in general Standard Oil was pumping money out with a muscular hand. The evidence suggests that Sibley in the House and Foraker in the Senate were the Rockefeller paymasters in Washington. Sibley, indeed, from time to time mentioned in his letters various friendly Representatives that were in dire need of "loans."

Foraker, the letters made clear, used money not only to defeat and to pass bills in the Senate, but also to influence decisions in the Ohio courts and actions by Ohio's legislative and administrative officers. Until Hearst made the first Foraker letters public, in 1908, it should be remembered that Foraker was a serious contender for the Republican Presidential nomination. He made the nominating speech for McKinley in 1896.

Under date of January 25, 1902, Foraker asked Archbold for $50,000 with which to acquire a secret share in the influential *Ohio State Journal* of Columbus, but the attempt on the Columbus newspaper failed. Foraker returned Archbold's bank draft.

The letters showed also large payments to Senators Boies Penrose and Mark Hanna; the latter Hearst had branded long before with the dollar mark. The entire correspondence was printed in all the Hearst newspapers and was a national scandal. No better springboard for this publicity could have been devised than its use in behalf of a third party against the parties of Bailey, McLaurin, Foraker, and Penrose.

Repeatedly it has been said that Hearst opposed our entry into the World War to curry favor with German and Irish readers in this country. This seems to me an inadequate explanation. Without attributing to him a prevision of the blunder's costliness in blood and treasure,

A Neglected Story

I am yet confident that, more astute than other publishers and politicians, he sensed, as they did not, the temper of the general mass, and knew it was pacific. Certainly he was the only major newspaper publisher not to be bamboozled by British propaganda. He knew the value, in Woodrow Wilson's second campaign, of such a slogan as "He Kept Us out of War"; he would have been pleased to use a slogan of that sort for the aggrandizement of himself and his journals, and he might have succeeded if there had not been an allied counter-propaganda more powerful than his. Walter Millis has described in "The Road to War" the breadth and subtlety of the movement to embroil us.

Hearst, whose voice had been loudest in demanding the rape of Spain, who had risked his life reporting a battle in Cuba after one of his correspondents had been wounded, who had planned to buy a steamer and sink it in the Suez Canal to prevent the Spanish fleet from getting through, turned a characteristic somersault in 1914. He demanded, in the name of peace, that the President embargo food, money, and munitions; he cried out against "wasting our wealth to continue a carnival of murder, to prolong an era of overwhelming disaster, to encourage the destruction of the white race, to tear down the achievements of civilization." He printed a cartoon of Japan, naked knife in hand, with the caption: "Look out, Uncle Sam, your neighbor is eagerly waiting an opportunity to strike you in the back." George Seldes tells us, in "Freedom of the Press," that in 1917 "millions of 'patriots' who read pro-Ally propaganda hated Hearst. With the post-bellum disillusion many said that if Hearst had succeeded in keeping us out of the war he would have ranked in our history in the vicinity of Abraham Lincoln."

More heartily than any other "patriot" on this side of the water, the British hated Hearst. Of what use to persuade Walter Hines Page, Ambassador at the Court of St. James's, to send a cablegram to President Wilson, warning that J. P. Morgan and Company were entangled in Allied finance and must be extricated (only a few newspapers have published this and Millis deleted it from his book), if this man Hearst was to arouse mass opinion against the obvious way of extricating the Wall Street house, by joining the Allies. The Empire's resources included a means of effective reprisal: as overlord of the world's cables, it was possible to supervise, even to censor, the news from Europe to the United States. After frequent interferences, the British, six months before the United States entered the war, closed the cables and the mails to Hearst material and expelled his correspondents. The French, Portuguese, and Japanese governments did likewise, as O. W. Riegel notes in "Mobilizing for Chaos."

Hearst's London representative was told gently that the prohibition could be averted or would be lifted on personal assurance from the publisher that all news would be printed verbatim as it went through the censors. He transmitted the message obediently to his chief. Now, Hearst had merely shrugged his shoulders when France, enraged at his temerity in printing the terms of an Anglo-French treaty, had expelled him from that country; but the British shutdown was a more serious matter.

"Tell them to go to hell," said he.

This left the Hearst chain and its International News Service, however, in the lurch for tidings of the greatest conflict in history. Victor Rosewater, in his "History of Coöperative News-gathering in the United States," says that Hearst's men filled in the gap by pirating news from rival press associations.

When it seemed inevitable that the United States would join the Allies, Hearst said that the people, who must fight the war, should decide about it, and demanded a referendum or at the least a majority vote in Congress. If he had succeeded in getting spontaneous Congressional action he would have accomplished a noteworthy overturn; for although the Constitution provides that Congress shall have sole power to declare war, it has never done more than recognize that a state of war existed, usually after that state had been engendered or superinduced by executive action. He did not succeed in either of his demands; and once we were in, he waved the flag as vigorously as any.

Instead of holding out the olive branch toward Japan, Hearst has been fairly consistent in trying to involve us in war with that country. In regard to Mexico he has shifted from side to side. He published a signed editorial in 1916 demanding that our troops occupy that country, arguing:

> Our flag should wave over Mexico as the symbol of the rehabilitation of that unhappy country and its redemption to humanity and civilization. Our right in Mexico is the right of humanity. If we have no right in Mexico we have no right in California or Texas, which we redeemed from Mexico.

But during the World War, when Carranza was dictator and a revolutionary movement against him got under way, the Hearst papers were loud in his defense. The explanation offered in some quarters for this change of front, and it was not incredible, was that Porfirio

Newspaper Crusaders

Diaz had given the Hearsts vast estates in Chihuahua, and that Carranza traded on this. In 1920 Carranza, like Madero before him, was murdered, and the Obregon-Calles combine achieved power. In 1927 Hearst bought from a dubious Mexican-American agent a series of forged documents, which had been rejected for good reason when offered elsewhere, pretending to show that Japan and Mexico had conspired against the United States and had paid huge bribes to certain senators, clergymen, and journalists. The publication of the material caused a sensation, and if it had been genuine might have provoked war; but a Senate investigating committee had no difficulty in exposing the forgeries.

If that ill-advised piece of sensationalism had not made the Hearst newspapers sufficiently ridiculous, their hysteria about radicalism would have completed the job. They have said, without warrant, that nine-tenths of the professors in our colleges and schools were teaching Communism; they have urged editorially that we throw "Reds" out of this country; they have professed to find Bolshevism or its heir in nearly every crook and cranny, and in particular among leaders of the Newspaper Guild. No editor has been so ardent as Hearst in his "red scares," none so tremulous in his simulated terror of the left wing.

When I spoke of the Hearst estates in Mexico as offering a credible explanation of his attitude for a time, I had in mind other items in his career. It was shown in 1898 that he had agreed in writing not to be unfriendly to the Southern Pacific Railroad for a payment of $1,000 a month; and as late as 1934 he agreed to supply American news to the Hitler press in Germany for $400,000 a year, after which his papers became kindly toward the dictatorship. Testimony before the National Labor Rela-

A Neglected Story

tions Board in 1937 revealed that the music critic on his tabloid picture paper, the *Daily Mirror*, got both a salary and a commission on advertising; that a column of travel notes was made up of publicity matter from steamship lines and railroads, and was signed with the name of an advertising solicitor; that a rewrite man prepared "blurbs" for department stores which bought advertising space; and that the same was true of employees who signed columns dealing with amusements and food.

Why a publisher as wealthy as Hearst should stoop to the Southern Pacific or the Hitler fee is a mystery; the petty venality of the *Daily Mirror* passes understanding. It is true that this property was said to be losing at the time some $30,000 a year; but then Hearst's New York *Journal*, which was still being published as an entity, was prosperous and had earned as much as three millions in a year; his California dailies had been known to gross more than five millions annually.

At the turn of this century Hearst owned two newspapers; by 1929 he counted twenty-eight, this country's largest chain, rated in value at ninety millions. They had a circulation twice as great as the Scripps-Howard chain, their nearest competitor; Hearst boasted that they reached twenty million readers. Since 1939, in a drastic process of paring, they have been put through a wringer with other Hearst properties. This fabulous engine of publicity and manufactory of opinion, both for good and ill, was entering an eclipse.

IV

Scripps: Bare-knuckle Fighter

EDWARD WYLLIS SCRIPPS was not born, as William Randolph Hearst was, with a silver spoon in his mouth. Son of a struggling Illinois farmer, he peddled ice and coal, sawed wood, went for a while to a night school, learned his first lessons about the press in the shop of the Detroit *News*, owned by his half brother, James, and from him imbibed the notion that large type and a small sales price might prove profitable. It was James and Ellen, a sister, who financed him in 1878 to the extent of $10,000 in founding the *Penny Press*, later the Cleveland *Press;* but the Cincinnati *Post* was the first daily in which he owned a controlling interest, and it was his best beloved. From the outset it was a crusading paper.

Walter Wellman, ever an adventurer as well as a journalist, had set up the *Penny Post* just when Scripps was starting the *Penny Press*. A campaign against organized gambling had so enraged the boss, then Thomas C. Campbell, that Pinkerton detectives had been employed to frame a blackmail case against Wellman and his brother Alfred, and subservient police had clapped them into jail. Walter Wellman appealed for help to the Scripps brothers; his plan was to pay a fine and give up his paper,

A Neglected Story

but E. W. Scripps insisted on fighting and salvaging the property. Afterward, at a cost of something more than $3,000, he came into direction of a smudgy, four-page sheet, heavily indebted, considering its negligible assets. James and Ellen were part owners and in time Milton McRae, working at first as an advertising solicitor at $25 a week, bought an interest.

The first campaign waged by that tiny paper was an oddity. It was due primarily to the fact that the staff included an unfrocked Methodist preacher, another man who had studied for the ministry, and a devout Swedenborgian. E. W. Scripps had no religious convictions to speak of, but regarded himself rather as an atheist; yet the others persuaded him to get behind a young evangelist who was preaching to growing crowds on corner lots; he perceived a certain novelty in the notion. Those advocating it made the point that if these were political rallies due attention would be paid to them; why not allot some space to the Lord's party? Gilson Gardner tells us, in "Lusty Scripps," that columns were devoted to the revival. The *Post* told elaborately how large the attendance was, what the evangelist said, how many souls were saved. "Nothing like the paper had ever been seen; probably nothing like it has ever been seen since."

Circulation jumped in a fashion to amaze Scripps. It doubled, tripled, quadrupled, and the readers did not fall away when the revivalist had gone. Thereafter the paper gave a great deal of notice to the doings of all creeds, and Scripps found himself, willy-nilly, enjoying the reputation in Cincinnati of a good and moral man. Certainly he was no hypocrite, but in that community at least he tried to live up to its opinion of him. Actually, as we learn from "Lusty Scripps," he was a hard drinker and overfond of women. One of the early items in the Cleveland *Penny Press* had recorded a fine imposed on him in police court for driving a horse (after it had cast a shoe) "while intoxicated." His instructions had been that the paper must print all the news regardless, and instead of firing the editor for printing this he gave him a raise in pay.

In Cincinnati a battle royal awaited Scripps, after the city came under the domination of George B. Cox, a boss who compared in stature and in methods with the worst in American municipal politics. Cox once said after a visit to New York that he had nothing to learn from the Tammany Society. From an office above the Mecca, his saloon at Dead Man's Corner, Cox ruled his satrapy. The condition of the streets was such that a man, after driving onto the sidewalk and killing two children, was acquitted of homicide on his plea that the paving made the accident unavoidable. There were few street signs and little lighting. The schools were starved, the police department venal, the fire department a laughing stock. Cox spent for the well-being of his subjects but a tiny fraction of the millions he levied from them in tribute.

Until the *Post* was established there was no newspaper opposition to those conditions. The *Enquirer* was the property of John R. McLean, son of a blacksmith who had speculated successfully in real estate, and himself a big investor in the city's public utilities. The *Commercial*, edited by Murat Halstead, was a party organ. The *Times-Star* had been bought for Charles P. Taft, half brother of William Howard Taft, by his new-rich father-in-law and was an auxiliary of the gang. It must be said in fairness that the future Chief Justice of the Supreme Court had no

A Neglected Story

stomach for its goings on; speaking in the 1905 State campaign on behalf of the Republican ticket, he reviled the Cox gang's "cohesive power of public plunder" in Cincinnati and Hamilton County, and urged that it be defeated. The State ticket, however, carried the county ticket with it to win.

This was just after Lincoln Steffens, in a magazine article, had spoken of Cincinnati as corrupt and contented, maintaining that it was the worst governed city in the United States. The *Post* reprinted that article and corroborated its findings editorially and in its news columns. Having tried earlier to silence Wellman with a blackmail charge, the gang tried libel against the *Post*. The firm of Bateman and Harper was retained to defend the action for criminal libel, which it did successfully. J. C. Harper, thereafter, became general counsel for the newspaper and organized an Honest Election Committee. Subsequently he became general manager of a group of Scripps properties, embracing the Terre Haute *Post* and half a dozen others. He proved one of the young publisher's most valuable counselors. "He was a crusader himself, although a lawyer," said Negley D. Cochran, a Scripps executive who saw him in action.

Although the Scripps paper in Cleveland uncovered racketeering in the building trades union and sent two men to the penitentiary, the general Scripps policy was to champion labor, right or wrong. E. W. held that the circulation and power of his papers was founded chiefly on the good will of the workers, that most dailies were published on behalf of the employer, and that many of this country's ills would be remedied if labor were better acquainted with its power and were made articulate. He entertained that idea when workingmen were mostly unorganized and when it was regarded as downright subversive to take that side.

William James, we may be sure, was not among the favorite authors of Scripps; it is safe to say that he was unacquainted with his familiar passage:

> Why should they [citizens] not blush with indignant shame if the community which owns them is vile in any way whatsoever? Individuals, daily more numerous, now feel this civic passion. It is only a question of blowing on the spark till the whole population gets incandescent, and on the ruins of the old morals of military honor, a stable system of morals of civic honor builds itself up. What the whole community comes to believe in grasps the individual as in a vice.

James was writing "The Moral Equivalent of War" when he said that, but what he wrote applied as well to the moral equivalent of disreputable government. Sensing this truth, the Cincinnati *Post* blew vigorously on the spark of civic passion, but it was a long while before the population got incandescent. The first effects were manifest in the State legislature, which was bipartisan, and which appointed in 1906 an investigating committee. Before the inquiry could be checked by subservient Cincinnati courts, a great deal of vicious material had come to light and had been duly displayed in the *Post*. Two judges testified that they took orders about how to decide cases from Boss Cox, and one, who said he must act according to the evidence and the law, was promptly ousted.

In Rud Hynicka, Boss Cox had an apt and eager disciple, who had grown to the stature of a lieutenant. He took his orders from the saloonkeeper at Dead Man's Corner but himself did not become a publican; instead, he turned later to theatrical enterprises.

A Neglected Story

Rudolph Kelker Hynicka attended during his young manhood strictly to the business of the Boss, and learned incidentally to read political weather signs; so that when the legislative investigation was pending he foresaw a squall and sought a storm cellar. He made a deal with counsel for the committee whereby, to forestall actions at law, he agreed to refund to the city "interest" which banks had paid him for the deposit of city and county funds, to persuade some of his pals to do likewise, and to give certain damaging testimony on the promise of immunity.

Thus nearly a quarter of a million dollars was siphoned from the pockets of grafters into the municipal till. Hynicka said jauntily on the witness stand that this was but a fraction of the annual rake-off, but that he hadn't the least notion where the rest went. Two years later, at another legislative inquiry, he adopted similar tactics, and as a consequence Cox thought it best to retire. Rud Hynicka ascended the throne.

Those revelations and the disgrace of the Boss did not shake the grip of the gang on Cincinnati and the county of which it was the capital, but they afforded the *Post* further opportunities to fan the civic spark; so that when Lincoln Steffens spoke of the city as corrupt and contented he somewhat overshot the mark. Many of its people were distinctly discontented. Indeed, at a meeting in 1923 of the Cincinnatus Association, a group of more than two score business and professional men, the tireless campaigning of the newspaper had a repercussion in its home town rather than in the Statehouse at Columbus.

The Cincinnatus Association had been formed in 1920 by a World War veteran to discuss public questions in a serious way; and on that evening the subject was municipal affairs, in particular a tax increase proposed by the authorities. One of the speakers was Murray Seasongood, a lawyer, who argued that the city government was archaic, inefficient, and wasteful, to employ no harsher language, and that to provide its officials with more money to squander was bad business. Since the members of the association were substantial and prominent, reporters for the morning papers, friendly to the machine, were present, and the proceedings were recorded.

Office holders under gang rule are seldom expert politicians, and those in Cincinnati, instead of letting the charges die there, retorted with a torrent of abuse. Members of the Cincinnatus Association replied in kind and demanded a new charter, such as twenty-seven other Ohio cities had adopted under a home-rule act. More, they demanded a small city council and a city-manager form of government.

The *Post* now had a double-barreled crusade on its hands: the old attack on an iniquitous system, plus a trenchant plea for nonpartisan, efficient management. It stuck to its guns although for years the merchants of the city had been withholding advertising, sometimes almost en masse. One may fancy the chuckles of Scripps at these attempts to coerce him. Gilson Gardner tells us that he loved to bully advertisers and would have preferred to get along without them. Perhaps no publisher had ever perceived more clearly the dangers inherent in that field. He doted on independence as much as he loved a rough and tumble fight, with no quarter asked or given. He continued to wage his fight for three years more, until a new charter was adopted and Murray Seasongood became Mayor.

A Neglected Story

Even so, the matter of mopping up required patience and skill. The man with the mop, ably seconded by the *Post*, was Colonel C. O. Sherill, a West Pointer with engineering and administrative experience. He put the city back on its feet and paid its debts while the tax rate was rapidly diminishing. It was the culmination of a long struggle and the end of forty years' domination by dishonest Republican control. "From the time Scripps became controlling owner," says Negley Cochran in his biography of the publisher, "the *Post* led the people of Cincinnati through a long hard fight against political corruption to many victories." Scripps himself, writing to the editor of his Seattle paper, said he had paid no attention during this struggle to the question whether his newspaper was making or losing money; "I felt that I would rather lose the *Post* as a business than possess it as a fat, greasy, prosperous prostitute."

Meanwhile the restless Scripps had been founding other papers here and there, and had left the Cincinnati fight largely in the hands of McRae, whom he took into partnership in 1890, and of his attorney editor, Harper. They wisely went about with bodyguards, as a rule, and the Chief, wherever he happened to be, was well armed, although he preferred bare knuckles. Each of the thirty dailies he founded was a scrapper, but not every one was a success. In St. Louis, for example, the *Chronicle* ate half a million dollars out of his pocket without gaining a solid foothold. "I was up against a better man," he explained candidly. "Joseph Pulitzer, who ran the *Post-Dispatch*, beat me at my own game." Both those men died as multimillionaires on their yachts, and eventually the

Newspaper Crusaders

Scripps property in the city of New York took over the dying *World* and merged it with the *Telegram*.

In other cities Scripps papers met less expert competition and got along better. It was so in Knoxville, where the *News*, in another double-barreled campaign, cleaned up the administration and established a city manager; it was so in Evansville, where the Republicans and Democrats were in corrupt combination and were ousted by the *Press* in favor of a city manager. These were bitter fights, but against no such odds as were encountered in Terre Haute.

J. C. Harper, who had promoted the Evansville *Press*, was made general manager in 1909 of the Terre Haute *Post*. In Cincinnati the fight had been against a Republican gang; in Terre Haute it was against the local Democratic gang, subsidiary to the State machine erected by Thomas Taggart of County Monyhan, Ireland, who had been brought to this country as a child; he had been mayor of Indianapolis for two terms, 1895–1901, and was a conspicuous figure, chairman of the Democratic National Committee, 1904–1908. His local henchmen were Don M. Roberts, first city engineer, then mayor of Terre Haute; and Crawford Fairbanks, head of the Terre Haute Brewing Company. The machine was efficient and well oiled.

As city engineer, Roberts took a census, primarily for the purpose of making up voting rolls; and in conventional fashion had listed names from tombstones and old rent lists, but had been unconventional in enumerating cats and dogs among the electorate. At the sudden access of population, business men smiled broadly; anyhow, they said, it would show that Terre Haute was prospering

A Neglected Story

and growing. For the most part they were friends of the brewer-boss, Fairbanks, who owned a newspaper among his other assets.

F. Romer Peters, who moved on with Harper from Evansville to become editor of the Terre Haute venture, set reporters to work looking into the voting lists, and found the padding which might have been expected. From a one-room flophouse, "The Red Onion," in the redlight district, a score of voters had been registered, and similar conditions were found galore. In a series of news stories the facts were set forth. Edward J. Meeman and George W. Clogston, then reporters but subsequently to become Scripps editors and executives, were assaulted by a thug with a police record, who was a follower of Roberts. Clogston was knocked unconscious in front of a crowded grandstand, while gathering facts about crooked gambling games operated there under the sponsorship of the gang; policemen who saw it happen made no arrests and the good burghers of Terre Haute manifested a singular indifference. No legal recourse could be procured.

After the *Post* had revealed the employment of violence and fraud in a Congressional election, however, an investigation was made by Federal authorities. A grand jury in Indianapolis, after being charged by Judge A. B. Anderson, summoned many Terre Haute residents as witnesses. Immediately Roberts directed that a Vigo County grand jury conduct its own inquiry, an old trick in the game, which had been employed, for example, by the Cincinnati gang before Scripps broke it up. The *Post* was not for a moment befuddled by the ruse. It printed on its first page a story with the headline:

Newspaper Crusaders

GANG PICKS
GRAND JURY
FOR PROBE

―――

Starts Election Investigation of Its Own With
Werneke's Uncle as Prosecutor and
Roberts Men on Grand Jury

―――

Only One of the Regular Panel Served

―――

In the introductory paragraph of that story it was said that five members of the grand jury had been selected "on an order from Eli Redman, who is now sitting on the circuit bench, and whose election is being contested on the ground of fraud." It was shown that but one man had been taken from the regular panel, and that the others were known tools of the Roberts-Fairbanks crowd, including the father of the rough who had slugged the two *Post* men.

Judge Redman issued a citation of contempt against Peters, on the ground that the information published was calculated to embarrass the court and the grand jury, as indeed it was, and to bring them into disrepute with the people. It happened that Peters was away, and that Clogston was in charge in his stead, so the warrant was promptly changed to accuse him. But this evidence of speed was as nothing to what followed. Clogston was arraigned before Judge Redman that afternoon, Thanksgiving Day, and a continuance was refused when his attorneys asked for it. A motion to quash was overruled and time to prepare an answer was denied. A fine of $50 and a sentence of ten days in jail were imposed. Straightway Clogston was thrown into a cell and was permitted to have no food that evening.

A Neglected Story

Scripps editors and reporters appeared to thrive in those days on unkindnesses of that sort. "Clogston spent two nights in jail without a whimper," Harper reported to E. W. Scripps on November 27, 1914, "and feels that he has had a great opportunity for public service. He has a wife and baby—she is as brave as he is." (That the prisoner did not remain longer in durance was owing to a writ of habeas corpus issued in Indianapolis by Judge Anderson, who characterized the proceedings as not due process of law in any civilized country in the world.) Harper wound up his report on a note of triumph:

> It really looks as if after all these years the Terre Haute *Post* was coming into its own, just as the Cincinnati *Post* came into its own. The local newspaper situation is ideal. The other afternoon paper is owned by the big brewer who has put up the money for the election corruption which has made Terre Haute a byword in the State. The other paper, the only morning paper, is . . . afraid to own its soul. The Terre Haute people seem to despise the coward even more than they do the knave.

That triumphant tone was justified, for the people of the town had begun to see that the machine was not omnipotent, since it might be defied by a struggling newspaper single-handed. Business men were no longer afraid to tell the truth when summoned into court, and they corroborated the exposures in the *Post*. Frank G. Dailey, the Federal prosecuring attorney in Indianapolis, caused the indictment of Judge Redman, Don Roberts, and half a dozen of their henchmen, and they were sent to Leavenworth penitentiary, while their underlings by the score were fined and jailed, mostly on pleas of guilty. Roberts refused to resign as mayor, and from the penitentiary continued to dictate the appointment of policemen and other matters, until he was impeached.

Newspaper Crusaders

It must not be supposed that the St. Louis venture was the only Scripps failure. Newspapers were purchased or founded elsewhere that proved costly experiments, but these did not dampen the ardor of the adventurer. At the urgent suggestion of McRae—this was while the chain was known as the Scripps-McRae group—the *World* of Kansas City was acquired, and it cost several hundred thousand dollars before it was abandoned. In Nashville and Pueblo there were losses, in the second town after several years of struggle. Other enterprises, as in Dallas, Memphis, and Houston, soon got themselves on a paying basis and so offset losses elsewhere.

Lest this give the impression that E. W. Scripps was a somewhat harum-scarum publisher, blown about by every wind, let me say that he was a man of exceptionally sound judgment in the direction of fiscal and editorial policies, no less than in his inspiration of crusades. In Cleveland, for example, where Robert F. Paine was editor of the *Press*, and at the outset had got himself an unexpected raise in wages by printing that item about his employer's being fined after an arrest while intoxicated, he justified the faith of Scripps by becoming one of his aces. He took an active interest in local politics, and as the paper grew in power his political power grew, until he was in virtual control. Better or worse, Scripps would have none of this. He issued an order, applicable to all his papers, forbidding any news or editorials in that paper which might affect an employee's political fortunes.

Writing in 1927, a year after the death of E. W. Scripps, about the chain of newspapers he had left, I said: "There is local autonomy and a fighting spirit. These are a heritage from Old Man Scripps. And it is

A Neglected Story

plain that under the present management the legacy is not being dissipated, but is being conserved." A former executive of the chain, who had read this, asked later whether I had been overoptimistic.

"Roy Howard has already begun to disavow and repudiate everything the Old Man stood for," he warned me.

Robert P. Scripps, eldest son, was titular head of the enterprises, and I pinned my faith to a letter his father had written, in which he said:

> It is my opinion that the value of the properties over which you exercise control might well increase manyfold if your chief aim were merely to cause increase in wealth.
>
> However, I repeat now what I told you when I first launched you in your career: That I would prefer that you should succeed in being in all things a gentleman, according to the real meaning of that word, than that you should vastly increase the money value of my estate. Being a gentleman, you cannot fail to devote your whole mind and energy to the service of the plain people who constitute the vast majority of the people of the United States . . . You are and can be, continually, entirely free from any temptation to cater to any class of your fellow citizens for profit. You have not had nor should you at any time ever have any ambition to secure political or social eminence.

The elder had become troubled about the management of the chain by his son, who lacked some of the Scripps fire and energy. "I am capable," he told Negley Cochran, "of destroying what I have created if I find it to be commercialized and its principles prostituted for gain after I am dead." If he had in mind setting up some safeguard in his will, as the elder Pulitzer had tried vainly to do, he failed to make the purpose effective.

Pulitzer provided that his newspapers should not be sold. Yet when the morning *World* died in 1931 the evening edition was sold to the *Telegram*. Despite the defeat of the will's provisions, there remained hope that the *World-Telegram* might carry on manfully in the Pulitzer-Scripps tradition, and the hope seemed justified when the

Pulitzer prize for meritorious service during 1932 was awarded to the merged property.

No single campaign waged by the paper merited that distinction, but by combining four of them it was justified. These were a drive to have a name written into the ballot in a New York Mayoralty campaign, which did not result in the candidate's election but drew votes away from the Tammany candidate; an exposure of irregularities in the administration of veterans' relief, which resulted in salutary action at Washington; an investigation of the mortgage situation, which resulted in a State law improving the status of investors; and an inquiry into lotteries conducted by fraternal orders, which caused the indictment of some officials.

Roy W. Howard said the award "is journalism's own answer to those skeptics who contend that appreciation of aggressively militant journalism has waned," and observed that "in no other city is the evaluation of a news story, an editorial, or a newspaper fight in the public interest appraised more fairly" than in New York. He promised that the *World-Telegram* would continue to be "a paper by, of, and for New Yorkers." Let us glance at the record and see whether he meant by that what the elder Scripps meant when he said that a newspaper "is not a fake or a snap for a day or two, or a scheme to bunco money out of fools' pockets. A reputation for honesty, and ability to give good service for money, is more necessary than a reputation for virtue in women"; and when he warned against seeking merely an increase in wealth.

Scripps, who looked down at the advertiser and ploughed back money into his papers because he feared

A Neglected Story

the effect of personal wealth on the freedom of his viewpoint, died an immensely rich man in spite of himself. His empire included, in addition to a continental spread of dailies, a profitable international news service, a feature organization supplying material to hundreds of papers beside his own, and an endowed agency to give the public information about scientific progress. Even before his death he was troubled by a shadow which fell athwart his news agency, owing to a premature and false report that an armistice had been signed ending the World War. This report was sent by Roy Howard, who has said that he accepted it in good faith on official authority. London newspapers, which heard the rumors, declined to print them. The New York *Globe*, which has since gone out of existence, characterized the United Press story as the most cruel hoax in journalistic history.

Arthur Hornblow, Jr., who was an American army intelligence officer at Brest, France, whence Howard sent the false message to this country, has given a detailed account of the circumstances in the old *Century Magazine*. From this it is clear that with the aid of an obliging French newspaperman at Brest the dispatch reached the transmitting office as though it had come from Paris, had passed the censors there, and must be all right. Hornblow's theory was that German secret agents put over the fake, and he said that "Howard did what any other skilled newspaperman would have done in similar circumstances"; then he asked:

> Who knows but that a still fight-hearted American people might have cried loudly for "On to Berlin!" had not the sweet branch of the olive tree been placed prematurely in their hands and found to be much, very much, to their liking?

Admiral Henry B. Wilson, commander of the American Navy in French waters, permitted Howard to use the false report. "The following morning," said Hornblow, "Admiral Wilson, every inch the gentleman, took upon his own shoulders complete responsibility for Howard's fateful cable." The Armistice was not signed until two days later.

Whether the false Armistice report was due to naïveté or was an abuse of public responsibility may never be determined. Excepting the profit in selling millions of extras, it has little bearing on the apprehension of Scripps lest his properties fall away from the standards of independence he had set for them. We get a better light on that by what happened after the merger of the *Evening Telegram* with the *World*. The new paper, on account of its increased circulation, announced an increase in advertising rates by three cents a line, and twelve large department stores withdrew their patronage. Scripps would have thumbed his nose at them if they were unwilling to pay a fair price for what they got. The *World-Telegram* sued for peace.

Another evidence of an altered attitude toward the advertiser came when the Scripps-Howard newspapers conducted a costly examination of the buying habits in certain cities. "We put sixteen major markets under a 'merchandise microscope'," they advertised; "here is an actual inventory of 53,124 homes, covering cosmetic, shaving and dental aids, food, radio, refrigerator, auto, tires, gas, and oil. It shows the brand and product preferences and point of purchase by income groups." The reader was urged to "write or phone your nearest Scripps-Howard National Advertising Office."

A Neglected Story

Promptly the Hearst chain countered with its own survey and advertised that "a good forty per cent daily read Hearst newspapers in fifteen great trading areas," enumerating cities from New York to Seattle. The family incomes of Hearst readers were impressively catalogued. "Isn't that what your own market analysts would call good?" the advertisement inquired. "Telephone today for one of our merchandise men." Thus the advertiser could reach daily more than 4,500,000 families, Sundays more than 6,500,000.

One may fancy that E. W. Scripps turned over in his grave at least once during this competition between his properties and the Hearst newspapers in scratching the advertiser's back. Doubtless there was another sepulchral revolution when Merlin H. Aylesworth, former director of the National Electric Lighting Association, became publisher of the *World-Telegram*, as a part of the paper's reactionary trend. He went to this post from the presidency of the National Broadcasting Company; and at a Princeton round-table discussion of the press he had threatened that the radio chains might enter the publishing business if the newspapers were to withdraw their daily free programs. This was after Richard Wormser, an advertising man, had said that a column of radio announcements in one thousand papers would cost, at card rates, $28,000 a day; in other words, that the newspapers, which were already beginning to throw out their free advertising for motion pictures, were giving a lot of free space to radio. It was a safe conclusion that once Aylesworth moved over to the *World-Telegram* it would do little crusading.

What about labor? The generous and belligerently helpful position of Scripps was manifest throughout his life; it was difficult to persuade him the worker could be wrong. When the American Newspaper Guild was formed, unionizing the editorial workers, its leaders supposed that the heirs to this tradition would be first to sign contracts establishing minimum pay and maximum hours for the underpaid and overworked members of the craft. To the contrary, it was found that Roy Howard was circulating anti-Guild propaganda among fellow publishers, and it was not long before its members were calling him "our No. 1 enemy." Not until April, 1937, did the *World-Telegram* sign a contract, which, however, omitted the preferential shop.

On August 29, 1938, this newspaper answered a question about the principal causes of industrial strikes in 1937 by saying: "Union organization issues, such as recognition, closed shop, and discrimination."

That reply gave the cue to the newspaper's attitude toward the Wagner Act and the National Labor Relations Board. From the first of July to the middle of November in 1938 it published fourteen editorials attacking them, jointly or separately. It had been equally critical of other progressive—whether or not mistaken—measures involved in the New Deal; and the tabloid *Daily News* had spoken of "the anti-New Deal Scripps-Howard chain." Thereupon Howard from his yacht dictated an editorial denying that there was "some sinister and mysterious control" behind publishers, and promising that "if or when the Scripps-Howard newspapers decide to part company with the New Deal, announcement of that fact will appear in these columns and no reader will find it necessary to seek elsewhere for the information." In the period I have mentioned sixty-five of seventy-one editorials were adverse to Franklin D. Roosevelt or to his measures and plans, yet no such announcement appeared in the paper.

In fairness it should be said that the *World-Telegram*, after Howard gained complete ascendancy, plugged hard for the Fusion movement which resulted in the election of Fiorello La Guardia as mayor of New York; that it supported Thomas E. Dewey in his exposure of racketeering and of the political protection of underworld characters; and that it was in part responsible for the adoption in New York of the savings-bank insurance plan inaugurated years before in Massachusetts through the efforts of Louis D. Brandeis. This cannot be called a glowing record, but it may have been the basis of Howard's assertion, in his Don Mellett Memorial Lecture on May 9, 1939, at Stanford University:

> To justify its long protected liberties and immunities, journalism has a great obligation. It must never lag. It cannot even run with the herd. It must inspire, and it must lead in every fight and in every movement for social advancement, if it is to justify the trust which the public has imposed in it.

Hardly had such glowing phrases been broadcast by the Scripps-Howard newspapers and the trade press when there appeared in the *Nation* of May 13 and May 20 two brilliantly written articles, "From Scripps to Howard," by Robert Bendiner and James Wechsler. The second of these quoted Howard's speech to the Denver Chamber of Commerce: "We come here simply as news merchants"; and asserted that the Scripps properties had "come under the control of chamber-of-commerce mentalities uninhibited by even a shred of liberal background or conviction." It cited chapter and verse of the suppression of articles by Heywood Broun and Westbrook Pegler, outspoken columnists for the chain. Not long before the articles appeared, Rollin Kirby, the distinguished liberal who had been serving the papers as cartoonist, had resigned in disgust.

The Scripps-Howard newspapers are owned by a holding company, and have attempted to dodge Federal taxes—quite within the law—like other corporate properties which employ this device. With what gusto the old Cincinnati *Post* had exposed tax dodgers, and with what contempt it had reviled these civic slackers! Like the Hearst chain, the Scripps-Howard chain has gloried in "red scares." Like Hearst, they have been going through a process of paring, by lopping off less profitable properties here and there; and in some instances it was clear that these newspapers had lost ground because they had ceased to be good crusaders and had "disavowed or repudiated" the Scripps policy. Roy Howard's illiberalism and his bootlicking of the advertiser were making money in some quarters, but they were curtailing the circulation, the prestige, and the influence of the Scripps papers.

V

Colonial Crusaders

T IS heartening to find that some of our earliest Colonial newspapers, long before the day of such stalwarts as Pulitzer, Hearst, and Scripps, were infused with the crusading spirit. Although "printed by authority" as a rule, they were so outspoken that they were suppressed more often than not, and one was officially burned in the public square "by the common hangman." Many crusaded against the Stamp Act and one was founded solely for that purpose. Samuel Adams, apparently the only notable rabble-rouser to emerge from that distinguished Massachusetts family, and James Franklin, elder brother of the philosophic Benjamin, employed early Boston publications to arouse the settlers against oppressive authority.

Although there was a deal of controversy and some crusading in early pamphlets and even in almanacs, the first tiny sheet to merit the name of a newspaper was *Publick Occurrences*, issued in Boston on September 25, 1690, seventy years after the Pilgrims landed at Plymouth Rock. It was established at the London Coffee House to give "an account of such considerable things as have arrived to our notice," and in order that its readers might "better understand the circumstances of public affairs."

Newspaper Crusaders

This statement, which took no account of comic strips, crossword puzzles, and fiction, nevertheless was a fair statement of what a newspaper ought to be and do.

Without following the quaint spelling, I may say that *Publick Occurrences*, in its only appearance, told (and thereby incurred the wrath of the authorities), about an expedition against the French and Indians. It stated that "when Capt. Mason was at Port Real he cut the faces and ripped the bellies of two Indians, and threw a third overboard in sight of the French, who informing the other Indians of it, they have in revenge barbarously butchered forty captives of ours that were in their hands."

By a printed order the Governor and Council suppressed the "pamphlet," because it had been published "without the least privy or countenance of authority," and added that, as "There is contained reflections of a very high nature: As also sundry doubtful and uncertain reports, [the officials] do hereby manifest and declare their high resentment and disallowance of said pamphlet, and order that the same be suppressed and called in, strictly forbidding any person or persons for the future to set forth anything in print without license first obtained from those that are or shall be appointed by the government to grant the same."

There ensued one of the most complete suppressions on record. The only original copy of *Publick Occurrences* is preserved in London. Chief Justice Samuel Sewall of the Massachusetts Bay Colony set down in his diary that the paper had been abolished because it was not licensed and because of the reference to the French King and the Maquas (Mohawks). A month after it appeared Cotton Mather, son of Increase Mather and like his father a Congregational preacher, wrote a sharp letter about it.

A Neglected Story

(Cotton Mather believed in putting down the troublesome; he was active in the persecution of Massachusetts witches.) In the face of these official and religious rebukes, no other attempt was made for fourteen years to issue a newspaper.

During that interval the Postmaster at Boston served as New England's newscaster. English papers, of which but few were obtained, gave some intelligence of official proclamations and new laws, but the Postmaster told his friends fully of these and in addition gave them the gossip of the coffee houses. Thus it was in order that on April 24, 1704, he should issue the first Boston *News-Letter*, but with a stipulation, surprising in these go-getting days, that no advertisement might be inserted at a cost of more than five shillings. This paper endured, occasionally under some other name, for seventy-two years; but it was namby-pamby from the first and was acceptable to the authorities, as non-crusading journals usually are. It was the only newspaper being printed in Boston during the British occupation, and died when the redcoats departed.

John Campbell, who published the *News-Letter*, was removed from office in 1719, and William Brooker, his successor, established the Boston *Gazette*. "It's sheets," said Campbell contemptuously, "smell stronger of beer than of midnight oil. It is not reading fit for people." Brooker replied with spirit and thus afforded our first example of two newspapers crusading against each other. A conformist, Campbell condemned his rival for one thing because Brooker printed some of the more fiery outgivings of Sam Adams about the Stamp Tax, the Boston Massacre, and the Tea Party. The British had their revenge. They taxed the crusading *Gazette* out of existence in 1724. Earlier, Adams had used the *Independent Advertiser* as an outlet, but it was short-lived.

It was from Sam Adams, so we are told, that Napoleon borrowed a phrase to apply to England, "a nation of shopkeepers."

James Franklin, the irrepressible, bobbed up on August 7, 1721, with the *New England Courant*, in which appeared the earliest writings of his younger brother, under various pen names. One of these was a tirade against hoopskirts, forerunner of many male protests against feminine fashions and foibles. Another burlesqued the trial of a fellow printer—Benjamin was an apprentice to his brother—and aroused the authorities, who jailed James overnight as a warning.

James Franklin was one of a group who frequented the London Coffee House, a focus of disaffection; Cotton Mather and others of the righteous dubbed these fellows the "Hell Fire Club." But not all the material in the *Courant* dealt with British oppression; it conducted a campaign against inoculating for smallpox, then raging in the town, while the *Gazette* earnestly advocated that treatment.

For the most part the *Courant* was critical and sarcastic about the government, sometimes none too pious in its tone. The General Court appointed a committee to consider the matter, and it reported that the paper's tendency was to mock government and religion, therefore that James Franklin be forbidden to print it further. In this emergency James Franklin ostensibly retired from its editorship and appointed Benjamin in his stead. Moreover he published a soft-soap salutatory, which said in part:

Long has the Press groaned in bringing forth an hateful brood of party pamphlets, malicious scribblers, and billingsgate ribaldry. The rancor and

A Neglected Story

bitterness it has unhappily infused into men's minds, and to what degree it has soured and leavened the tempers of persons formerly esteemed some of the most sweet and affable, is too well known here to need any further proof or presentation of the matter.

No generous and impartial person, then, can blame the present undertaking, which is designed purely for the diversion and merriment of the reader. Pieces of pleasantry and mirth have a secret charm in them to allay the heats and tumors of our spirits and to make man forget his restless resentments. They have a strange power in them to hush disorders of the soul, and reduce us to a serene and placid state of mind.

Not long thereafter Benjamin Franklin, who found his brother a hard taskmaster, moved on toward Philadelphia; but for three years the *Courant* continued with his name at the masthead, unmolested. Toward the end it became less obstreperous and lost popularity. It seems to have died of inanition in 1727. John Franklin, another of the brothers, invited James to Newport, and he moved his printing press to that settlement.

Most mettlesome from first to last of those early Boston papers was the *Massachusetts Spy*, founded by Isaiah Thomas when he was twenty-seven. Under a Charleston date line it said, in its second issue, August 14, 1770, that if the Non-Importation Agreement against Britain, adopted by all the colonies except Georgia, failed of effect, they would cease commerce with the West Indies unless they also entered; and presently it was saying, in a letter from Williamsburg, Virginia, that a boycott had been adopted there on British paper, glass, paints, and tea, because of the tax. Such items set the tone of the paper.

Thomas spread across his little sheet on July 7, 1774, what he called a "new device," a dragon and snake cut into eight parts, with a motto beneath: "Join or Die." The dragon represented Britain, and the snake the dis-

Newspaper Crusaders

united colonies. The head and throat were labeled as New England, crying, "Unite and Conquer!"; other sections denoted various colonies and settlements. This famous cartoon, probably the first to be used on this continent for crusading purposes, is attributed by Princeton's *Public Opinion Quarterly* of July, 1937, to Benjamin Franklin; certainly it appeared in his *Pennsylvania Gazette* on May 9, 1754, and was widely copied. Actually its initial issue was in the *Constitutional Courant* of Burlington, New Jersey. The paper was instantly suppressed as seditious and did not reappear.

The *Spy* had the citizenry of Boston on its side, and printed the cartoon with impunity. More, it was full of such items as this: "We learn from Providence that last Thursday fortnight [the item appeared March 17, 1775] a great number of the inhabitants assembled in the market place there, and after kindling a large fire, they threw in about 500 weight of tea, as a free will offering of that precious herb collected from the several inhabitants."

This was some two years after the Boston Tea Party. John Hyde Preston, in "Revolution, 1776," gives credit for that adventure to Sam Adams, who was a failure in the law and in various business attempts but a past-master of propaganda. He was a "born rebel," Mr. Preston says. First he seized on the Boston Massacre, which occurred when British customs officers tried to collect duty on a shipload of Madeira wine smuggled in by John Hancock. Most New England merchants were smugglers in those days, but our schoolbooks fail to tell us about it. They neglect also to inform us that the first armed rebellion against Britain in New England was not at Lexington or Concord but at Newcastle, New Hampshire, where the colonists took over Fort William and Mary on Decem-

A Neglected Story

ber 14, 1774, and removed the powder and guns to Durham. The first Tea Party, according to a New Hampshire guide book compiled by Works Progress Administration writers, was at Exeter.

As for the Boston Massacre, Sam Adams persuaded Paul Revere, who was an engraver and silversmith, to make a cartoon showing orderly citizens—not a riotous mob—being mowed down by a firing squad. This was broadcast as a handbill, not in the papers. It proved effective anti-British publicity, quite in the picture of the methods of Adams.

Thanks largely to the Colonial boycott on tea, the East India Company was near bankruptcy and determined to relieve itself of its overstock by building warehouses in Boston, Philadelphia, and New York, so as to undersell the Holland tea smuggled in by the settlers. This caused a great to-do; Hancock and his fellow merchants in those cities had warehouses well stocked, and feared that the value of their illicit goods would be cut in half.

"Abstract ideas about liberty and greed for commercial profits were so intermingled in the minds of the 'patriots'," says Mr. Preston, "that it is hard to be certain which was stronger. But only a few artists of rebellion, like Sam Adams, wanted independence for its own sake; and even he was not entirely selfless. Revolution would bring him fame, and his hunger for fame was all-consuming." He hails Adams as the father of the revolution.

More than any one else, Adams inflamed the colonists against the British plan to undersell local merchants. Three British ships arrived at Boston with cargoes of tea valued at $75,000; and it was he who encouraged fifty Bostonians of the first families to paint and costume themselves as Indians and raid the crates of tea on the docks. Some at least were thrown into the harbor; there are reports that some were taken to shops and homes.

Unblushingly the *Gazette* printed an item about the Tea Party, which was a sort of glorified ruffianism. The *Spy* was discreetly silent on that point, but continued to berate the British. Government authorities attempted to silence it by libel actions, but found that they could not enroll grand juries which would indict. By order, the paper was publicly burned, but Isaiah Thomas went ahead undaunted. In North Carolina, loyalists hanged him in effigy but did not quench his spirit. He was the first to write a history of journalism in this country, or at least a history of printing, which appeared in 1810. In it he said:

> Common sense in common language is necessary to influence one class of citizens as much as learning and elegance are to produce an effect upon another. The cause of America is just; and it is only necessary to state this cause in a clear and impressive manner to unite the American people in its support.

So clearly and impressively did Thomas state that cause, before the Revolution, that the cautious John Adams urged him to abate his vehemence. The British put a price on his head; and on the eve of the outbreak of hostilities he fled. He found General Joseph Warren of Worcester in Boston with his oxcart, and persuaded him to move his heavy press, type case, and "make-up" stone. This Warren—who was killed at Bunker Hill— agreed to do; and the relics are now in the library of the American Antiquarian Society in Worcester. A room there is devoted to the ancient pieces. The press presents but little if any improvement over the press utilized by Gutenberg, credited with having invented printing,

A Neglected Story

when he struck off a page from movable type two and a half centuries earlier.

In Worcester the first issue of the *Spy* appeared on May 3, 1775. In the following year Thomas announced the Declaration of Independence dramatically to the town. Hancock had sent it by mounted messenger to George Washington in New York, with a request that it be relayed to the other colonies; and the courier taking a copy to Gen. Artemas Ward in Boston reached Worcester on July 14, which was a Sunday. When he pulled up in front of the King's Arms tavern and went inside for food and drink, Thomas espied him and obeyed his nose for news. From the messenger he obtained the document, and sent friends around to help gather the populace at one of the churches. From the porch that afternoon—for on a Sabbath no newspaper could be printed—he imparted the news by reading the Declaration impressively. He did not print it until the eighteenth, and the *Courant* in Boston had beaten him by three days. But John Dunlap of the *Pennsylvania Packet* had broadcast it as a poster on July 5, and Benjamin Towne on the next day published the text on pages One and Two of the *Pennsylvania Evening Post*.

How the colonists received the news, for which their more courageous papers had been campaigning and preparing them, may be judged from the account written by an eye witness of the reading by Thomas, now preserved by the Antiquarian Society in Worcester. The news was acclaimed "by demonstrations of joy and confidence," and "we were all so happy we did not know exactly what we did." The King's arms were torn from the tavern and from the court house, and were burned. There was a deal of punch drinking and merrymaking;

for the New Englanders, a God-fearing folk, were not averse to rum on occasion.

If I appear to have devoted undue attention to the Boston newspapers, it is because that town boasted seven pre-Revolutionary journals, while New York had but four, Virginia but two, some of the colonies but one, during that period; even when the Stamp Act was enacted, New Jersey and Delaware had none; furthermore, the tocsin call to freedom was sounded first in Boston, and most clearly. There, as elsewhere, both sides were represented; there were Whig and Tory organs, distinctly a "party press," notwithstanding the general notion that such a division did not come into being until after the birth of the Federalist party. The conflict between these groups was as distinctly forensic and political as though they represented major parties; and the names they adopted were political terms borrowed from their oppressors.

In England the Tories had been the successors of the Cavaliers; and they opposed the exclusion from the crown of the Duke of York, a Roman Catholic. The Whigs applied the nickname to identify them with outlawed Irish Papists, bullies, and ruffians. The term Whig likewise had a religious origin, having been applied in derision to Presbyterian rebels in Scotland, perhaps derived from the initials of the Covenanters' motto: "We Hope in God." It was a form also of the Scots Gaelic word for horse thieves. Henry Adams appears to have been justified when he defined politics as the organization of hatreds.

Not only political terms and institutions but literary manners were pilfered unblushingly by the colonists from

A Neglected Story

the empire whose yoke they meant to throw off. The flavor of Addison and Steele could be discerned in the essays, articles, and editorials contributed to Colonial journals by Sam and John Adams, Jonathan Mayhew, James Otis, Joseph Warren, Benjamin Austin, Jr., Thomas Cushing, Oxenbridge Thatcher, Samuel Dexter, Josiah Quincy, and Samuel Cooper.

That these brilliant rebels and their followers might have accomplished a revolution in time even without the help of crusading newspapers I would be the last to deny. It could have been done by word of mouth. It was so that Bacon's Rebellion in Virginia, the first civil war this country witnessed, was accomplished. Nathaniel Bacon, an English lawyer who had emigrated and settled on the upper James River, became a member of the cabinet of Governor William Berkeley, who thanked God there were no free schools and no printing, because they spread disobedience and heresy, and who hoped there would be none for another century. The Governor was, as Dr. Charles A. Beard and Mrs. Beard say in "The Rise of American Civilization," a man "frankly coarse and brutal." Bacon opposed his policy toward the Indians and was supported by the colonists; he demanded the abolition of exorbitant taxes, repeal of the new restrictions on the suffrage, and fought other evils. An expedition under his command in 1676 captured and destroyed Jamestown, but the uprising was put down with great severity by Berkeley. "The old fool," said Charles II when he learned of the executions; "he has taken more lives in that naked country than I for the murder of my father."

That, to be sure, was an isolated instance of armed resistance against the most callous and arrogant of the Colonial Governors; but it serves to illustrate what can be accomplished by an eloquent and determined leader with a good cause. The journals that fomented the Revolution supported such leaders and probably in some instances created them; but as a whole their grievance was not the brutality of a single executive; it was, to state it in general terms, the British mercantilist theory as applied to the colonies. That theory, as crystallized in law, is thus expressed by Charles M. Andrews in the fourth volume of his "The Colonial Period of American History":

> As far as they [the Colonies] could contribute to England's national stock of wealth and add to her strength and prosperity they were required to do so; and whether that contribution were important or otherwise, they were expected to conform to the principle, laid down in the very dawn of their history, that whatever of value a colony might furnish was to redound to the advantage of the State under whose aegis it had been established.

Therefore an act was passed in 1660 providing that the American and other colonies could neither import goods nor export them except in British bottoms; this was to build up the British merchant marine and afford customs revenues. As regards the settlers on this continent, the plan was never quite successful. Edward Randolph, chief surveyor of customs for expenses and a salary of one hundred pounds annually, journeyed wearily through the New World and reported endless violations of the law, ranging from smuggling to disregard of the acts of trade, the unlawful manufacture of woolen, and the felling of trees reserved for the navy. He made seventeen journeys across the Atlantic in an effort to arouse London, but his inefficient superiors gave him little help.

Meanwhile the colonists were asserting their rights more and more in their local legislatures and assemblies; and, abetted by their newspapers, they were outraged

A Neglected Story

when direct taxes were imposed to replace the indirect revenue through trade regulations. Primary among these was the Stamp Act, which bore upon the press rather than upon the merchants. But the newspapers did their share also in regard to the taxes on tea and other commodities, and encouraged wholesale boycotts.

Enacted in 1765, the British Stamp Tax on the American press was in imitation of an earlier English levy on newspapers there. It required printing on stamped paper costing a half-penny more, and taxed each advertisement two shillings. Printers here organized mobs to seize the stamped paper, and journals were issued on some occasions without the name of the publisher, on unstamped paper. William Bradford issued his *Pennsylvania Journal* on October 31 of that year with an array of skulls and crossbones across the top and with the column rules turned, to make them heavily black. He said the paper had died of "a stamp in its vitals." In 1760 there were but eighteen papers in the colonies, by 1770 there were thirty. Alfred McClung Lee, in "The Newspaper in America," attributes the increase mainly to the desire to fight this and other oppressive measures.

One objection to the Stamp Act was that it interfered with trial by jury in providing that any offender against it was to be tried in a royal marine or admiralty court, wherever complaint might be lodged, without regard to distance from the place of publication. One of the first to protest against it was Patrick Henry, who introduced into the Virginia House of Burgesses his resolution that the State alone had power to lay taxes, and charged that whoever maintained Britain had such a right was an enemy of the colony. It was in this speech, which the newspapers spread rapidly through the settlements, that Henry offered his celebrated peroration, amid cries of "Treason!" that "Caesar had his Brutus; Charles had his Cromwell; and George the Third may profit by their example. If that be treason, Sir, make the most of it."

With slight modifications, the resolution was adopted and Governor Fauquier in alarm prorogued the House. It was too late. The next issue of the *Maryland Gazette*, of which Charles Carroll of Carrollton was the moving spirit, carried the resolution in full, with an editorial of approval. Benjamin Franklin's *Pennsylvania Gazette* followed suit. Then the *Newport Mercury* joined the chorus, and was promptly suppressed for its pains. In Charleston the *South Carolina Gazette*, the *American General Gazette*, and the *Gazette and Country Journal* (three gazettes, mind you, the last established just for this action, in one town!) published the resolutions. New York got it from the *Gazette and Post-boy*. In Boston the same thing happened, and an editorial by John Adams in the *Gazette* there was printed in pamphlet form for circulation in London. It was moved in Parliament that the pamphlet be suppressed as traitorous. The motion was lost by a decisive vote. The Stamp Act roused such a furore that when it expired by limitation, May 1, 1757, it was not renewed.

Among the Tory papers was the New York *Gazetteer*, later the *Royal Gazette*, under the editorship of James Rivington, who lied loyally in editorials and in news reports. Among the contributors to his paper were Myles Cooper, president of Kings, later Columbia, College; the Rev. John Vardill, a satirist of talent; Isaac Wilkins, a writer of influence; and Attorney General Seabury. Its circulation is said to have reached 3,600—for it numbered loyalists in all the colonies among its subscribers—and

A Neglected Story

this, if true, was quite as large as any newspaper then enjoyed, even in England. John Jay and Philip Livingston called on Rivington for the source of his false statements but got no satisfaction, nor did he mend his ways. Later, to be sure, he apologized to the Continental Congress; but in the meantime he violently assailed Isaac Sears, one of the more zealous of the Sons of Liberty, who had moved from New York to enlist a company of infantry at New Haven.

In retaliation, Sears rode into New York with his men, armed to the teeth, recruited some reinforcements, demolished Rivington's plant, and carried away the type to be melted later for bullets. At this, one may be certain, there was a great loyalist outcry about an invasion of the freedom of the press.

John Mein, editor of the subsidized Boston *Chronicle*, a Tory organ, poked fun at the sour-faced Puritans and lambasted the Whigs with a will. Sometimes he filled an entire page of his paper with advertisements of his own books. He was subjected to various indignities and finally, under a charge of having insulted the populace, was compelled to leave the country. Ezekiel Russell, of the Portsmouth *Mercury* in New Hampshire, was paid by the British to attack the "patriots," and his paper lasted only three years after it was founded in 1765. In Boston the *Evening Post*, published by Thomas Fleet and then by his sons, attempted to carry water on both shoulders, so as to avoid prosecution and still gain a circulation, and, for some forty years, carried on; it went out of existence almost immediately after the Revolution became a fact.

Tory papers, however, were in the minority. It cannot be said that they were without influence, because even after overt hostilities had begun there was a large body of sentiment on this continent sympathetic with Britain, and strongly in favor of the monarchic form of government. The pro-British editors did not fulminate in vain, and their work required as much courage as the Whigs needed; for they faced the wrath of the colonists, whereas the protagonists of rebellion faced authorities who often were weak or timid.

Our most noteworthy instance of the freedom of the press arose in the case of John Peter Zenger, editor of the New York *Weekly Journal* and a Crusader of authentic type. The paper was established November 5, 1733, in opposition to Bradford's *Gazette*, the Tory organ. From the first it was replete with animadversions upon Governor Cosby and his henchmen, and on November 6, 1734, the Governor issued a proclamation that it contained "divers scandalous, virulent, false, and seditious reflections," offering a reward of fifty pounds for information as to the authors of these pieces. He directed that certain copies be burned by the hangman near the pillory. Finally after Zenger had criticized him for permitting a French man-of-war to anchor in the harbor, he brought an action for libel to silence the editor.

This case, described by Gouverneur Morris as "the dawn of that liberty which afterwards revolutionized America," has been the subject of so much attention that I need do no more than summarize it here. Zenger was thrown into jail because he could not meet unreasonable bond requirements, and continued to get out his paper from prison. When New York lawyers were too fearful of authority to defend him, Andrew Hamilton of Philadelphia, an exceptionally able man and a friend of Benjamin Franklin, took over the case successfully.

A Neglected Story

Zenger was acquitted, largely through his lawyer's skill and eloquence; Hamilton was feted, escorted with huzzahs to his boat, and received a salute of ordnance as he was ferried across the river. The editor remained at his desk until near death, and passed on his paper to his son.

The "Virginia-Centinel Papers," published in the *Virginia Gazette* in 1756, were widely reprinted; so were other papers denouncing the Mutiny Act, which the English Parliament re-enacted annually after 1689 to provide for cases of mutiny or desertion in the colonies. Tom Paine appeared in the *Pennsylvania Journal* of January 4, 1775, with an imaginary dialogue between General Wolfe and General Gage, Wolfe rebuking Gage for leading redcoats against Americans.

Until 1758 the Colonial post-riders carried newspapers free. Then a rate was imposed, on the ground that "the newspapers of the several colonies on this continent, heretofore permitted to be sent by the post free of charge, are of late years so much increased as to be extremely burthensome to the riders." Gradually the rates were increased, on both letters and papers, until to send but a single letter sheet from New York to Philadelphia cost 12½ cents, to Baltimore 18¾ cents, to Richmond 25 cents. This closed correspondence by mail to all but the well-to-do and limited newspaper circulation, although the varying rates in that department were not so severe. Daniel Webster offered a resolution in the Senate in 1840 to reorganize the system, but vainly. The zoning method continued until 1847, when after seven years of windy debate Congress consented to the use of stamps. Indeed, the zoning system as applied to books, one of our avenues of communication and culture, continued until 1938, when it was terminated, at least temporarily, by executive order. The post-office record of this country is bespotted with incidents as backward as this, or worse.

Campaigning by pre-Revolutionary editors undoubtedly hastened the overthrow of British rule, perhaps made it possible. As the Beards put it in their "Rise of American Civilization":

> The political and cultural significance of this early American journalism, crude as it appears to the sophisticated of modern times, can hardly be overestimated. If narrow in its range, it was wider and freer than the pulpit and the classroom and it was an art open to any person, group, faction, or party that could buy a press and exercise enough literary skill to evade the heavy hand of colonial authorities . . . Clearly the institution of the press, operating, at least in a measure, on a national scale, was prepared to serve the lawyers and politicians who were to kindle the flames of revolution.

VI

Constitution and Amendments

THOMAS JEFFERSON and Alexander Hamilton have served as convenient symbols of opposed political thought when this republic was in the making. We think of them as statesmen, which they were, but they exercised a deep journalistic influence also. Both of them wrote for their party organs, but not under their own names. Jefferson, moreover, was responsible for the Bill of Rights, guaranteeing freedom of the press, which Hamilton ridiculed. Hamilton's faction (over his protest) was responsible for the Sedition Act, an attempt to gag the press.

Philip Freneau was editor of the *National Gazette*, Jefferson's principal organ; John Fenno had charge of the *United States Gazette*, chief mouthpiece for Hamilton and his Federalist followers, although they promoted also the New York *Evening Post*. Freneau was a crusader for democratic processes, Fenno for a highly centralized government; and both of them were more severe in their criticism of opponents than partisan editors nowadays are likely to be.

Jefferson said Fenno's paper was "strong for a king, Lords, and Commons." That view was repeated in a paragraph which appeared in Freneau's paper during the candidacy of John Adams for the presidency in 1792:

> The mask is at last torn from the monarchical party, who have, but with too much success, imposed themselves upon the public for the sincere friends of our republican constitution. Whatever may be the event of the competition for the vice-presidency, it has been the happy occasion of ascertaining the two following important truths: first, that the name of Federalist has been assumed by men who approve the constitution merely as "a promising essay towards a well ordered government"; that is to say, as a step towards a government of kings, Lords, and Commons. Secondly, that the spirit of the people continues firmly republican, and if the monarchical features of the party had been sooner held up to the public view, would have universally marked the division between two candidates (equally unassailed in their private characters) one of whom is as much attached to the equal principles of liberty entertained by the great mass of his fellow citizens, as the other is devoted to the hereditary titles, orders, and balances, which they abhor as an insult to the rights and dignity of man.

It seems highly probable that Jefferson wrote that orotund paragraph. Freneau admitted in his later life, although he had denied it earlier, that Jefferson dictated or penned many of the articles and editorials directed against Washington, Hamilton, and other Federalists; he even exhibited a file in which the contributions were marked. Jefferson, while his part in the campaign was still in the dark, said that the *National Gazette* had "saved our Constitution, which was galloping fast into monarchy." This was when Washington indicated that he would like to have his Secretary of State discharge Freneau, who was a translating clerk in his department. "I will not do it," Jefferson said.

Let it be said at once that the newspapers of that day did not report the proceedings of the Constitutional Convention in Philadelphia in 1787. The Founding Fathers assembled there "for the sole purpose of revising

A Neglected Story

the Articles of Confederation," under which this nation was drifting rapidly, as John Adams observed, toward "convulsion and anarchy." Since the intention was to throw those articles out of the window and frame a new document, the delegates met behind locked doors, with an armed sentry on duty; and when the elderly Ben Franklin took a walk another delegate accompanied him, lest his garrulity betray the true purpose of the Convention.

Rhode Island was not represented, and Massachusetts took care not to send the turbulent Sam Adams. Jefferson was in France as our ambassador, Tom Paine was in England on a business mission, and Patrick Henry, who was elected a delegate, refused to attend because, he explained, he "smelt a rat." The liberal wing of colonial opinion was but feebly in evidence, and the document as drawn safeguarded no civil liberties save the right of habeas corpus.

All but six of the fifty-five delegates had been soundly educated in the colonies or abroad, and they were familiar with the history and structure of government since the days of ancient Greece and Rome. For the most part they were well read in Montesquieu and were much impressed by his admiration of the English system of checks and balances. They merit the high praise which has been accorded to their statesmanship. Their deliberations are known, thanks to the fact that James Madison took copious notes of them.

The newspaper fight began after the Constitution had been framed, with the provision that it should become effective when ratified by nine of the thirteen States, as among those nine. It was a stiff fight, for sixteen of the delegates failed to sign, and it became bruited about that Hamilton and his followers favored an elective monarchy.

Although dissatisfied, Hamilton agreed to do what he could "to prop the frail and worthless document"; at least it was better than "convulsion and anarchy"; and Jefferson, who had returned from France, was persuaded to lend his support on condition that a Bill of Rights would be tacked on as amendments and adopted. Not all the States could be persuaded to enter the Union until the first ten amendments had been passed.

Noah Webster thought his editorials in the *Mercury* of New York were the mainspring in ratifying the Constitution; John Hancock thought that Major Benjamin Russell's *Centinel* in Boston had turned the tide, certainly in Massachusetts. The real power was the "Federalist," a series of eighty-six able papers written by Hamilton, John Jay, and James Madison and first printed in newspapers friendly to them. It was in one of these contributions, while Jefferson's amendments were pending—the first safeguarding freedom of speech, conscience, and the press—that Hamilton said:

> What signifies a declaration, that "the liberty of the press shall be inviolably preserved"? What is the liberty of the press? Who can give it any definition which would not leave the utmost latitude for evasion? I hold it to be impracticable; and from this I infer that its security, whatever fine declarations may be inserted in any constitution respecting it, must altogether depend on public opinion, and on the general spirit of the people and the government. And here, after all, as is intimated upon another occasion, we must seek for the only solid basis of all our rights.

Doubtless the ablest sustained political crusading ever witnessed in this country arose in the fight for and against the Constitution and Jefferson's amendments. Two of the amendments written by him, the first relating to the apportionment of representatives in the House and the second to the pay of members of both houses, were defeated, so that the Bill of Rights, as it was called then and is called now, consisted of the third to the twelfth clauses he submitted.

Opposition in the Continental Congress and among the informed public to the Constitution, on the ground that it did not safeguard State sovereignty nor civil liberties, led to an agreement regarding the amendments but did not prevent Hamilton and his followers from picking flaws in them, in their newspaper outgivings. Both sides won, for the Constitution was adopted and so were the amendments.

Hamilton wrote the bulk of the papers advocating ratification. The first, which he wrote, was published in the *Independent Journal* in New York, October 27, 1787, and was followed by seventy-five more, until April 2, 1788, all signed "Publius." Madison and Jay wrote part of them, and it has been said that a few more were contributed by William Alexander Duer, a brother of John Duer, president of Columbia College. William Duer was author of "Constitutional Jurisprudence in the United States," and an able lawyer.

The *Daily Advertiser* in New York printed all the articles, and it was this paper, apparently, which Madison read, for he kept a file. Other newspapers followed suit when they were friendly to Hamilton and his group, so that the essays were spread well through the States which were to pass on the question in convention. The *Independent Journal*, which had taken the lead, was printed by J. and A. McLean at 41 Hanover Square; and the brothers collected the papers into two volumes called "The Federalist."

Isaiah Thomas, in his "History of Printing," set down a table of the newspaper line-up during the controversy, without regard to a few which maintained a middle-of-the-road attitude. In New Hampshire, eight were for the Constitution and two against it; in Massachusetts, the score was twenty to eleven; in Rhode Island, four to three; in Connecticut, ten to one; in Vermont, nine to six; in New York, twenty-nine to twenty-seven; in New Jersey, three to five, yet this State was third to ratify, by unanimous vote; in Pennsylvania, thirty-four to twenty-nine; in Delaware, none were in favor and two opposed, yet Delawate was first to adopt the Constitution by unanimous vote of its convention; in Maryland, nine to eleven; in the District of Columbia, two to three; in Virginia, seven to fifteen; in South Carolina, four to four; in Georgia, three to seven; in Kentucky, two to fourteen; in Tennessee, one to five; in Mississippi, one to one; in the "Territory of Orleans," five to one. The tabulation, if correct, gave a total of 151 newspapers in favor of ratification to 137 against it.

In Massachusetts no newspaper maintained a more constant fire for the Constitution than Major Russell's *Centinel*. Hudson suggests in his history that its energy and persistence gave the cue to Bennett's New York *Herald* in later years, when campaigning for some important measure. Major Russell called meetings of mechanics to adopt resolutions and send them to the State convention, and announced in triumph ratifications in other States. He himself reported the proceedings of the convention in Boston, and at first sat in the pulpit of the church where it was held, but was voted out of it, owing to "puritanical notions." A stand was fitted up for him in another place. When word came that Virginia had accepted the Constitution, "there was a most extraordinary outbreak of rejoicing," Major Russell reported. "It

A Neglected Story

seemed as if the meeting-house would burst with the acclamation."

Isaiah Thomas in the *Massachusetts Spy* supported the Constitution also, but he was earnest in advocating the use of titles, and spoke of George Washington as "His Highness the President General." John Dickinson, founder of the college bearing his name, who had been a member of the Colonial Congress in 1765, of the Continental Congress in 1774, and then of the Constitutional Convention, wrote his advocacy of the document under the pen name of "Fabius."

Foremost among the New York newspapers opposing the Constitution was the *Journal and Daily Patriotic Register*, of which Thomas Greenleaf was editor. He had learned to set type in the shop of the *Spy*, for a time had worked on the *Independent Chronicle* in Boston, and was a son of that Joseph Greenleaf whose pre-Revolutionary writings had incensed the royal authorities. By tradition and by preference he was suspicious of those who leaned toward monarchy and centralized government; under the name of "Brutus" in the *Journal* he wrote a series of articles answering those which went to make up "The Federalist," expressing the same fear as Jefferson, that the presidency would become a hereditary monarchy, and that the States would be submerged. When New York ratified the Constitution, and held a parade to celebrate the event, Greenleaf devoted a column of his paper to ridicule of the pageant, and aroused such resentment that a mob broke into his office, in spite of his firing twice at the oncomers, and destroyed the plant. His paper is credited with having been the first to espouse Jeffersonian theories in this country.

Newspaper Crusaders

Benjamin Austin, Jr., of the Boston *Chronicle* carried on in that city against the *Centinel*, and once sued Major Russell successfully for damages. In Providence, a town predominantly Federalist, the *Phoenix*, opposing the Constitution, attracted more attention that the *Gazette*, which favored it, because the *Phoenix* was a livelier and better edited paper.

B. F. Bache's *General Advertiser* in Philadelphia, later called the *Aurora*, was another of the outstanding journals in opposition, and once called a Federalist organ "a sink of prostitution." The phrase is quoted as showing that the newspapers campaigning against the Constitution ran rather to epithet than to the forensic dignity of the "Federalist" essays. As a fact, their weakness lay in their having no acceptable substitute to offer, provided Jefferson's Amendments were accepted; for under the Articles of Confederation there was no executive head of the States, Congress had authority to appropriate money but no power to raise funds by levying taxes, and the States, issuing floods of continental currency, which soon became worthless, were raising tariff barriers against each other. "Convulsion and anarchy" loomed in the immediate offing unless drastic action were taken, and the Constitution provided a drastic change.

George Henry Payne, who discerned clearly the influence of Jefferson and Hamilton, says in his "History of Journalism":

For the next twenty years [after the Revolution] the press of the country was practically under the dominance of two men; and though both would have indignantly resented the suggestion that their activities brought them within the classification of active journalists, of one of them, at least, Alexander Hamilton, it is true that his public career after the war was as

A Neglected Story

closely identified with the journalism of the country as were the men who actually earned their living by writing for and printing the newspapers.

With the prejudices against the trade—prejudices inherited from England, the social ideas of which still dominated the nation—it was understandable that men who prided themselves on being "gentlemen" should disown too close an association with a calling such as "Printing," which had yet to live down its early stigma.

Jefferson, to be sure, contributed to Freneau's paper; but Hamilton and Jay, not contented with the *Gazette of the United States*, promoted the New York *Evening Post* (it was the third incarnation of that name, each paper independent of its predecessors), started the Baltimore *Anti-Democrat*, and subsidized other dailies. James Melvin Lee estimates that the Federalists controlled three-fourths of the press in this country in 1800.

Once the Constitution had been adopted, the Amendments ratified, and Washington elected President, the newspapers which sympathized with the Jefferson group opened their fire on the administration. Washington said that Freneau's *National Gazette* and Bache's *General Advertiser* were "outrages on common decency" and that the opposition press in general upbraided the treaty with England, after the Revolution, "in such exaggerated and indecent terms as could scarcely be applied to a Nero, to a notorious defaulter, or even to a common pickpocket." After Washington had retired to Mount Vernon, Bache rejoiced that he was no longer in the capital "to give currency to political iniquity and to legalize corruption."

It must not be supposed that the Federalist press was kindlier toward Jefferson; its editors denounced him as an agrarian, a leveler, an atheist, a demagogue, and an anarchist. He had remained in France until after the revolution began there and he was one of those who welcomed Citizen Genêt as minister to this country, in

December, 1792. He and those who agreed with him were denounced by Hamilton, Washington, and the others of their faction as Jacobins, this being the name of the French revolutionary group which had set up the Reign of Terror. Even in that day there was a "red scare" in this country. Washington accused Jacobin sympathizers in this country of fomenting the Whiskey Rebellion in western Pennsylvania.

Genêt's chief mission was to enlist this country in a war against England. When Washington, in part at least by reason of Hamilton's advice, refused to enter any "entangling alliances," the French Minister appealed over his head through the opposition newspapers to the public. Vermont farmers planted "liberty trees" in honor of the Paris government, and in New York young "reds" wore long trousers to indicate how they stood. Thereupon Hamilton wrote a series of articles under the pen name of "No Jacobin," which were printed in the *Daily Advertiser* and copied in Fenno's paper. Washington, in as great concern as any ever inspired by the Bolsheviki or the Stalinists, demanded the recall of Citizen Genêt.

In those days the Senate met behind closed doors. This aroused Freneau, who demanded that the sessions be open to the public. "The Peers of America," he said editorially, "disdain to be seen by vulgar eyes . . . Secrecy is necessary to design and a masque to treachery." He kept up that sort of thing until the doors of the Senate were opened. From the first the House admitted "shorthand reporters" for newspapers in the capital, on the thrifty policy of requiring copies for the *Congressional Record;* but during the very first session, in 1789, Aedanus Burke of South Carolina introduced a resolution that the reporters had "misrepresented these debates in the most

A Neglected Story

glaring deviations from truth." A prolonged debate ensued. One Representative said he would rather "submit to all the inconveniences of ridicule than sacrifice a valuable publication of useful and interesting information to his constituents." Burke finally withdrew his resolution, but said contemptuously that he could not approve of "sacrificing the honor and dignity of the House by putting it in the power of the printers." It was not until the day of the elder James Gordon Bennett, as a result of a campaign he waged in the *Herald*, that reporters for newspapers outside Washington were admitted to the House. It is clear from the whole record that the Founding Fathers were chary about taking into their confidence the people, whom Hamilton described as "a great beast."

Not the Constitution, which by its provision for an Electoral College repudiated majority rule, and which was ratified, it has been estimated, by about one-sixth of the adult white males in the thirteen States, but the amendments, bespeak the will of the people whom Hamilton despised and whose "passions" and "turbullence" stirred the fear of most of the other delegates to the Philadelphia convention. If we except the three "reconstruction clauses," and the Eighteenth and the Twenty-first Amendments, which cancel, the process of change in the original document has been a process of liberalization. More than half the amendments as they stand were written by Jefferson, and these ten were adopted in part by reason of prior verbal agreements, in part by a vigorous but scattering support in the colonial press. They were limitations on the powers of Congress, not of the States.

The Thirteenth, Fourteenth and Fifteenth were the "reconstruction amendments," and they were ratified under duress by some of the southern States while under military rule, as the price of their return into the Union. The necessary three-fourths vote was procured by force of arms, without the need of a journalistic crusade. It is true that for years Connecticut, New Jersey, Pennsylvania, Ohio, and other northern States disregarded their provisions for enfranchisement and protection of the Negro as flagrantly as ever the prohibition amendment was flouted. It is true, too, that newspapers have commented acidly on the twisting of the Fourteenth Amendment, under the Supreme Court's interpretation of the "due process" clause that corporations are persons, into a meaning which could not have been foreseen by multitudes who voted for it in Congress and out. But none of them have been the subject of an organized newspaper campaign.

The Eighteenth Amendment was the fruit of a century-long newspaper crusade, supplemented in its later stages by a powerful lobby at Washington. Its repeal likewise was due mainly to agitation in the press. All the amendments since the Fifteenth have been ratified with the help of powerful newspaper support. After the Supreme Court had overridden the will of Congress in passing an act taxing incomes, by declaring it unconstitutional, the electorate, by a long and difficult process, made possible by the Sixteenth Amendment this levy, which is in strict accord with ability to pay.

The next amendment, stipulating that United States senators should be elected by popular vote, quite altered the complexion of the upper House and appeared to put an end to such bosses as Mark Hanna. The Nineteenth, giving suffrage to women, became effective in August, 1920; we should have taken this progressive step much earlier. The Twentieth, altering the terms of the President and Vice President and of members of Congress, abolished the "lame duck" sessions which had been an impediment to democratic processes.

Although the operation of the Electoral College was altered by the Twelfth Amendment, the College remains in the Constitution like a vermiform appendix. Possibly the next amendment will be an appendectomy. The device was an expression of the distrust cherished by the Founding Fathers of "the people," and more than once has made President a candidate who had received a minority of the votes, while according to other candidates a much poorer showing than the balloting justified. It is a cumbrous relic of the day when horror would have greeted any suggestion of a government of the people, for the people, and by the people. (Lincoln was a minority candidate, who owed his election to the Electoral College.) The pious intention of the Founding Fathers was that the College should be a gathering of the best minds, free to choose at will a good executive. That intention has come to naught. The electors now are little more than clerks, who sign on the dotted line. As early as 1876, when James Russell Lowell was an elector during the contest between Hayes and Tilden, it was suggested that he vote for Tilden and he was horrified; he had been sent there to vote for Hayes.

Admittedly there are objections to altering an institution, however mistaken, once the political machines and the electorate have become accustomed to it; but this is the sort of campaign which might be undertaken successfully by the daily press, or by a chain of newspapers, such as the Hearst properties. Abolishment of the Electoral College, for one thing, would result assuredly in a successful attempt to get more and more voters to the polls, which is sadly needed.

It remains to take note of a series of proposed amendments which failed ignominiously because no competent newspaper campaign was undertaken in their behalf. They were framed at the Hartford Convention, which met December 15, 1814, behind locked doors, and adjourned the following January 5. In response to a call by the Massachusetts legislature, twelve delegates from that State including George Cabot, who presided; seven from Connecticut and four from Rhode Island, named by their legislatures; two from New Hampshire and one from Vermont, representing county organizations, framed a report protesting against the War of 1812 and complaining that the United States had refused to meet the expense of defending Massachusetts and Connecticut because these two had refused to lend their militia to the government forces. All the delegates were Federalists, and Madison, whom they opposed, was President.

The call for the convention said that it was "for the purpose of devising proper measures to procure the united efforts of the commercial States, to obtain such amendments and explanations of the Constitution as will secure them from further evils." It was, then, a line-up of the commercial northeastern States against the planting and agricultural southern and western States, which were politically in the saddle. Agrarian majorities dominated both Houses of Congress. The delegates drew up a series of amendments to the Constitution, one providing that slaves should not be counted in Congressional representation, that a two-thirds vote be required for the admission of new States (for the new units then being created were agricultural), for an embargo on foreign commerce, or for a resolution to declare war, save in case of invasion. The report embodying these amendments ended on a threat of nullification and secession. It was futile; the amendments did not get even to a popular vote.

In some quarters that secret convention was regarded as treasonable. Even among the Federalist newspapers it did not win wide support. It is true that Theodore Dwight, editor of the *Daily Advertiser* in New York, acted as secretary of the proceedings and advocated the resolutions in his paper; but, although William Coleman, editor of the New York *Evening Post*, a stout Federalist organ, went to Hartford to find out what he could of the news, his vigorous opposition was credited with having prevented New York from sending delegates, and he was unsparing in his arguments against the proposed amendments. As the spokesman for Hamilton and Jay, his word carried weight. Other less influential Federalist journals were hardly less emphatic. As for the opposition papers, although in the minority, they were torn between derision and high indignation. The Civil War and secession were less than half a century distant, yet we find the Richmond *Enquirer* saying:

> No man, no association of men, no State or set of States has a right to withdraw itself from this union of its own accord . . . The majority of States which form the union must consent to the withdrawal of any one branch of it. Until that consent has been obtained, any attempt to dissolve the union or to obstruct the efficacy of its constitutional laws, is Treason—Treason to all intents and purposes.

Newspaper Crusaders

This in general was the response in southern newspapers, which for the most part had supported the Kentucky and Virginia Resolutions, calling for nullification and secession, in spirit much like the resolutions adopted at Hartford. Centrifugal forces in the North and South, tending to disrupt the nation, found expression and were opposed at different times by the editors of both those sections.

VII

Suppression and Warfare

OHN ADAMS went in a coach and six to the Capitol to deliver his inaugural and like Washington, his predecessor, was accused of speaking as if from the throne. He once described Washington as "one-third Whig; one-third Tory; the rest mongrel."

Advocating "government by an aristocracy of talents and wealth," and convinced that the Federalists enjoyed a monopoly of those blessings, Adams won by three votes in the Electoral College. He was no orator and no campaigner, but his party was heavily preponderant. As Jefferson, the opposing candidate, was second in the poll, he became Vice President. From the first Adams put on so much side that he was subjected to the jeers of hostile editors, but not until he signed the Alien and Sedition Acts did a real newspaper storm break out.

The Alien Act, empowering the President in case of war to imprison or deport persons of foreign birth, caused a deal of resentment, but it was not put to use and need not concern us here. The Sedition Act was meant to silence orators and newspapers who ventured to criticize the administration. A fine of $5,000 and imprisonment for five years were the maximum penalties imposed for opposing any Federal measure, impeding the operation of any law, writing, printing, publishing, or quoting any false, scandalous, or malicious sentiments which might bring into disrepute the government, its officers, or either House of Congress. This was not a war measure. Hamilton warned his fellow Federalists: "Let us not establish a tyranny. Energy is a very different thing from violence."

In this new country there were then some two hundred newspapers, of which not more than twenty-five were militantly opposed to Adams; but he, haughty and thin-skinned, could not tolerate their shafts. He vowed that the Sedition Act was not his doing, but the work of Hamilton, and his prior record seemed to many to bear out his protest. He had signed the Declaration of Independence and so subscribed to "certain unalienable Rights." In paying tribute to Edes and Gill, printers of the Boston *Gazette*, he had said:

> None of the means of communication are more sacred, or have been cherished with more tenderness and care by the settlers of America than the press. Care should be taken that the art of printing should be encouraged, and that it should be easy and cheap and safe for any person to communicate his thoughts to the public . . . Be not intimidated, therefore, by any terrors, from publishing with the utmost freedom . . .

Yet after signing the Sedition Act, a gesture which spoke volumes, Adams indicated in a letter to Timothy Pickering, his Secretary of State, that it was not enough to silence William Duane, successor to Benjamin Franklin Bache as editor of the rambunctious *Aurora*. "The matchless effrontery of this Duane," he wrote, "merits the execution of the Alien Law. I am very willing to try its strength on him."

To deport Duane was impossible, because he had been born near Lake Champlain in New York. He was indicted for seditious editorials, severely beaten by admirers of Adams, and sent to prison. His sponsor, Dr. Thomas Cooper, author, lecturer, and clergyman, also was arrested for sedition, because he had criticized Adams in the *Sunbury and Northumberland Gazette;* he was fined and jailed.

In Boston, the *Independent Chronicle* was outspoken against the Alien and Sedition Acts and praised a member of the Massachusetts legislature who held the same views. This was construed as a libel on the legislature, and Thomas Adams, the editor, was indicted; he was ill and Abijah Adams, his bookkeeper, was arrested. His counsel contended that the English common law, under which the libel act was framed, was inconsistent with the Constitution of the State. Judge Dana, a good Federalist, declared from the bench that the English common law was "the birthright of every American." Adams was fined costs, sent to jail for thirty days, and put under bond for one year. The *Chronicle* printed a paragraph when he was liberated: "Yesterday, Mr. Abijah Adams was discharged from his imprisonment, after partaking of an *adequate proportion* of his 'birthright' by a confinement of thirty days under the operation of the Common Law of England."

James Thompson Callender, who had worked for Bache on the *Aurora*, set up the Richmond *Examiner* to fight the Federalists and was especially vigorous in denunciation of the Sedition Act. He was tried before Judge Samuel Chase (afterward elevated to the Supreme Court), who charged the Marshal not to let any of those "rascally Democrats" get on the jury, and sentenced Callender to nine months in prison. While there, the editor continued his attacks on the President.

Ten editors and printers were convicted under the Sedition Act; some were acquitted.

Jefferson drafted a set of resolutions, declaring the Alien and Sedition Acts in violation of the Constitution, therefore null and void. The Kentucky legislature passed the resolutions and the Governor signed them; then James Madison, who had assisted in drafting them, got them through the Virginia legislature, inviting other States to cooperate. The Massachusetts legislature, in disapproval of this, declared the Acts constitutional, and that it was the business of the Supreme Court to pass on such matters. Thereupon Kentucky proclaimed the revolutionary doctrine that a State could review an act of Congress and nullify it if unconstitutional, and Virginia appropriated funds for arms and supplies. The issue of the Alien and Sedition Acts became a factor in the campaign which ensued and caused the overthrow of the Federalists.

Jefferson, made President by what he liked to call "the great revolution of 1800," (he thought that a revolution of some sort was necessary every once in so often) remitted the penalties of the editors who had crusaded against Adams and the Sedition Act, and in most cases Congress reimbursed them. The President set afoot the impeachment of Judge Chase, by now an associate justice of the Supreme Court. No one who reads the record can doubt that the impeachment was merited, but the Federalist majority in the Senate made the effort abortive.

Jefferson's inaugural, which ran to but 1400 words, was printed the next day in the newspapers at the capital and in due season, for mails traveled slowly in those days, in the hostile New York *Evening Post*. The *Post*, however, contained no comment on it for three days, perhaps because William Coleman was awaiting editorial advice from Hamilton and Governor John Jay; and then it took the form of a letter to the editor, signed "Lucius Crassus." Afterward, Coleman's comment was vigorous enough.

Jefferson's Republicans, termed Democrats in that day as an epithet but later to adopt the name as a party designation, were smarting under the severity of Federalist judges, such as Dana and Chase, before whom their editors had been arraigned. John Adams had sat up until after midnight on his last day in office, signing commissions for Federalists to take office, many of them in the courts. If ousters were impossible, as in the case of Chase, there remained another recourse: the law creating the judgeships was repealed despite the outraged cries of Federalist editors and Senators that this was an "assault upon the judiciary" and would wreck the Constitution. A new law was enacted, and Republican (or Democratic) judges were put on the bench.

If the War of 1812 could properly be entitled "the second war for independence," as it sometimes is, it would be difficult to understand why a large part of the press fought stoutly, and with impunity, against waging it. It is true that the slogan most generally heard in that day was "Free Trade and Sailors' Rights"; it is true that English frigates and merchantmen had captured American ships, searched them, and impressed some of their sailors into service; it is true that a great to-do was made about depredations on our merchant marine. But

Julius W. Pratt and Charles A. Beard have demonstrated satisfactorily by their researches that these were not the underlying causes of the war.

New England shipowners, upon whom our high-seas losses fell most heavily, were strongly opposed as a group against taking up arms. For one thing, they thought an attack on the British would help Napoleon, who was anathema to them; for another thing, and this was more important, they feared the admission of additional agricultural States, through the acquisition of new territory, and the loss of commercial power in Congress and in the government.

Those advocating the war were southern planters who wanted more land and frontiersmen who were angered because the English were lending aid to their traditional enemies, the Indians. The principal "war hawks" in Congress were John C. Calhoun of South Carolina, who wanted to annex the Floridas and Mexico, and Henry Clay of Kentucky who, although he spoke for the frontiersmen, proposed that we take Canada. The senators and representatives who voted to "recognize" a state of war did not represent commercial or industrial interests; they represented the South and the border States.

Thus it was that the New England newspapers generally opposed the war, which indeed reflected in the outcome no great credit upon their country except in seamanship and valor; while southern newspapers, as well as newspapers in the States then under settlement through the westward movement, were strongly in its favor. There were a few exceptions, two of which deserve attention.

A Neglected Story

One of these was the Albany *Argus* established by New York Democrats particularly to support the war party. Martin Van Buren and William L. Marcy were contributors to its columns. Subsequently Marcy, as United States senator from New York, was credited with having coined the phrase, "To the Victor Belong the Spoils." They were central figures of what was known as the Albany Regency, and controlled the politics of the State. Jesse Buel, who had no such weapons in his verbal armory as those two and others of the Regency, was editor of the *Argus* but seems mostly to have been a figurehead. The paper got the national patronage and became State printer; it was issued as a semi-weekly until a decade after the war had been concluded with a sorry peace.

The other journal was the *Federal Republican*, which denounced the war although published in Baltimore, whose people were violently in favor of it. Alexander Hanson, its editor, was then twenty-six years old; in spite of statements on the floor of Congress that all opposition to the conflict must cease, he declared that he would speak as freely against Madison's administration as he chose, although the party he represented had knuckled down to the Sedition Act during the administration of John Adams. Madison, who had been a Hamiltonian until after he went to Washington, had shifted over to the Jeffersonians. Like Jefferson, he was of peaceful intention, and would not have permitted warlike measures if he had controlled Congress; nevertheless, this was called by his opponents "Madison's war," and Hanson felt justified no doubt in calling him to account for it.

"We mean to represent," said Hanson's *Federal Republican*, "in as strong colors as we are capable, that the war is unnecessary, inexpedient, and entered into from partial, personal and, as we believe, false motives bearing upon their front marks of undisguised foreign influence which cannot be mistaken."

That statement appeared on a Saturday; on the following Monday a mob demolished the newspaper office. Hanson, determined to continue printing, reestablished editorial and publishing offices in the basement of a friend's home, but printed his paper in Georgetown. This provoked more violence, and the officers of the city appeared to offer no resistance when another mob attacked the improvised publishing office. Gen. Henry Lee mapped a plan of defense and offered to take command of it; in this he was joined by other survivors of the Revolution who were of the Federalist faith; all were armed and provisioned.

The second mob, after stoning the building, forced the door open and were subjected to gunfire as they went up the stair. One was killed, several wounded. A troop of mounted militia was ordered to the scene, and the commander, with the mayor of the city, persuaded the defenders of the house to go to jail. Assurances were given that they would be protected, and that the house would not be molested. As soon as the party was on its way the residence was rifled. The next night a crowd gathered about the jail and the turnkey permitted the rioters to enter. Some of the prisoners escaped, others were beaten, and Gen. Lee was crippled for life, while one of his associates died under torture. Magistrates who made an investigation put the blame on the publishers of the *Federal Republican*.

A Neglected Story

Although the two-party system developed promptly in this new nation, the turbulence of those early days was not solely political. Newspaper editors represented not only the partisan views of their readers but economic interests and personal prejudices. Their divisions thus took on the air of crusades.

VIII

For and Against Slavery

JOHN ROLFE of Jamestown, Virginia, recorded in 1619: "Came in a Dutch man of warre that sold us twenty Negars." A year later the Pilgrims landed in Massachusetts, and presently they began trying, with but poor results, to enslave Indian captives. Thus were laid the bases of a conflict, marked often by violence and sometimes by homicide, which divided the newspapers of this country into two crusading groups.

On the eve of the Revolution, Charles A. Beard and Mrs. Beard tell us in "The Rise of American Civilization," there were half a million slaves in the colonies, constituting one-fifth of the population in Pennsylvania and Delaware, one-sixth in New York. In New England, where Negroes were unsuited to the climate and to outdoor labor, they were used as domestic servants and numbered but one in fifty of the people. Indentured white servants, in reality peons, were found more satisfactory for farm work.

Although Quakers in Virginia and Pennsylvania began agitating against slavery as early as 1696, nearly a century elapsed, as best I can find, before there was a journalistic utterance against the institution. This was in Noah Webster's *Minerva*, in December, 1793, in an editorial "intended to demonstrate that the labor of slaves in any country is less productive than that of freemen." The paper was not established, however, as an abolitionist organ. Webster was induced by Federalists to give up his law practice in Hartford and edit the daily in answer to critics of George Washington as President.

Under Quaker influence, the Manumission Society of Tennessee was formed in 1814 and established the *Manumission Journal* as its mouthpiece, but this was a quarterly, not a newspaper. Not until 1817 was the *Philanthropist* set up with the avowed purpose of opposing slavery. It was followed by the *Emancipator* in Jonesborough, Tennessee, edited by Elihu Embree, a Quaker; and in the following year Benjamin Lundy, another of the faith, established the *Genius of Universal Emancipation*. Neither made much stir; but William Lloyd Garrison wrote for Lundy's paper an article in which he named a New Englander who, so he said, had permitted one of his ships to be used in the coastwise slave trade. For his impertinence he was jailed, and determined while a prisoner to devote his life to the cause. "I owe everything to Benjamin Lundy," he subsequently declared.

On returning to Boston, Garrison established the *Liberator*. He was not without previous editorial experience, for he had worked with the *National Philanthropist*, our first temperance paper, the forerunner of those campaigners which brought the blessings of the Eighteenth Amendment and prohibition; and afterward he had edited at Bennington a journal equally opposed—as he thought natural—to intemperance and to slavery. His unbridled verbal violence made him more enemies than friends, and but few converts. "Gentlemen of property and standing" mobbed him in his office.

Other antislavery publications of that period were the *Abolition Intelligencer* in Kentucky, the Edwardsville *Spectator* and Illinois *Intelligencer*, the *African Observer* in Philadelphia, *Freedom's Journal* in New York, the *Investigator* in Providence, the *Free Press* in Bennington, and the *Liberalist* in New Orleans. Sectional boundaries, it is clear, did not govern them. The last of the list made its appearance in 1828.

Long before this some of the so-called "slave States" had turned against the institution. Virginia prohibited the trade in 1778; and, since most of the indentured servants there and in the other colonies had been kidnaped, was the first State to make kidnaping a capital offense. James Oglethorpe, when he made the first settlement of his new colony at Savannah, forbade the sale of rum in the interest of good order and banned slavery—he was like Garrison in linking the two—because he did not want a province "void of white inhabitants, filled with blacks, the precarious property of a few." But within a decade he had to wink at trading in intoxicants, and clergymen were advising settlers that "if you take slaves in faith and with the intent of conducting them to Christ, the action will not be a sin, but may prove a benediction." Under such pressure the trustees of the colonies removed the ban.

New Englanders, too, found ample Biblical justification for slavery and for holding indentured servants. And had not Cromwell, who signed the death warrant of Charles I, sold into slavery all of the garrison not slain in the Drogheda massacre? It was not surprising, therefore, when Roger Williams founded a settlement at

A Neglected Story

Providence and Anne Hutchinson at Portsmouth, that Rhode Island should become a center of the slave trade. The settlers, in vessels they built, journeyed to the West Indies, distilled molasses into rum, and traded the rum for slaves to bring back to the colonies. Providence and Boston were the chief ports of the iniquitous traffic.

Benjamin Franklin, who first called his Philadelphia paper the *Universal Instructor in All the Arts and Sciences*, presently changed this to Pennsylvania *Gazette*, and in its columns encouraged, in 1775, his Society for Promoting the Abolition of Slavery. Massachusetts forbade slavery in 1780, at least by implication, and Pennsylvania provided for gradual emancipation. New York stipulated in 1799 that children of slaves, born after July 4 of that year, should be apprentices for a time and then liberated.

Despite this widespread revolution against bondage, North and South, the framers of the Constitution could not bring themselves to abolish it. For one thing, most of them were slave owners; there were then 40,000 bondmen in the North. It is true that George Washington, who presided, had arranged to liberate his Negroes, but not during the lifetime of Martha Washington. Thomas Jefferson, who said that he trembled at the thought of slavery "when I remember that God is just," was not present at the convention. James Madison, usually credited with the actual phrasing of the Constitution, explained that the word "slavery" was avoided because it was considered unseemly to acknowledge property rights in human chattels. The institution, however, was recognized and to some extent safeguarded. It was even provided that slaves were to be reckoned in Congressional representation, on a three-fifths ratio, and the States were forbidden to enact laws interfering with the recovery of runaways. Further importation of slaves after twenty years was forbidden; even this concession was granted only with the understanding that the stock on hand would multiply. Garrison denounced the document in the *Liberator* as "a covenant with death and an agreement with hell."

More redoubtable than Garrison, and doubtless more influential, was James Gillespie Birney. A Kentuckian, he was graduated from Princeton and a little later determined to liberate his slaves, move to Illinois—"the best site in the whole world for taking a stand against slavery," he said—and set up the *Philanthropist*. This was in 1836. Birney attacked not only the institution but the methods of the slave owners as threatening the freedom of the press, reprinted editorials from their organs, and undertook to refute speeches by southern Governors. At once the Cincinnati *Post*, the *Whig*, and the *Republican* centered their fire upon him, and more than once his plant was destroyed by infuriated proslavery mobs, the first time within three weeks of its sounding.

Charles Hammond of the Cincinnati *Gazette* courageously defended the newcomer. He was a member of Lundy's abolition society, a lawyer, a man of independence and of excellent education. "He spoke at the bar as good English as Addison wrote in the *Spectator*," one of his contemporaries said. Hammond helped make Birney a national figure by reason of his wide influence editorially. Thus it came about that Birney became the presidential candidate of a third party, in 1840 and 1844. This was the Liberty Party, which opposed the annexation of Texas but was dedicated primarily to abolition. In the 1844 election Birney polled more than 62,000

A Neglected Story

votes, and took the electoral vote of New York, thus defeating Henry Clay and causing the election of James K. Polk.

Birney's *Philanthropist*, withstanding storms of violence, continued until 1847, when he merged it with the *National Era* in Washington, edited by Dr. Gamaliel Bailey, a Methodist clergyman. Here Harriet Beecher Stowe's "Uncle Tom's Cabin" was printed serially in 1851–1852, prior to book publication in Boston, in which form it sold millions of copies here and abroad. As a melodrama it wrung tears from audiences in the New York Bowery and for years throughout this country. The South retorted with fourteen novels, such as "Uncle Robin in His Cabin in Virginia," and "New England Chattels."

Birney's part in the election of Polk to the presidency appears more significant when we consider the methods employed by some of the newspapers opposed to the successful candidate. During that campaign the Ithaca *Chronicle* printed what purported to be the diary of a traveler named Roorback, on a tour of the South, in which he described an imaginary auction of slaves. "Forty-three of these unfortunate beings had been purchased, I am informed," said the fake story, "of the Hon. J. K. Polk, the present Speaker of the House of Representatives, the marks of the branding iron, with the initials of his name, on their shoulders distinguishing them from the rest."

That precious bit of campaigning was reprinted by the Albany *Patriot*, and then by the *Evening Journal* of that town. The latter was edited by Thurlow Weed, a personal and political ally of William H. Seward and Millard Fillmore. When the Albany *Argus* exposed the hoax, and accused the *Journal* of mendacity, Weed undertook to exculpate himself by saying: "This charge is utterly and unqualifiedly false. The extract in question was taken, precisely as it appeared in the *Journal*, from an exchange paper and was published by us without a doubt of its genuineness."

On both sides of the controversy there was resort to violence. Elijah Lovejoy was one of the victims. He established an abolitionist paper, the *Observer*, in St. Louis, and moved it across the river to Alton, Illinois, under threats of attack. When his press arrived there, a mob destroyed it. Another was procured, and a year later, after an editorial had been printed calling for the formation of an antislavery society, this machine and the type in the shop were ruined. Still a third press was purchased, and was placed for safekeeping in the hands of the Mayor, who had it stored, but seemed to offer no resistance to a mob which threw parts of it into the river. Undaunted, Lovejoy got his fourth press; it was delivered in St. Louis, and he was shot dead when he called at a warehouse for it.

Arthur and Lewis Tappan, brothers and prosperous silk merchants in New York, financed the *Journal of Commerce*, in its beginning an abolitionist organ, and for a time edited it. In October, 1823, they organized a meeting of "the friends of immediate abolition of slavery in the United States" at Clinton Hall, and a riotous mob broke it up. Associated with them were two clergymen, the Reverend Dr. F. F. Cox and the Reverend J. M. Ludlow, who appealed to Negroes in the North for support and advocated intermarriage.

Although New Yorkers wept over Topsy and Little Eva on the stage, in "Uncle Tom's Cabin," the town,

A Neglected Story

then comprising a quarter of a million population, was for the most part in favor of slavery. The *Evening Post*, later strong in support of emancipation, regarded the movement at that stage as "mad and absurd." The *Courier and Enquirer* called for public meetings to protest against abolitionism and berated the *Journal of Commerce* as "the organ of fanaticism and hypocrisy."

A group of Negroes who went to the Chatham Street chapel to celebrate the Fourth of July came to fisticuffs with a singing society of whites who claimed precedence in the use of the hall. "There was fault on both sides," said the *Evening Post* the next afternoon, "and especially on that of the whites. . . . Those who are now trying to get up an excitement against the Negroes will have much to answer for, should their efforts be successful."

There was much to answer for. On July 9 a mob formed, broke the windows of the Tappan shop, and sacked the homes of the brothers. They demolished the furnishings of the clergymen who had called for intermarriage, and made bonfires of furniture, church organs, parlor pianos. Then they moved on to Five Points, the Negro quarter, where in 1740 fourteen blacks had been burned during a so-called insurrection. There they destroyed three churches and a schoolhouse, and beat inoffensive colored folk into insensibility, while hordes fled to the open fields for safety. Infantry and cavalry arrived on the scene toward midnight and put a stop to the outrages, but attempted no arrests or discipline.

John C. Calhoun's mouthpiece, the *United States Telegraph* in Washington, had been fanning the flames of southern wrath meanwhile. New Orleans indicted the Tappans and made a demand, which was ignored,

Newspaper Crusaders

for their extradition, then offered large rewards for their bodies. The postmaster at Charleston, South Carolina, refused to deliver newspapers favoring abolition on the ground that they were insurrectionary. This was during the proslavery administration of Andrew Jackson, and Amos Kendall was Postmaster General. He upheld his Charleston subordinate, and encouraged others in the South to follow his example, which they did. Only three influential newspapers were outspoken in their criticism of the Postmaster General: the Boston *Courier*, the Cincinnati *Gazette*, and the New York *Evening Post*. In spite of their stand, President Jackson boldly asked Congress to enact a law excluding from the mails "incendiary" matter dealing with the slavery question.

It was at this point that Augustus Baldwin Longstreet became editor of the *State Rights Centinel* in Augusta, Georgia. He advocated nullification even before John C. Calhoun got round to it, and followed it to its logical end, a proposal of secession. In addition to being editor of that newspaper from 1832 to 1836, he was a lawyer, college and university president, politician, and clergyman; he would have no fellowship with Methodists in the North who believed in abolition, and was a prime mover in the split of his denomination into two branches.

Before establishing the *State Rights Centinel*, Longstreet had spoken and written against the "tariff of abominations" of 1828, which southerners felt discriminated against them in favor of northern industries; and when South Carolina, in 1832, called a convention which declared the tariff unconstitutional, proclaimed it void in that State and warned the Federal authorities that secession from the Union would follow any attempt at coercion, Longstreet took up the battle in his newspaper with gusto. He regarded Calhoun, leading spirit of the South Carolina defiance, as "above William Pitt, or any other premier who ever lived before or since his day." In defense of slavery, he argued as a preacher rather than as an editor or economist; his editorials treated it as a moral question, to be answered exclusively on the authority of the Bible.

While Longstreet was plugging valiantly for slavery, the elder James Gordon Bennett espoused the cause in the New York *Herald*, which he founded in 1835. He had worked for a time under James Watson Webb on the pro-slave *Courier and Enquirer*, and had been grounded in the theory that the institution was economically sound. He published a long article about the condition of industrial workers in Liverpool, contrasting their misery with the lives of slaves in the southern States, and asserting that by comparison the slaves lived like "princes." This argument, that wage earners suffered greater insecurity, hardship, and poverty than the blacks, who enjoyed as a rule life tenure and the assurance of food and care when ill or incapacitated, was taken up in the South with great fanfare, and was reiterated in newspaper editorials there.

In the wake of Longstreet, ten years before the Civil War, Robert Barnwell Rhett began demanding secession in the columns of the Charleston *Mercury*, and was abetted by the *Courier* in that South Carolina town. It is an ironic circumstance that in its early days the *Courier* had been a Federalist organ, strong for a centralized government so powerful as to be impregnable to revolt.

Rhett exercised wide influence prior to the conflict. So did George D. Prentice of the Louisville *Courier*, but in the opposite direction. The *Courier*, which was to become Henry Watterson's *Courier-Journal*, tried to keep Kentucky on the side of the North, but succeeded only in keeping her neutral. Prentice is credited with having at least prevented secession.

"If the cotton States shall decide that they can do better out of the Union than in it," said Horace Greeley in the *Tribune*, "we insist on letting them go in peace. The right to secede may be revolutionary but it exists nevertheless." Greeley changed his mind, however, and later joined the coercionists.

The "Barnburners"—so called on the theory that this faction would destroy the Democratic Party to avert slavery in the territories—bolted and nominated Martin Van Buren. The New York *Evening Post* threw in its lot with this wing and on election day said editorially:

> Shall the great republic of the western hemisphere, the greatest which has yet blessed the anxious hope of nations, to which the eyes of millions, now engaged in a desperate struggle for emancipation in Europe, turn as their only encouragement and solace, the republic which was founded by Washington and nourished into vigor by Jefferson and Jackson—shall this republic make itself a byword and a reproach wherever its name is heard? Shall the United States no longer be known as the home of the free and the asylum of the oppressed, but as the home of the slave and the oppressor of the poor?
>
> All good men have an interest in answering these questions. But above all others, the laboring man has a deeper interest. The greatest disgrace inflicted upon labor is inflicted by the institution of slavery. Those who support it—we mean the Negro-owners, or the Negro-drivers of the South—openly declare that he who works with his hands is on the level with the slave . . .

That excerpt, quoted by Allan Nevins in his history of the *Evening Post*, is reminiscent, in its last phrase, of a speech John Adams had made to the Continental Congress in 1777.

A Neglected Story

> It is of no consequence [he said] by what name you call the people, whether by that of freemen or slaves; in some countries the laboring poor are called freemen, in others they are called slaves; but the difference as to the state is imaginary only. What matters it whether a landlord employing ten laborers on his farm gives them annually as much money as will buy them the necessaries of life or gives them those necessities at short hand? . . . The condition of the laboring poor in most countries—that of the fishermen particularly in the Northern States—is as abject as that of slavery.

There was a voice from Massachusetts, the voice of a president-to-be, laying publicly the groundwork of an economic argument subsequently exploited by James Gordon Bennett in the *Herald* and southern orators as well as editors.

It must not be supposed that an article describing Liverpool "wage slaves" was Bennett's only contribution to this campaign. When an abolition convention was to be held in the Wall Street district, the *Herald* said:

> What business have all the religious lunatics of the free States to gather in this commercial city for purposes which, if carried into effect, would ruin and destroy its prosperity? . . . Public opinion should be regulated. These abolitionists should not be allowed to misrepresent New York . . . When free discussion does not promote the public good it has no more right to exist than a bad government that is dangerous and oppressive to the common weal. It should be overthrown. On the question of the usefulness to the public of the packed, organized meetings of these abolitionists, socialists, Sabbath-breakers, and anarchists, there can be but one result arrived at by prudence and patriotism. They are dangerous assemblies—calculated for mischief, unreasonable in their character and purposes . . . That a half dozen madmen should manufacture opinion for the whole community is not to be tolerated.

In opposition to sentiments such as that, a group of abolitionist publicists in New England, as the movement waxed there, used its newspapers to spread their views. John G. Whittier, who said one of the proudest acts of his life was to sign the 1833 antislavery proclamation, was one of the leaders of a noteworthy company:

Edmund Quincy, Jonathan Sewall, Theodore Parker, Thomas Wentworth Higginson, Henry Ward Beecher, Wendell Phillips, Charles Sumner, James Russell Lowell. In New York, Gerrit Smith helped keep the torch alight; in Philadelphia, Lucretia Mott; in South Carolina the Grimké sisters.

No such devotion as flamed in those breasts animated Daniel Webster, and his vacillation proved his undoing. For a time he gave frank expression to his antipathy to slavery; but State Street in Boston was of the same mind as Wall Street in New York, and regarded the institution as a basis of prosperity. Thus Webster came to say that the Constitution recognized slavery as prevailing in certain States by reason of local laws, and that Congress had no right to interfere with them; but that in new territories Federal law was operative, and could forbid slavery if Congress saw fit. His attitude toward the immunity of slavery where established, and his implication in the Fugitive Slave Law, which his newspaper critics made much of, gravely damaged him. "Sir," he said in the Senate, and the words were broadcast through the press, "the principle of the restitution of runaway slaves is not objectionable unless the Constitution is objectionable."

Both sides took up that sentence for newspaper comment. The truth was that Webster was torn between his own ideals and the interests of those who had helped him into the Senate. "Presidential ambitions and runaway slaves," says Vernon Louis Parrington in the second volume of "Main Currents in American Thought," "were stewing in a common political pot with abolition societies and northern mercantile interests." The intellectuals of Boston quickly repudiated their former idol.

A Neglected Story

Said Emerson: "The word 'liberty' in the mouth of Mr. Webster sounds like the word 'love' in the mouth of a courtesan."

So fully documented are the effects of slavery on political fortunes and sometimes on the fortunes of editors that there is little excuse to do more here than enumerate some of the less familiar phases. While editors in the North were calling for the hanging of Jefferson Davis on a sour apple tree, editors in the South were accusing Northerners of all the outrages ascribed to "Huns" during the World War. It is not to be expected that in such crises the press will maintain a Parnassian calm. As yet few newspapers can exhibit detachment even in a national political campaign. Yet it is worth noting that there had been distinct improvement in that regard.

IX

The Ku Klux Klan

Born after the Civil War as a club for merriment and masquerade, the Ku Klux Klan was perverted from innocent to evil purposes. That it is widely discredited, and in most places is an object of ridicule, is due to the drubbing administered to it by the newspapers. It is by no means dead, even now, and in backward States like Florida continues to threaten Negroes; in Indiana it makes meaningless election threats, reminiscent of its political power there in other days. But for the most part its leaders have abandoned their malicious racial and religious activities, and pose only as enemies of Communism and Fascism. We have even witnessed the spectacle of its Imperial Wizard, Hiram W. Evans, as an invited guest at the dedication of a Roman Catholic Co-Cathedral of Christ in Atlanta, erected on the site of the Klan's former national headquarters. In that transformation the press had been the chief agency.

Commenting on the Atlanta phenomenon, the New York *Herald Tribune* noted that the Klan's "fantastic flummery and bizarre rituals" had spread to nearly every part of this country, and that men of prominence recalled with shame that once they had joined it.

A Neglected Story

"Time," it said, "often favorably spoken of as the Great Healer, has outdone itself in its beneficent ministrations." Time and the sound common sense of the American public had been but the allies of the newspapers in emasculating the old Klan. And time had been the minor factor, for only fifteen years before this happened the hooded "knights" had been at the height of their power.

Between 1920 and 1925 the Ku Klux Klan boasted a membership of six millions, and national figures courted its favors. Its warning parades, its violence, its tarring and feathering, its actual homicides, constituted a grave problem. Against this the daily press directed its crusades. It was not unanimous; it seldom is, even when the issue seems to an outsider clearly a choice between black and white. In States where the organization wielded its greatest power some newspapers still truckled to it. But instances such as this were infrequent.

The most noteworthy of the crusades against the Klan was conducted by the New York *World*, which for one thing tabulated its illegal actions during the single year beginning in October, 1920: "four killings, one mutilation, one branding with acid, forty-one floggings, twenty-seven tar-and-feather parties, five kidnapings, forty-three persons warned to leave town or otherwise threatened, fourteen communities threatened by warning posters, sixteen parades by masked men with warning placards."

On September 6, 1921, the *World* began a series of twenty-one articles about the Klan, its origin, its activities, and its money-making aspects. "Colonel" William Joseph Simmons, then Imperial Wizard of the Fiery Cross, was living in an Atlanta palace which cost more than a million dollars of Klan funds. On September 18 the article dealt with the moral turpitude of Edward Young Clarke and Mrs. Elizabeth Tyler, press agents hired by Simmons, and cited police-court records. The revelations were widely quoted and stirred other newspapers to action. A Pulitzer prize was given to the *World* for its excellent work.

One of the editors who joined the campaign was George R. Dale of the Muncie, Indiana, *Post-Democrat*. His experience illustrates the methods employed by Klansmen under attack. Circuit Judge Clarence Dearth seized the papers newsboys were delivering, containing an attack on him as part of the exposures, and threatened the carriers with jail. Dale demanded that he be impeached and was threatened with contempt proceedings, but persisted until the House in Washington voted with but one dissent for the trial. In the Senate, impeachment failed by but three votes of the required two-thirds.

That was in 1922. Dale was set upon by three masked Klansmen who beat him severely while he was urging the impeachment, and he asked for a police investigation. Instead, the Muncie authorities arrested him, charging him with carrying a concealed weapon, with violation of the liquor law, with libel, and with contempt of court. Not until 1926 did the Supreme Court of the State vindicate him.

In the fight against corrupted and intimidated officials, the Indianapolis *Times* supported Dale, for it was engaged already in the campaign. It had brought charges against D. C. Stephenson, political boss of the State and a former Grand Dragon, which resulted in his conviction on a charge of second-degree murder; and it had forced an investigation which besmirched two

A Neglected Story

United States senators. It had ousted from office the mayor of Indianapolis and the city comptroller, his brother-in-law, both Klansmen.

The Vincennes *Commercial* was another of the Indiana newspapers in that crusade. Thomas W. Adams, its editor, was not assaulted, but he felt the power of the Klan in his paper's treasury, for advertising fell off heavily. The Indianapolis *Times* lost 15,000 of its circulation during the fight. Not only personal courage but a willingness to face financial losses was necessary in any editor who joined the fray.

While these things were happening the Dallas *News* and the Houston *Press*, among many other scattered dailies in the Lone Star State, were fighting the Klan. Sam Acheson says, in "35,000 Days in Texas," that the *Press* got the greater credit for the campaign, but expresses the opinion that the *News* deserved the larger share. Both merit praise, for Texas was then a stronghold of the Klan. In Tennessee, another stronghold, the Memphis *Commercial Appeal*, with C. J. P. Mooney as managing editor, berated the organization in news stories, in cartoons, and in editorials, and won a Pulitzer award. In Georgia, where the Klan had been born in its modern guise, Julian Harris of the Columbus *Enquirer-Sun*, as it was known at that time, demanded justice for the Negro, denounced lynching, and upbraided public officials who bootlicked Klansmen. The newspaper lost a fifth of its circulation and nearly half of its advertising, because the Klan dominated the community; but it stuck manfully to its guns and succeeded finally in winning over its audience to a certain degree of decency. These instances will suffice for those not familiar with the campaigns.

In its origin the Klan was a social organization of a few former Confederate officers in Pulaski, Tennessee. On Christmas Eve of 1865, defeated and penniless, they decided to have a little social club and try to cheer up their mothers and sweethearts over the holiday. Later, when a formal meeting was held, someone suggested as a name the Greek word "Kuklio," meaning a band or circle; and since most of the men were of Scotch-Irish descent it was decided to add the word "Klan." As the main purpose was merriment, why not wear costumes? Thus it was that they made their first appearance swathed in sheets and with pillowcases over their heads.

Merriment there was aplenty, when these Klansmen rode for the first time, sheets hiding their horses as well as themselves; but there was no amusement among the superstitious Negroes recently set free. The blacks thought these were the ghosts of Confederate Cavalry officers, and some of them, who had been insolently idle, returned in fright to their work in the fields. Thus an idea was suggested to the social club: they could use their weird get-up to intimidate the former slaves into usefulness. From that point the club progressed to intimidation of northern interlopers during the reconstruction era, the carpetbaggers and their assistants, the scalawags among the "po' white trash."

Among the Negroes there were Union Leagues, formed under the encouragement of Union League Clubs in northern cities, to terrorize the whites and to shelter members guilty of crime. "Rape is the foul daughter of Reconstruction," says Claude G. Bowers in "The Tragic Era." There was desperate need for such activities as the earlier Klansmen undertook, and the organization spread amazingly. It could not have spread so rapidly and widely by word of mouth alone. No, the southern newspapers campaigned for it editorially and lent their news columns to its support. They printed, for example, "General Orders" such as:

Shrouded Brotherhood! Murdered Heroes!
Fling the bloody shirt that covers you to the four winds . . . Strike with the red-hot spear . . . The skies shall be blackened. A single Star shall look down upon horrible deeds. The night owl shall hoot a requiem over ghostly corpses . . .

Literate Negroes repeated or read these horrendous outgivings to their fellows, and shuddered in their cabins. The carpetbaggers did not believe the Klansmen to be ghosts and were somewhat more difficult to handle, but as a rule they listened to warnings to get out without making violence necessary. In its beginnings the Klan seldom used force, and was under the leadership of noteworthy and admirable men. In the spring of 1867, Mr. Bowers tells us, the first national gathering was held in Nashville; by then the organization embraced practically all the adult white males of substance in the South.

As was inevitable, a secret and masked organization drew to it a lawless element and many men who were animated by vengeance rather than a desire to protect property and their women. In the autumn of 1869 Gen. N. B. Forrest, who headed the organization with Lee's approval, denounced the base element but without avail, and presently the Klan was formally dissolved.

Before the Klan went out of existence, the newspapers of the North were crusading as vigorously against it as the newspapers in the South had favored it in its early days. Horace Greeley declared in the New York *Tribune* that the "five thousand victims of the Ku-Klux outrages in the South are Republicans." Other newspapers demanded that Congress take action, and Congress did.

After six weeks of debate, Congress enacted a force bill, as it was commonly called, "more despotic," Claude Bowers declares, "than any known since the first Sedition Law of the first Adams Administration, which wrought the political revolution of 1800." In spite of the opposition of the greatest Constitutional lawyers in the Senate, such as Lyman Trumbull and Allen G. Thurman, it set aside Constitutional guaranties, turned over to Federal instead of State courts those accused of assault and robbery, and even provided for packed juries. It provided for martial law and the suspension of the writ of habeas corpus. Wendell Phillips told a huge audience in Steinway Hall in New York that the way to handle the South was "to march thirty million of men to the Gulf . . . and hang a few Generals." Ben Butler told a Boston audience that any comparison of the white and black races in the South would prove the Negroes far better fit to rule. Newspapers made such utterances the texts for editorials. Once the bill was law, a new reign of terror began.

Efforts to test the constitutionality of the anti-Ku-Klux Law were futile. The Supreme Court of the United States dismissed one suit on a technicality and was divided in another. One action was withdrawn and another was abandoned while pending.

In those early days the Klan boasted no friends on the Supreme Court. But in modern times a newspaper campaign directed against Hugo L. Black just before he became a member of the Supreme Court of the United States, on account of his having been a member of the Ku Klux in its later form, aroused countrywide con-

A Neglected Story

troversy. Ray Sprigle of the Pittsburgh *Post-Gazette* won a Pulitzer prize by writing a series of articles showing that Mr. Black, who had been a prosecuting attorney and police judge in Birmingham, Alabama, had joined the Klan in 1923 and had resigned two years later; that his resignation was not accepted; and that later he attended a Klan meeting with Governor Bibb and accepted the "gold passport" of life membership. He was quoted as acknowledging Klan support in his successful race for the United States Senate, at a time when the organization was at the height of its power.

When President F. D. Roosevelt sent to the Senate for confirmation Mr. Black's nomination to the highest bench, Senator Copeland of New York raised the question of his membership in the Klan but was silenced by Senator Borah, although Borah voted later against confirmation. The vote in its favor was 63 to 16. Subsequently Mr. Justice Black said in a radio talk that he had resigned from the Klan. "I never rejoined. What appeared then, or what appears now, on the records of the organization, I do not know."

Paul Block, owner of the *Post-Gazette*, assigned Sprigle to investigate the Klan charges, and the reporter went to Alabama. Apologists for the new Justice, among newspapers favorable to the Administration, said that the articles were the outcome of a "conspiracy" between William Randolph Hearst and big business. The *New Republic*, which joined that chorus, said joining the Klan "was much like what joining Rotary or Kiwanis is in some small midwestern town." Among newspaper editorials, some asserted that Mr. Black had joined the order without realizing its full significance. "The inference being," said Dorothy Thompson, "that he was not a rascal, but only a sap." The controversy raged inconclusively in newspapers and magazines alike.

The force bill of 1871, aimed at the Klan, made it a felony to deprive persons of their civil rights. It is still a blot upon our Federal statute books, but it was invoked for a good purpose by Federal officials against the feudal overlords of the coal dynasty in Harlan County, Kentucky, on the ground that they had conspired to defraud citizens of constitutional or statutory rights. Like the "due process" clause of the Fourteenth Amendment, the force bill was put to uses of ironical import, which certainly could not have been foreseen by its framers. Several States, beginning with Tennessee, had enacted anti-Klan laws; in New York state the old measure was resurrected against the president and five directors of the German-American Settlement League, Inc., charged with owning and operating a Nazi camp at Yaphank, Long Island; for the old law required secret organizations to register the names of their officials and members.

It was almost half a century after the first Klan was obliterated that a new Ku Klux was organized at Atlanta by Simmons in 1915. Excepting for its name and a credo of Nordic supremacy, it has nothing in common with its predecessor. For a time it made little headway, but after Simmons employed Clarke and Mrs. Tyler as press agents its appeal was widened to include fundamentalist religious beliefs. Free publicity matter was printed in newspapers far and wide of a nationalist and dogmatic nature, and as the organization spread into the North it became anti-Catholic, anti-Jewish, and anti-Bolshevist. The *World's* exposé caused the retirement of Simmons; Evans, a Dallas dentist, became the Imperial Wizard.

In Alabama, Arkansas, and Georgia, as was to be expected, the Klan took an important part in politics; it was nearly as powerful in Oregon, Connecticut, Indiana, and Oklahoma. I have said that national figures curried favor with it. Tom Watson, a brilliant Georgian, who as a member of the State legislature had demanded abolition of the vicious convict-lease system and later had stood for justice to the Negro, went afterward into the Klan camp and was largely responsible, by his incitements, for the lynching of Leo M. Frank in 1915. Another Watson—James E. Watson of Indiana—sat in that "smoke-filled room" where Warren G. Harding was chosen as Republican candidate for the presidency. The Indiana Watson spoke with the voice of the Klan, but this does not mean that Harding was a Klan candidate; for cheek by jowl were Senators Henry Cabot Lodge of Massachusetts and James W. Wadsworth of New York, and Joseph R. Grundy, who represented Senator Boies Penrose of Pennsylvania and the Manufacturers' Association of that State.

At the Democratic national convention of 1924, John W. Davis, attorney for the House of Morgan, was chosen as standard-bearer, according to Ferdinand Lundberg in "America's 60 Families," "as a compromise after a convention deadlock between the Ku Klux Klan, which backed William G. McAdoo, and the Roman Catholic Church, which backed Alfred E. Smith." When Smith got the nomination, in 1928, it was commonly understood that the Klan worked vigorously against him in the South and even in the North, contributing to his defeat.

Newspaper Crusaders

In Florida, as late as 1938, men in Klan regalia, carrying burning crosses, visited Negro sections with warnings not to vote; there were reports that a few defied the threat, but doubtless it was largely effective. In Indiana, Walter E. Bossert, a former chieftain of the Klan and a leader in eighteen States, said his followers would see that he got the Republican senatorial nomination. Politicians, recalling that the Klan in its heyday numbered some 35,000 in Indianapolis alone and more than 400,000 in the State, were fearful that there might be some substance in the boast, but their apprehension was ungrounded. The same Watson who had helped nominate Harding was an opposition candidate for the nomination, but he had the good sense to say nothing about his former influence with the tribe. In spite of his silence, the voters appeared not to have forgot; for Raymond E. Willis, publisher of a weekly village newspaper, got the nomination.

It must be confessed that the Ku Klux Klan expressed a psychological trait not uncommon among citizens of the United States. The West produced its vigilantes, and the type is still indigenous to some extent to southern California. The Know-Nothings at the middle of the last century, who called themselves the American Party, were active when immigration was heavy and manifested the same inordinate nationalist and nativistic notions as the Klan. The American Protective Association expressed similar sentiments. These were like the Klan in their arrogant stress on Nordic superiority ("Saxon civilization," Senator Josiah W. Bailey of North Carolina calls it), and in their efforts to regulate the deportment of their neighbors as well as to bulldoze officials. The kinship with Nazi ideals is striking; and so it was not inappropriate that in one case at least an anti-Klan law was invoked against a Nazi camp at Yaphank.

It is true that the National Security League and scores of other organizations manifest a repulsion toward "foreigners" and proclaim the superiority of the native born. Secret fraternal orders, moreover, afford a color, a sense of mystery, and an attractive ritual for their members. But none of these has been so intolerant toward "inferior" alien stock as the Klan.

Lawlessness, as expressed by the Ku Klux, did not cease to find expression throughout the nation when the Klan was no longer a formidable factor in national affairs. Lynchings were more frequent in the South but were not peculiar to that region. A measure was introduced in Congress to make public officials responsible for lynchings within their jurisdiction, and to lay them liable, if they had not exercised diligent effort, to a fine as high as $5,000 or to prison for five years, or both. A bloc of southern senators, toward the end of that session in 1938, conducted a filibuster against the Wagner-Van Nuys bill which lasted twenty-nine days, and defeated it. The arguments of these senators was that the legislation would be an invasion of State rights; as the Richmond *Times-Dispatch* noted, they seemed more concerned about a "right to lynch."

No better commentary on the spirit animating that legal but shameless filibuster occurs to me than an excerpt from John Jay Chapman's talk about an earlier lynching at Coatesville, Pennsylvania, to which I referred in the first chapter. Mr. Chapman was holding a memorial prayer meeting at the scene of the crime. In part he said:

Newspaper Crusaders

When I read in the newspapers of August 14, a year ago, about the burning alive of a human being, and how a few desperate, fiend-minded men had been permitted to torture a man chained to an iron bedstead, burning alive, thrust back by pitchforks when he struggled out of it, while around stood hundreds of well-dressed American citizens, both from the vicinity and from afar, coming on foot and in wagons, assembling on telephone call, as if by magic, silent, whether from terror or indifference, fascinated and impotent, hundreds of persons watching this awful sight and making no attempt to stay the wickedness, and no one man among them all who was inspired to risk his life in an attempt to stop it, no one man to speak in the name of Christ, of humanity, of government . . . I seemed to get a glimpse into the unconscious soul of this country. I saw a seldom revealed picture of the American heart and of the American nature. I seemed to be looking into the heart of the criminal—a cold thing, an awful thing . . .

To look on at the agony of a fellow being and remain aloof means death in the heart of the onlooker. Religious fanaticism has sometimes lifted men to the frenzy of such cruelty, political passion has sometimes done it, the excitement of the amphitheater in the degenerate days of Roman luxury could do it. But here an audience chosen by chance in America has stood spellbound through an improvised *auto-da-fé*, irregular, illegal, having no religious significance, not sanctioned by custom, having no immediate provocation, the audience standing by in cold dislike.

I saw during one moment something beyond all argument in the depth of its significance. You might call it the paralysis of the nerves about the heart of a people habitually and unconsciously given over to selfish aims, an ignorant people who knew not what spectacle they were providing, or what part they were playing in a judgment-play which history was exhibiting that day.

No theories about the race problem, no statistics, legislation or mere educational endeavor, can quite meet the lack which that day revealed in the American people. For what we saw was death. The people stood like blighted things, like ghosts about Acheron, waiting for someone or something to determine their destiny for them . . .

The subject is not local. This great wickedness is not the wickedness of Coatesville nor of today. It is the wickedness of all America . . . This whole matter has been an historic episode; but it is a part, not only of our national history, but of the personal history of each one of us.

The bloc of southern senators who filibustered against the antilynching bill not only made this a part of their personal and political history, but riveted the attention

A Neglected Story

of the entire country upon the fact that only in the South could Senators be produced who would oppose a legal effort to obliterate the ugliest stain on our present life, a stain such as no contemporary European country need confess.

In the forefront of the filibuster were Senator Tom Connally of Texas and Senator Josiah W. Bailey of North Carolina.

As a fact those Senators did not represent their States or their section. A careful poll by the Gallup Institute of Public Opinion, whose surveys have been remarkably accurate, showed that fifty-seven per cent of the people south of the Mason and Dixon Line favored the antilynching bill. The filibusterers knew not only that the bill would pass the Senate as it had already passed the House, but that the majority of the people they were sworn to represent were in its favor.

Newspapers generally campaigned for passage of the Wagner-Van Nuys bill. It was noteworthy that the most influential journals in the South were among them. Although the Richmond *Times-Dispatch* was not the first of these, my inquiries show that it was the most active and made itself most widely felt among Southerners.

Federal agents had been sent into Florida to solve the kidnaping and murder of five-year-old James Bailey Cash, Jr., without protest that this was an invasion of State rights. Commenting on this, the *Times-Dispatch* recalled that Senator Claude Pepper had been one of the filibusterers against the antilynching bill.

> Where is that great devotee of States' rights, Senator Pepper of Florida? [it inquired]. He objected loudly on the floor of the Senate to the Federal antilynching bill, which provided for the entry of Federal G-men into the various States to secure evidence against sheriffs and their deputies who allow

lynchings to take place. And where are the many other Floridians who echoed his sentiments on this issue? Has a single one of them been heard to argue that Federal agents have no business solving the Cash kidnaping?

The *Times-Dispatch* was one of nine Virginia newspapers to campaign for passage of the antilynching bill. Among the other leaders of opinion in the South were the Greensboro *News* in North Carolina, the Louisville *Courier-Journal*, the Norfolk *Virginian-Pilot*, the Chattanooga *Times*, the New Orleans *Tribune*, the San Antonio *Express*, and the Miami *Daily News* in Senator Pepper's home State. Doubtless their influence was responsible for the predominance of sentiment favorable to the measure. Each of them deserves an accolade, for each has won its spurs as a knight in a good cause.

This country's banner year in lynching was 1892, when 69 whites and 162 Negroes were thus put to death; in 1938 the number was nine, all Negroes. In that year mobs were frustrated in forty-four instances by officers of the law, five in northern States and thirty-nine south of the Line, sometimes with force of arms; in all, seven white persons and seventy-two Negroes were saved from mass murder. While the Wagner-Van Nuys bill was being debated for six months there was not one lynching; soon after it had been defeated there were lynchings at Rolling Fork, Mississippi, and at Arabi, Georgia; the Negro victims were burned to death; apparently the mob spirit had been fanned by the group of filibusterers.

Virginia had an antilynching law before the Federal measure was introduced. It was enacted in 1928, and defined a mob as "a collection of people assembled for the purpose and with the intention of committing assault and/or battery upon any person, without authority of

A Neglected Story

the law." I cannot find that this was any more effective than the early Federal force bill, but it also was put to a strange use. Under its provisions strikers who engaged in a brawl on July 7, 1937, at a gate of the Industrial Ryan Corporation at Covington—a melee which resulted in nothing worse than scratches and bruises—were sentenced, one to four years in the penitentiary, another to three years, a third to two years. The cases were not tried in Covington, a town of eight thousand, but were taken to Highland County, which is non-industrial and without a mile of railroad. When a fourth striker was put on trial the *Times-Dispatch* sent a staff correspondent to the county seat, and revealed what had not been understood by the public, that the antilynch law had been invoked. It protested so vigorously, and other newspapers followed suit so effectively, that this striker was sentenced to but nine months.

Neither the *Times-Dispatch* nor the other newspapers which had joined its campaign stopped there, however; they aroused public opinion which caused the charges against twelve other strikers to be dropped. Still not satisfied, they pilloried Judge Benjamin Haden, who had imposed the sentences. He charged the men with contempt of court for violating an injunction he had issued against picketing, and sentenced them to serve from six to nine months in jail, not the penitentiary. By this time newspapers outside Virginia were aroused, and the jurist decided that if the defendants would serve the jail sentences he would suspend the penitentiary terms.

While the men were still in jail—the longest time served was less than two months, and its length was due to indecision of the part of the prisoner whether he should appeal his case—the Virginia legislature amended the antilynching law which had been perverted from its real purpose, so that it could no longer be utilized against troublesome strikers.

In no public issue have the newspapers of this country exhibited sounder editorial sense than in regard to the Ku Klux Klan. In few instances have they worked more effectively and boldly for the general good. It is in recognition of this fact that the Pulitzer prize has been awarded so frequently to anti-Klan crusaders. The work of the Ku Klux in this country has revealed a more rotten spot at the core of its people, vividly described by John Jay Chapman, than ever the pogroms of Europe have manifested. Newspaper crusades have pared away a part of the rottenness; that the daily press will continue its good work seems to be assured.

X

Trying to Tame Tammany

NO CAMPAIGN against political corruption is more famous than that by which New York newspapers deposed Boss Tweed from his Tammany throne. Few journalistic exploits have been described oftener or with greater pride; yet it merits a brief repetition here because of the magnitude of the stake involved, because it came at the apex of municipal pilfering, because it dried up for a time the springs of graft, and because, although the Tiger afterward roved the political jungle and at times waxed plump, he was so crippled in the fight that he had a permanent limp. "There has been nothing equal to the result thus obtained in the history of journalism," said Frederick Hudson; but he abstained from details because, when he wrote his history, he regarded the facts as too fresh in the public mind.

William Marcy Tweed, chairmaker, city fireman, ward boss, grand sachem, got himself made a member in 1857 of the County Board of Supervisors, which levied local taxes and supervised expenditures for buildings and improvements. In a short while he was worth three millions, and rejoiced that his horses at Greenwich, Connecticut, enjoyed mahogany stalls. He remained on that Board thirteen years, and served four terms as its president. As one example of the method he and his companions adopted to get rich quick, it may be said that a county courthouse which was to have cost a quarter of a million really cost eight millions, with chairs at $470 each. The thefts of the gang have been estimated as high as a hundred millions.

By 1869 the Tweed gang had made A. Oakley Hall mayor and controlled the council, district-attorney, and municipal judges; more, they had made John T. Hoffman governor and dominated the legislature, to which Tweed went as State senator. Their ambition, so M. R. Werner assures us in "Tammany Hall," was to send Tweed to the United States Senate, make Oakley Hall governor, and promote Hoffman to the presidency.

In those days the New York *Times* was owned and edited by Henry J. Raymond, a political associate of Thurlow Weed and William H. Seward, the latter subsequently governor and Secretary of State during the Civil War. The *Times* boasted on May 7, 1870, of "reforms made possible by the recent legislation at Albany," referring to laws passed by the Tweed-Republican coalition. A year later (on August 12, 1871, to be exact), the *Evening Post* said that a bargain had been struck "between the most prominent factions of the two parties, the Seward-Weed Republicans and the Tammany Democrats, by which the offices were divided between them," and continued:

Tammany managed the city vote, in accordance with this bargain; Mr. A. Oakley Hall, the counsel of the combination, drew up the laws which were needed to carry it out; Mr. Thurlow Weed and his lobby friends passed them through the legislature, and the New York *Times* gave them all the respectability they could get from its hearty support, in the name of the Republican party.

A Neglected Story

The *Evening Post* was now well launched in its crusade against Tammany, and continued it, mostly through the medium of epithets with no specific proof of its charges, until the fall of 1871, when Charles Nordhoff retired as its managing editor, and it ceased firing. In the meantime the *Times* had passed out of Raymond's hands to George Jones, who had helped finance it and who took up where the *Evening Post* left off. Tweed, in a shabby office on Duane street where he had hung out a shingle as a lawyer, chuckled at the denunciation. It was a matter of common knowledge that the city was being plundered. Newspapers which he controlled had nothing but praise for the administration; many of their editors, as a fact, were on the city pay roll. He did not expect to be hurt by the mouthings of one or two outlanders. By this time William Cullen Bryant, editor of the *Evening Post*, was ready to discharge, and did, a city editor who printed stuff unkindly to Tweed. Horace Greeley of the *Tribune* closed his eyes to the iniquities of the gang.

Tweed's reckoning took no account of a disgruntled former companion in graft. James O'Brien, as sheriff, had received no salary but had collected an average of $100,000 a year in fees; this he had thrown around regally, so that when he left the office he was as poor as when he took it. In the spring of 1871 he submitted to the Board of Audit a claim for $200,000 as "extras," confident that it would be paid as such fraudulent demands customarily were. The Board thought O'Brien was a has-been and overrode his demand. Not long after this a friend of his got employment in the city auditor's office, and diligently copied for him page after page of the accounts, which reeked with dishonesty. These O'Brien took to the *Times*.

Here was ammunition aplenty to substantiate the charges that the Tweed ring was the forty thieves, and George Jones assumed the role of a later Ali Baba. Soberly, day after day, he made public the "Open, Sesame."

Awakened from an illusion of security, Tweed at first was resentful and defiant. "What are you going to do about it?" he asked. His surly bravado aroused the anger of citizens who before had been complaisant or resigned. Alarmed at last, Tweed thought he would buy the *Times* to silence it, and one of his organs announced:

> We are informed that negotiations are in progress for the sale of the New York *Times*, to a company in which Peter Cooper, Moses Taylor, Cyrus W. Field, A. Oakley Hall, James Fisk, Jr., Jay Gould, Peter B. Sweeney, and William M. Tweed are to be the principal stockholders. The present managers of the establishment will leave as soon as the purchase is completed . . . We learn, also, that the first overtures for this transaction were made by George Jones, through a third party.

Sweeney was high in Tweed's councils. That men of the standing of Peter Cooper, Moses Taylor, James Fisk, Jr., and Jay Gould suffered their names to be used in such a connection need surprise no one. At a meeting in Tammany Hall not long before this, August Belmont had presided and Horatio Seymour had sat on the platform beside Samuel J. Tilden; a little later Tweed was to appoint a committee of six leading citizens, including John Jacob Astor, to look over the city accounts and refute the *Times;* the committee reported that the deportment of the administration was "correct and faithful." The explanation given afterward was that Tweed saw to it that these men escaped taxation, but threatened heavy levies if they were troublesome.

The *Times* denounced the published story about the sale as "a fabrication from beginning to end," and

A Neglected Story

Tweed cast about for some other recourse. City advertising at high rates, which served as a sop to other papers, was of no use because Jones consistently refused to accept it. Lawyers for Tweed attacked the newspaper's title to its building but failed because the title was sound; they tried in vain to get an indictment for criminal libel or a ruling of contempt of court. Well, there was always a sure resort, according to Tammany practices: bribery would turn the trick.

Thus it happened that an eminent lawyer, a friend of Jones, invited him to a business consultation. Jones found in the office Comptroller "Slippery Dick" Connolly of the Tweed gang, who wasted no time beating about the bush of his business. He offered Jones five million flat to stop publishing those figures.

"I don't think," said Jones, "that the Devil will ever bid higher for me than that."

Encouraged, Connolly painted to Jones a picture of life in Europe with all that money. He could "live like a prince."

To Jones that picture did not seem attractive. He refused to take the money, and Connolly returned to Tweed with the incredible news.

As New Yorkers returned to town from their summer vacations they found the *Times* still nursing its campaign and publishing figures of expenditures for "general purposes," repairs on uncompleted buildings, and so on. A mass meeting at Cooper Union overflowed into an impromptu mob in Astor Place—memorials to Peter Cooper and John Jacob Astor, whom Tweed had found useful—and at both there were cries of "Hang them!" At the next election the machine was thrown out of power, and then Tweed was indicted on more than a hundred counts, four for felonies, three for forgeries, two for grand larceny, one for false pretences, one for conspiracy. His companions had either fled or turned State's evidence, and he stood alone. In his battery of able lawyers was Elihu Root, then a young man. The sentence was twelve years in prison and a fine of $12,500; meantime a suit had been filed to recover six millions.

Tweed, escaping from jail through connivance, fled to Spain, was rearrested there, and brought back in a naval cruiser. In his last days, until he died in jail, he was a pathetic figure. Perhaps it was pity for him at this stage which led Henry L. Mencken to say that "the famous war upon William M. Tweed shook the whole nation, for he was a man of tremendous power, he was a brave and enterprising antagonist, and his fall carried a multitude of other men with him." To Mencken, George Jones of the *Times* was "an accomplished mobmaster."

Although "Honest John" Kelly, former sheriff, who succeeded Tweed, managed to amass a fortune of half a million, he kept Tammany Hall free of charges of graft. During his regime, as a fact, Jacob Sharp bribed the Board of Aldermen to give him free a franchise for a street railway on Broadway (for which an honest bidder vainly offered a million), and most of the aldermen who did not flee were convicted, but there was no proof that "Honest John" or his followers had a finger in the pie. An able organizer, Kelly transformed a horde of guerilla bandits into a trained army, and the overoptimistic, observing the good results, thought the Tiger might have changed his stripes.

Certainly a breathing spell was needed for honest development. The town was growing prodigiously. In

A Neglected Story

1870, when Tweed was Commissioner of Public Works (and saw to it that he got his share), the first apartment house had been erected, amid wonder and admiration, at 142 East Eighteenth Street, with suites of six rooms and a bath renting at $1,500 for the first floor to $1,080 for the topmost, for it was a walk-up. The *Evening Post*, so Allan Nevins tells us in his history of that newspaper, urged that elevators be installed, arguing that thus as much rent could be charged for the upper flats as for the lower. Presently another house provided a porter who lighted the halls, removed garbage, and sent up fuel on a dumbwaiter, at monthly rentals of $40 to $75 a month; and then at Fifth Avenue and Sixty-eighth Street, overlooking Central Park, a tenant could get eight rooms, a bath, elevator service, his own kitchen range, and a water heater for $75 to $150 a month. By 1874 the *Evening Post* thought that this new development "may now be considered almost perfect."

In other parts of New York there were 220,000 persons in a square mile of tenements, of which 4,000 buildings had no sewer connections. In two decades prior to 1870 the population had doubled, to a million, and half the city's children lived in slums of indescribable squalor. During Kelly's overlordship, which began in 1871, conditions were somewhat improved; but when his successors, Croker and Murphy, came into power, it was discovered that although the Tiger limped slightly, he had not changed his stripes.

Richard Croker of County Cork, Ireland, had been a protégé of "Honest John," and was schooled in a political atmosphere clean enough. In his boyhood he had asserted leadership by commanding the Fourth Avenue Tunnel Gang of toughs; and in his young manhood he was charged with the murder of a political enemy's henchman but escaped, thanks to a hung jury. He proclaimed that he regarded the Democratic Party as the place for young men, and when he was twenty-two voted seventeen times for his candidate for constable in Greenpoint. Comptroller "Slippery Dick" Connolly, who had proffered the five-million-dollar bribe during the Tweed days, perceived that Croker might be useful and put him on the city pay roll at $1,200 a year. Then Kelly made him, first city marshal, later coroner at $15,000 a year. Kelly helped him escape from the murder charge by employing expert defense counsel.

After Croker became Grand Sachem he elected to the mayoralty his friend Hugh J. Grant, the first Tammany man to hold the office since Tweed's day. Almost immediately the Republicans set afoot an investigation of the administration, which showed clearly enough that Croker was not following in the footsteps of "Honest John." Bourke Cockran and Joseph H. Choate, of counsel for the Tammany leaders, tried to discredit the testimony, but it left Croker with a black eye, nevertheless. Other inquiries were to follow, including a grand-jury report that Grant's administration as sheriff (before Croker made him mayor) had been "tainted and corrupt," with "an utter subversion of the public interests to personal gain," and that it had been "mercenary, slovenly, and wholly indecent."

Although Croker's graft seems cautious and picayunish in comparison with Tweed's reckless swashbuckling, we find M. R. Werner telling us, in "Tammany Hall," that he rose to be "the most powerful leader New York politics had ever known," and that he demoralized the city "more systematically and more efficiently than it has ever been done before or has ever been done since." Yet after the municipal election of 1901, in which the newspapers were largely instrumental in defeating the whole Tammany ticket, Croker thought it best to "abdicate," and to turn over the ostensible direction of Tammany to Lewis Nixon, an Annapolis man and naval builder, who promised, amid knowing smiles, to reform the Hall.

Seth Low was elected mayor in that campaign, with William Travers Jerome as his district attorney. They charged that P. A. P. Widener, Thomas Fortune Ryan, William C. Whitney, and others of the Metropolitan Street Railway Company were cheating their stockholders of millions, and that they were the real power behind the Tammany throne. Jerome, so Gustavus Myers reminds us in "the History of Tammany Hall," said he knew that in attacking this group "I am arraying myself against the most dangerous, the most vindictive, and the most powerful influences at work in this community," but charged—and subsequently proved—that these men were corrupting legislators not only in New York but in Albany.

Although Croker had retreated to his estate in England, he was still the boss, and Nixon, realizing that he was being made a laughingstock, resigned. A triumvirate headed by Charles F. Murphy, who soon assumed sole power, succeeded him and ousted the chief. Like Croker, Murphy had been a gang leader and successful with his fists; he became a saloonkeeper and Tammany district captain before he gained control, and as dock commissioner under Mayor Robert C. Van Wyck he had doubled his substantial fortune, so that he was a millionaire. During the Seth Low administration, when he acceded to power, the newspapers, which were fairly solid in support of better local government, told circumstantially about the relations between the Tammany gang, the police, and the underworld, but the system remained intact. Even as late as 1939 there were proofs that Tammany leaders lent protection to racketeers.

Thomas E. Dewey, who successfully prosecuted a Tammany district leader for his complicity with a racketeer, credited the newspapers with gains along this salient, despite Tammany's discomfiture. He said that municipal corruption and racketeering could not stand "the powerful exposure to public opinion which only a free and courageous press can provide," and credited to this instrumentality the defeat in 1937 of the Tammany ticket. It still remained to be seen whether the Tiger, lamed and shell-torn, was as powerful as his enemies.

Von Moltke said that whipping Russia was like beating a feather pillow. Tammany had proved to be a political feather pillow.

XI

Other Augean Stables

ALMOST as celebrated as the overthrow of Tweed were the campaigns in which William Lorimer's bribery to procure a seat in the United States Senate was exposed and in which Abraham Ruef was dethroned in San Francisco. Each reverberated loudly, although the first was not of comparable value or importance to the other and will therefore be dismissed in short order.

While senators were still being elected by State legislatures, Lorimer was elected from Illinois in 1910. His chief backer was a rich lumberman who was in disfavor with the main section of the Republican organ in the State, a fact which has been offered as an explanation of the Chicago *Tribune's* interest in presenting proof that he had bought his seat with $100,000 in bribes. Whatever the motive, the effect politically was salutary: Lorimer lost his seat in the upper branch. Despite the fact that his shame was recounted in every newspaper in this country, he did not lose his position as a financial manipulator and became president of the LaSalle Street National Bank in Chicago. (That city has given evidence more than once that it considers political bribery a peccadillo.) When the bank was drifting toward the rocks

Lorimer wished to make it over into a State institution, and to do this required a million and a quarter in cash. He borrowed a check for that amount from Charles Gates Dawes, soon to become Calvin Coolidge's Vice-president but then president of the Central Trust of Chicago. The Central Trust was held partly responsible when the Lorimer bank failed. Afterward Lorimer organized still another bank and borrowed millions from the Hoover Reconstruction Finance Corporation. Apparently Washington had somewhat the same attitude as Chicago toward the financier's political knavery.

So far as newspaper crusading is concerned, the Lorimer record is more malodorous than significant. It threw certain interesting sidelights, and it made a great noise at the time, but it is hardly worth further attention.

Fremont Olbor's victory over Abe Ruef was of a different caliber, and a newspaper exploit of distinction. Ruef was cardticing all the tricks of Tweed's infamous trape; he extorted money indiscriminately from brothels, prizefight promoters, gambling hells, business big and little. The *Bulletin* and the *Call*, subsequently merged, were then part of the Loring Pickering estate; and when Older became managing editor of the *Bulletin* it was as dishonest as the other San Francisco papers, which were owned or controlled by the Southern Pacific Railroad.

In common with the Southern Pacific, the utilities and other large corporations in San Francisco had their way with the daily press then functioning there. In the city and thorughout the State, with the chief Cerberus of the citizen muzzled thus, injustice and corruption were the order of the day.

A Neglected Story

The fact that we were taking money [Older says in "My Own Story," a chronicle of his journalistic struggles] from the railroad, the gas company, and other public-looting corporations, was known in the business office. As a result, that department had become permeated with an atmosphere of chicanery and dishonesty . . . *Bulletin* men, by various shady pretexts, were getting rugs, pianos, bicycles, furniture, jewelry, everything they could lay hold of, in trade for advertisements. The books were juggled.

Older had to begin a house cleaning at home before he could undertake municipal reform, and he had a fight on his hands, not wholly successful. Time and again when he was exposing Abe Ruef, the enemy countered with proof of malfeasance in his own office. And he encountered "danger, financial reprisal, the cold stare of former friends and acquaintances." But he persisted, enlisted the aid of underworld characters in his exposures, trapped senatorial boodlers, and put Ruef in stripes. He had carried on the fight for five years before he enlisted the help of Francis J. Heney in the prosecutions. He had been boycotted and ostracized. A gunman had been told he could have $10,000 if he would kill Older, and the home of a witness for the *Bulletin* had been dynamited.

Older began, nevertheless, undertaking the reform of criminals and printing their life stories in the *Bulletin*. One of them was Jack Black, a convicted bank robber and a drug addict, whose sentence Older got commuted to one year; Black turned straight, gave up drugs altogether, and became an extremely useful citizen. Lemuel Parton of the New York *Sun*, however, has said that Older's greatest work was on behalf of Tom Mooney, unjustly imprisoned for a Preparedness Day bomb explosion in San Francisco. Parton was with the *Bulletin* during that campaign, when Older printed documentary evidence that the testimony against Mooney had been perjured. To this case, Older devotes little attention in his autobiography, and he did not live to see Mooney finally free and exonerated.

"My Own Story," dictated to a stenographer not long before Older died, is an exciting but inadequate book. It tells, however, about his efforts, which were successful, to get Ruef paroled from the prison to which Older had sent him; Parton explains that Older had become saturated with Tolstoyan ideas about crime and punishment. The book throws highlights on one of the most noteworthy Crusaders, and one of the most contradictory personalities in American journalism.

Older's crusade on behalf of Tom Mooney was one against political corruption, engendered in part by public utilities which stood behind the district attorney and other officials. The intention was to discipline Socialist labor agitators like Mooney and Warren K. Billings. Ten persons were killed and forty hurt in the bombing, and it seemed an auspicious moment to make an example of troublesome leaders. At the outset Older supposed Mooney was guilty; as for Billings, he had been convicted earlier of bombing power-line towers. But when proof fell into Older's hands that Frank Oxman, "the honest cattleman" who had identified Mooney and Billings, was a perjurer and had tried to induce a friend to follow his course, Older began a campaign which continued until his death. He proved that other witnesses had lied, that the convicted men were martyrs, and procured intervention by President Woodrow Wilson, so that Mooney's death sentence was commuted to life imprisonment. He printed statements by the Judge who had presided at the trial and by each of the jurors that they believed Mooney and Billings innocent. But the Supreme Court of the United States found legal technicalities against establish-

A Neglected Story

ing justice in the case, and one Governor after another refused to act, one on the ground that the move for pardon was "corruptly inspired." Mooney served twenty-two years and was fifty-six when liberated by a Governor who had made the promise to do this a part of his campaign. A second offender, Billings could not be freed under the California law.

More than once, when newspapers have been indolent, negligent, or ineffective, groups of citizens have taken the initiative in combating crime conditions, but always they have sought and ultimately have gained the help of the press. In the vanguard of these was the Baltimore Criminal Justice Commission, which came into being after William B. Norris, a building contractor, was shot to death and robbed of a $7,000 pay roll in 1922. There was a partnership in crime between policemen, certain lawyers, court officers, bondsmen, and politicians; embezzlements, larcenies, and manslaughter were at disturbingly high figures, and the chances were five to one that offenders either would not be caught or would go unwhipped of justice. Aroused, Baltimore's business and professional men determined to finance their own campaign to end these conditions.

Ultimately, the Baltimore Crime Commission embraced eighteen organizations, but at the outset it was subjected to derision by the *Sun*, which opposed its recommendations and for a time was severely critical, editorially, of its proposed moves. The commission paid no attention but went ahead with James Merritt Hepbron, an expert criminologist, as managing director. It undertook to present a factual picture of the situation, showing how much crime there was, how many offenses resulted in arrest, and how many in reprisal, how many of the accused were dismissed by magistrates, what the grand juries did, what the State and district attorneys did, what court action was taken, and so on to parole.

As the facts were divulged the *Sun* veered around, and the Hearst papers, the *American* and the *News-Post*, never actively unfriendly, lent a hand heartily. Whether Mr. Hepbron and his compact staff could have accomplished their remarkable cleanup without this assistance is doubtful. Plugging away steadily, the commission had one of the worst criminal lawyers disbarred, ousted a police commissioner installed for political purposes, put the courts on their mettle, cleared their dockets and streamlined their trials, brought convictions for five-sixths of all defendants, got a constitutional amendment to enable a budgeting system, reformed the system of bonding, and won the earnest cooperation even of politicians and the police force.

These heartening results encouraged other cities to emulate the Baltimore commission. Thus in New York, a Citizens Committee on Control of Crime, organized with a substantial fund, was chiefly responsible for a fruitful investigation of conditions in Brooklyn. Chicago, Philadelphia, Los Angeles, Cleveland, Memphis, Kansas City, Washington, and Evanston were other towns to set the good work afoot, almost always with generous newspaper support. States in some instances have followed suit: New York, Illinois, Kentucky, Kansas, Massachusetts, Missouri, Nebraska, Pennsylvania, and New Jersey. By this process the dark hints of newspaper reporters, usually "in the know" about such matters but often powerless to divulge them, have been reduced to statistics and personalities.

A Neglected Story

No group of citizens was needed to prod the press of New Bedford, Massachusetts. In that city of considerably more than 100,000 the *Standard-Times* and the *Mercury*, under a single ownership, investigated for more than six months officially protected vice and gambling before beginning the publication of a series of stories in the *Standard-Times*. They imported for the purpose an experienced outside newspaper man who worked under the name of William A. Purcell and who reported secretly at intervals, usually in near-by towns, to his superiors, who were Basil Brewer, publisher; Charles J. Lewin, editor in chief; and Charles E. Carll, managing editor.

Purcell, who signed his stories with that name and whose identity was kept secret throughout, went to New Bedford on January 7, 1938, and registered at a dubious hotel, where drinks were sold at all hours and where he saw at the outset other evidences of vice which would not escape any wideawake reporter. Several days later he made his first bet at the Silver Dollar, "a cafe and bar just off Baylies Square at the intersection of Eugenia and Front Streets," where, he learned, "the bartender was City Councilman William M. Cabral."

Publication of the articles did not begin until the following September. In the first of them Purcell said that "gaming, lottery, vice seemingly had a 'go' sign that flashed most of the time in New Bedford," and that, although the men in charge of dice and card games, the numbers racket, "books" on horse races, slot machines, and lotteries complained that the depression hurt their business, "the city's gambling business alone can be estimated conservatively at more than $1,000,000 yearly."

The series ran on the first page of the *Standard-Times* day after day, often accompanied by a first-page editorial. Gambling rooms were described in detail and their location given as a rule more minutely than the Silver Dollar's. The four men higher up in the ring were named, with the statement that they were part of an intercity group which included Boston. Their system of "grapevine" communication was described and their principal telephone number was given. How they moved their quarters on information that the police were about to make a raid as a matter of policy, how they assisted at times in these farces, how school children gambled on slot machines near the schools, was set forth circumstantially. Thus Purcell said that one game was shifted twice, and added:

> The location of the "spots" in the order of the moves follows:
> Middle Street and Acushnet Avenue, with entrance just off the Elm Street parking lot.
> Sawyer Street, just off Acushnet Avenue, with entrance behind that of the place of business of a Chinese laundry.
> Number 8 Hazard Street, second floor.

Specific as Purcell's statements were, with names, addresses, descriptions of lookouts and principals, and the amounts wagered, there were those in New Bedford who made a personal issue of the drive and declared that the paper was hitting at the Mayor, Leo E. J. Carney. Among merchants and professional folk the reaction to the campaign was generally favorable. It may have been that the Mayor was as ignorant of what was going on as I believe President Warren G. Harding to have been about the facts of Teapot Dome. Thirty days after taking office, and while Purcell was investigating, he had said that the city was "as clean as it has ever been," and had abolished a special squad of police to deal with vice and liquor

A Neglected Story

violations; later he had reinstated the squad but not, he explained, because he thought conditions any worse.

In a first-page editorial, signed jointly by the *Standard-Times* and the *Mercury*, the matter of a remedy was put squarely up to the people of the city. "Where Purcell left off is where New Bedford must begin in the solution of this problem." It posed for its readers a series of questions and concluded: "New Bedford's good name and future depend in part on its ability to find the answers to these questions."

When a grand jury was impaneled, the newspaper discontinued its series lest it be accused of trying to influence action. Indictments were returned against forty-five persons, including the mayor and seventeen other city officials. While under indictment the mayor was reelected and later was acquitted of bribery. Nevertheless gambling and vice, if not abolished, were driven to cover and deprived of official protection.

San Francisco, Chicago, New Bedford; we have crossed a continent and have ranged from knavish gang rule on a large scale through national politics to house cleaning in a city of medium size, but we have not exhausted the subject. There is a certain sameness about crusades against political corruption, even in the methods employed; but other examples shall be noted, as evidence that the daily press has been alert in recent years and is still on guard.

While the *Standard-Times* was exposing conditions in New Bedford, New England neighbors were bestirring themselves. The Bridgeport *Post-Telegram* revealed the unreasonable prices paid for parts of the Merritt Parkway right of way through Connecticut, and the Waterbury *American* and *Republican* exposed "a million-dollar conspiracy" to defraud that city.

In the parkway case it was shown that plots of land cost the State at the rate of $6,000 an acre; several realty men were indicted; one State official was ousted and another charged with felony. After that the State Highway Department condemned property, as was its right from the first, and got it at an average of $250 an acre instead of thousands. In the Waterbury case, Governor Wilbur Cross demanded the resignation of one official after another, including his Lieutenant Governor, who was mayor of the city, and who was indicted with twenty-one other persons. Two State Senators and a former Representative, who had been his party's leader in the House, were compelled to relinquish profitable political posts. The State's attorney resigned when charged in a grand jury report with having countenanced gambling on a large scale in Waterbury. Subsequently a lottery ring was smashed by sixty arrests.

In its repercussions the Waterbury crusade was useful. Both major parties felt the effect in the 1938 State election. Jasper McLevy, Socialist mayor of Bridgeport, cut deeply into the strength of the two old-line organizations. He polled more than 160,000 votes for governor, a remarkable achievement for a Socialist in staid New England. In Waterbury he put both the major parties to rout and carried the city.

In Philadelphia the *Evening Ledger*, never famous for muddying the waters, assigned a woman reporter in 1932 to investigate the "numbers game," on the basis of reports from churchgoers that the poorer part of the population was losing $100,000 daily in the racket. As the

A Neglected Story

result of a ten-day crusade there were 132 arrests, and seventy-eight men were sentenced to terms ranging from thirty days to two years, while thirty-seven others were fined and put on probation. During the crusade the *Ledger's* reporter told how the winning numbers were selected and gave an illustration. Her fancied figure was backed heavily by readers of the paper; it happened to be right, and as a consequence seven "banks" failed to pay their scores. The police, who had vowed they could do nothing about the racket, were summoned to protect the gamesters against angry crowds.

Although the "numbers game" was suspected thereafter, gambling and vice continued unabated in the city, and S. Davis Wilson, the mayor, adopted a familiar stratagem in 1937 when, to quiet public dissatisfaction, he named prominent clergymen as members of a commission of inquiry. To his discomfiture, the group reported that crime was rampant and that the courts were politically controlled. It asked the district attorney to make a grand-jury investigation, but at first he refused; later, when the mayor had turned against his political party, he complied, but the mayor had him ousted in favor of the attorney general, whose assistants took charge of the grand jury. The jury indicted the mayor on twenty-one counts, and on other charges indicted four police officials, the chief of the gambling ring, and 140 other persons.

Political influence in the courts was exposed by the Philadelphia *Record* in a series of twenty articles, after William F. Hawkes, the managing editor, learned that a court sentence of ten to twenty years had been listed by the clerk as six months. The series gave specific instances of political power in getting the sentences of offenders reconsidered and in effecting the parole of men with long police records. As a result of the exposure, the system of probation and paroles and the methods of reconsidering sentences was revamped, so that Philadelphia was put on a judicial footing with more honest communities.

Powerful New York newspapers were silent while the Long Island *Chronicle* crusaded for two years against political corruption in Long Beach. When Frank Frankel was elected mayor there, in November, 1929, the *Chronicle*, a weekly paper, reported that "floaters" had been imported from New York to vote for him at $5 a head; twelve young men were arrested, and one naïvely confessed, whereas the others were tried and acquitted promptly. The mayor appointed as chief of police a man described by the *Chronicle* as a former bodyguard of Brooklyn beer-runners, under an agreement, according to the weekly, that liquors could be unloaded at Long Beach for the metropolitan market. Federal authorities investigated the rumrunning in 1930 but did not make a successful case.

At first the *Chronicle* was the recipient of city advertising, and gave the proceeds to the Long Beach Hospital; this revenue was taken away, not from the paper but from the hospital, and such pressure was brought to bear on other advertisers that they withdrew from its columns. Circulation fell from more than seven to a little more than one thousand, but Charles Gold, owner and publisher, and James G. Blake, editor, kept up the fight. Gold, retired head of a house on the New York Curb Exchange, had started the paper as a hobby and appeared willing to lose money in the fight. It cost him additional fat sums in legal fees, for he and Blake were indicted, together and individually, for criminal libel; they could never get one of the cases to trial, as they tried to do in order to present

A Neglected Story

in court record further evidences of skulduggeries. They wanted, for one thing, to describe the fourteen pieces of property owned by the mayor on which gambling games flourished. Their persistent campaign of publicity, however, resulted finally in closing 100 gambling places and restoring to the community at least a semblance of honesty in government.

In St. Paul, Howard Kahn, editor of the *Daily News*, owned by the Ridder family, consulted leading citizens before he launched a campaign against crime conditions, but was not spurred into it by them. His charges in first-page editorials and the news brought a grand-jury investigation in March, 1934, but it gave the police department a clean bill of health. The foreman of the grand jury, explaining in a radio talk that St. Paul was not a gangsters' headquarters, did not know that while he was talking John Dillinger and a companion were shooting their way out of a trap there set by Federal agents. Readers of the *News* learned about the broadcast and the concurrent gunfire the next morning, and a group of them pledged $60,000 to Kahn to carry on his crusade. He flew to Washington; and what he said caused Attorney General Homer S. Cummings to describe St. Paul as "the nation's poison-spot of crime."

Yet the fact was that for a while comparatively little crime was committed in the city. It was a base of operations, under an agreement that racketeers and gunmen would not be molested if they would practice their arts elsewhere. For a time the promise was observed; but presently the gangsters began killing one another, then they succumbed to the temptation to rob and kidnap on the home grounds.

Newspaper Crusaders

Kahn returned from Washington with eight Federal secret agents, who soon sensed that high police officials were involved and tapped their telephone wires. Conversations, nine-tenths of them incriminating, were transcribed by stenographers and recorded also on metal disks. In a second grand-jury investigation no whitewash was attempted. Many police officials were removed from office, others were imprisoned. The city amended its character, in order to take those posts out of politics, and achieved a high standing, as regarded criminal offenses, among cities of its size. Kidnaping and gang murders ceased, the city's "fences" were closed, and robberies greatly diminished.

Atlantic City, established in the public mind as a health resort and glamorous playground, held no glamour for reporters of Hearst's New York *Journal and American*, who twice surveyed it. The first investigation, in 1930, revealed protected vice and resulted in prison sentences for a score. The second, in 1936, showed that many of these were "back in the brothels and gambling joints." Enoch L. Johnson, boss of the city and county, was described by the *Journal and American* as "the bald-headed Belshazzar of the Boardwalk." On July 16, 1936, it said:

> Not only does Kitty Harris, notorious brothel keeper, enjoy full political patronage and protection in this city, but a corporation controlled by Enoch L. (Nocky) Johnson sold her a house in which she and her coterie of imported women ply their trade. Queen Kitty did not have funds enough to buy this property outright. So the above-mentioned corporation aided her by taking a $4,800 mortgage on the property, which is . . . a few doors from another bagnio she operates.
>
> Kitty blandly boasts that she is "personally acquainted with all the big boys in Atlantic City."

A Neglected Story

As a result of these and other charges, the Federal Bureau of Investigation stepped in, there was a second roundup and more convictions.

Hand in hand with conditions of that sort go high taxes, but it was not until 1939 that the Chamber of Commerce began a campaign in its local newspapers, the *Evening Union* and the *Morning Press*, to reduce the rates. It bought advertising space to impress on the city that property owners were not the only citizens taxed but that a man earning $100 a month must pay $231 a year in hidden taxes on bread and bacon as well as on tobacco and tea. The Chamber asserted that Atlantic City had "the highest adjusted tax rate of any city in America."

In Miami, another playground and health resort, the *Daily News* waged for nearly two years a drive to oust the mayor and city commissioners. The fight began when the commissioners voted themselves double pay, and continued in news stories and first-page editorials declaring that the "termite" officials were destroying the foundations of local good government. The editor organized a group, Citizens and Taxpayers, Inc., to work for recall of the commission and finance the legal steps necessary. On March 1, 1939, the campaign was crowned by the ousting of the officials in a five-to-one vote.

Another southern city with a courageous newspaper was Mobile, where the *Press-Register* undertook to get rid of a lottery ring. Henry P. Ewald, executive editor, who directed the fight, said in an editorial:

> The only apparent reason nothing is being done against the gamblers is that the gamblers have a great deal of the political power and are generous contributors to campaign funds and are energetic workers at election times.

Ewald was lured into a house and there beaten with blackjacks and a revolver butt. On his description four persons were arrested, one a politician, prizefight promoter, and gambler, another a saloonkeeper who served as his lieutenant. When their attorney tried, on March 8, 1939, to get a reduction of their heavy bonds from a United States Commissioner, before whom they were arraigned, he said: "I know this: the charge is unusual, extraordinary, and extremely important. It is a question whether a man can write newspaper editorials—not only in Mobile but throughout the country—without being interfered with."

The bail was not reduced. The *Press-Register* announced that it would "not permit blackmail or political pressure to make it desist from this campaign." The reference to blackmail arose from the fact that Ewald had been decoyed into the house where he was assaulted with that in view; to avoid embarrassing the paper, he had resigned.

In the winter of 1928–1929 two newspapers in Augusta, Georgia, the *Chronicle* and the *Herald*, ordinarily competitors and bitterly antagonistic, forgot their differences and joined hands to reform the city administration and save it from threatened bankruptcy. They found they could see "eye to eye," as they expressed it, about the hospital and school boards, both politically dominated, and about the need for retrenchment. As a result the boards were freed of political pressure and the city's floating debt was reduced by one-fifth. A Citizens Good Government Committee was formed and a movement set under way for a city manager.

Concurrently the *Press* and the *Observer-Dispatch* in Utica, New York—not rivals, these, but under joint

A Neglected Story

ownership—printed news stories of widespread crime in that county, of connections between politicians and the underworld, of lotteries and other rackets, and of election frauds. The diversion of five millions in taxes on illicit liquor was charged. Federal agents took a hand in the investigation, and a grand jury returned more than two hundred indictments, naming among others seventy election inspectors. The mayor resigned.

Slot machines were wiped out of Holyoke, Massachusetts, through the efforts in 1938 of the *Transcript-Telegram*. William Dwight, the managing editor, heard reports occasionally that a few had been brought into the town over a weekend, but found that the fear of publicity kept them at a minimum. A disgruntled former welfare commissioner sued for libel on the ground that certain statements in the newspaper reflected on him, although they did not mention his name; he lost his action.

In setting down this record I have noted dates, in order to correct a prevalent impression that latter-day newspapers are indolent and neglectful. It may not be amiss to note briefly certain other crusades since the beginning of 1930:

In Denver the daily newspapers combined to compel an investigation of vice and improved the atmosphere; in Springfield, Missouri, the mayor and chief of police were indicted after a campaign by the *News* and the *Leader;* in San Francisco the chief of police assisted the daily newspapers in their fight on crime; in Cedar Rapids, Iowa, the *Gazette* exposed misgovernment and corruption, winning a Pulitzer prize; the award had gone earlier to the Atlanta *Constitution* for its fight against municipal graft; the Atlanta *Journal*, observing that the cleanup was not complete, told of the protection of bootleggers and gamblers, and elected a reform mayor; in Newark, New Jersey, the *Evening News* forced election frauds into the open, in spite of the theft of records from the City Hall and the Essex County Hall, so that sixty city employees and members of election boards were arrested; in Kansas City, Missouri, the *Journal-Post* crusaded successfully against vandalism and racketeering; in Cleveland the *Plain Dealer* exposed election frauds and in New Orleans the *Times-Picayune* did the same thing, at the same time; in Columbus, Ohio, the *Citizen* proved that a judge and four others had conspired in blackmailing; in Pensacola, Florida, the daily press overthrew the municipal machine; in Grand Rapids, Michigan, the *Press*, and in Elmira, New York, the *Star-Gazette*, supplanted a city machine with the city-manager form of administration.

Those instances, although not a complete record, should suffice to silence the skeptic.

In many of the crusades against political corruption, the outcome is the establishment of a city manager. This form of administration, inaugurated in Dayton, Ohio, in 1914, is now enjoyed by hundreds of cities, principally as a result of newspaper campaigns. It is not a panacea, but it has a good record in taking the sting out of politics, promoting efficiency, and averting waste. As a rule the city manager has had training as an engineer and competent fiscal experience; and where he has been unhindered in discharging dubious city employees, installing a merit system, and paring to a budget, the results have been gratifying. Statistics show that in Saginaw, Michigan the annual cost to each citizen under this plan is $17.15, whereas in other municipalities of the same size not so blessed the average is $45.83. Cincinnati has lower taxes than any other city of like population.

By proportional representation the city-manager plan hamstrings the machine, which is engendered by our political system. That organized minorities have power in municipal, State, and national government is due partly to the inertia of a large part of the electorate. Their apathy is not due, whatever they may say, to a repulsion against "a dirty game," but to an unwillingness to study and master the intricacies of primaries, caucuses, district, ward, and State organizations, the spoils system and log-rolling. Obscure politicians who breathe this atmosphere from their youth and become acquainted with its daedal inner workings, finally acquire authority as boss or a lieutenant.

Hearst, Pulitzer, Scripps, and Older, among others, have overthrown particular bosses and damaged special machines, but they have not done away with the machine system. By the adoption of proportional representation and the installation of nonpartisan administration, the city-manager plan has thrown a monkey wrench into the machinery. By the same devices, it has disarmed partisan newspapers. John Dana Wise, publisher of the Richmond *Times-Dispatch*, has said that partisanship was one of the greatest dangers to a free press, which "through indirection and coloring of news to conform to a newspaper policy, extends a hearty invitation to the public for corrective measures"; and Harrison Robertson, after sixty years of service for the Louisville *Courier-Journal*, has observed: "The independent newspaper nowadays gets the respect of the people. The day of the partisan paper is over. You can't run a paper successfully now as an organ of a party or a faction."

Newspaper Crusaders

A daily press alive to political developments and implications, but tied to the apron strings of no party, might do much to end the machine system. In some schools and colleges a serious attempt has been made in recent years to teach the functions and structure of politics on a realistic basis; this is useful. But the daily press has been more successful in getting out the vote when most it was needed. Its record as an enemy of governmental dishonesty is conspicuously good.

XII

For Safer Traffic

NGENUITY and persistence have been manifested by newspapers throughout this country in promoting traffic safety. They have been the chief contributors to a movement which has decreased the ratio of fatalities from automobile accidents. They have arranged frequent examinations of cars, encouraged careful driving with offers of free license plates, oil, and gas, devised "Safety-grams," a "Hall of Shame," and a "Dial of Death," printed editorials, cartoons, news, statistics, photographs, and maps. Although the motor remains a lethal instrument, the daily press and the agencies cooperating with it have succeeded at least in making their public safety-conscious.

From a toll of 1,291 deaths in 1911—exclusive of collisions with trains and streetcars—the rate increased steadily to 9,103 in 1920, when newspapers began bestirring themselves. The registration of motor vehicles in 1920 was less than ten millions; by 1938 it had tripled, with a geometrical increase in congestion and the hazards of a hurried civilization. In 1937 the loss of life was more than 40,000, and an insurance company noted warningly that in six major wars since the birth of the United States, conflicts aggregating fifteen years, the number of soldiers who were killed in action and who died of their wounds was about half the number slain by automobiles in a similar period. The motor was twice as deadly as warfare!

To combat this condition, newspapers began printing lists of victims and clocks or dials with hands pointing to the number killed during the preceding month or year. Some ran at the head of each story about an automobile accident the number of deaths in the community or the nation. The Indianapolis *Star* published an analysis of the automobile traffic problem and the *News* of that city printed daily for nearly two months pictures of dangerous corners. Prizes were offered for efficiency in preventing accidents and for safe driving. Detroit newspapers cooperated in a campaign to make the streets safer for drivers and passengers and pedestrians. The *Free Press*, the *Times*, and the *News* sponsored a better traffic ordinance, gave prizes for practicable suggestions, and arranged for the free inspection of brakes and gear. Clubs were organized elsewhere for safe drivers and stickers attached to their cars, better traffic control through lighting systems was devised, grade crossings were abolished, and municipal courts were brought to more effective discipline. These were among the opening guns.

The city editor of a Philadelphia newspaper observed that there were no warning signs for motorists near the school his child attended, and began a campaign, in which other newspapers joined, for the protection of 350,000 pupils. The *Courier-Post* ran six full-page weekly advertisements, financed by filling stations and garages, urging drivers to have their machines inspected periodically, and supplied seals, stamps, and duplicate sheets so

A Neglected Story

that records might be maintained at the garages. Inspection was free and no repairs were made save by request; the garages were repaid for their investment by an increase in their business. The *Ledger*, in news, editorials, and cartoons, reminded its readers of Frankenstein and the monster he had created. The *Inquirer* printed a map showing 300 street intersections where there had been ten or more accidents during the preceding year. The *Bulletin* printed daily articles on the subject and throughout the year a "Dial of Death." The *Record* published daily a box headed "Traffic Toll," and gave space to features as well as to editorials. The *Daily News* attacked hit-run drivers and negligent officials. All these papers supported the Automobile Club and the police in a three-month campaign for a traffic safety car, equipped with a loud speaker, addressing school children in particular.

In nearby Camden the *Courier and Post* organized a "Save a Life Club," which provided, among its services, free inspection of cars.

In Minneapolis the *Star* promoted another safety club, and the *Tribune* printed material supplied by the State Safety Council. The two collaborated in promoting a parade, in which some twenty cars wrecked recently were displayed, with seventy high-school students, in black hoods and cloaks, to represent the fatalities of the year. At the annual convention there of the State automobile club a life-size dummy dressed as a woman and stuffed with wheat was swung on a trolley across a street and hit by cars at speeds varying from twenty to sixty miles. In St. Paul the proceedings of the traffic court were put on the radio once a week and fully reported by the press; throughout the State, newspapers published

"Safetygrams," telling each day of a traffic violation to avoid. In that year, 1935, there was a fifteen per cent drop in accidents.

For two years, beginning in 1933, the San Francisco *News* ran daily an article dealing with highway safety, and at the end of the first reported a decrease by eighteen deaths. The articles were supplemented by cartoons and editorials and photographs, and by myriad windshield stickers, "Safety—or Else." The paper sent letters to drivers, owners, and organizations, conducted contests, distributed driving rules and pledges to be signed, called conferences of officials, and inaugurated an annual safety week. The San Francisco *Call-Bulletin* paid for 100 license plates to be given to careful drivers, based on photographs snapped by its cameramen. Daily pictures were published showing motorists exercising caution.

Cleveland had the second worse traffic fatality record in this country in 1937 when the *Plain Dealer* undertook a safety crusade. The city was surpassed only by Los Angeles, described by Chads O. Skinner of the *Plain Dealer* staff as "that municipality of mad motorists." A citizens' committee had explored the situation and had recommended detailed improvements, but its report had attracted only cursory notice. One of the purposes of the campaign was to abolish the approach to the traffic problem "by the method of cracker-barrel opinion."

Skinner was sent first to Evanston, Illinois, to study the advanced methods evolved there by the Traffic Safety Institute of Northwestern University; then to Milwaukee. His articles appeared on the first page and were cogently supported in editorials. The head of the safety institute at Northwestern was sent to Cleveland to study the situation and recommend a new technique

A Neglected Story

in control. The police department, which had never until then heard of such a thing as a traffic engineer, employed one and established a training academy for its traffic officers. The *Plain Dealer*, as part of its drive, organized an inter-precinct police safety contest, with an award, which further stimulated the members of the force. Its efforts were rewarded not only by the awakening of the police and other municipal departments but by galvanizing motorists themselves into a sense of their responsibility.

The result was a reduction by half in the rate of deaths from motor accidents.

In Oakland, California, the *Tribune* opened a drive with an eight-column banner and a five-column picture layout. It offered stickers to drivers who would sign a safety pledge and had to work its job printing plant overtime to supply the demand.

In Albany, New York, the *Times-Union* ran daily for a week on its first page an article devoted to the traffic problem and to safety, with an eight-column picture layout and photo-diagrams. It persuaded the governor to issue a proclamation on behalf of the campaign, and enlisted the aid of local and State police. Five gallons of gasoline and a quart of oil were given daily at its expense to the four best drivers of that day, and a "safety lane" was set up where cars were inspected without charge. Casualties were reduced by one-third, and traffic court cases declined by half.

In New Orleans the *Item* drove home to its readers the horrors of traffic accidents by printing gruesome pictures and factual descriptions. For years the *Times-Picayune* had displayed automobile fatalities prominently, with statistics in blackface at the top. In Memphis, too, the *Commercial Appeal* and the *Press-Scimitar* minced no words in their campaign, and the latter gave a full page of photographs of victims, many taken at hospital bedsides.

In Worcester, Massachusetts, the *Evening Post* named a dangerous thirteen-mile stretch of express highway the "Death Pike," and demanded that it be reconstructed. Heeding the protest, the governor saw to it that the road was rebuilt.

Unremitting attention and unflagging enthusiasm brought results but did not deprive the automobile of its deadliness. The newspaper campaign was compared at times with the fight for a safe-and-sane Fourth, but that dealt with one day instead of 365, and with an ebullient toy rather than a luxury which had been converted first into a convenience and then almost a necessity. By 1939, however, forty cities in which the campaign had been waged with especial vigor reported marked improvements. The president of the National Safety Council reported that during the first half of 1938 there were 3,670 fewer deaths from traffic accidents than during the same period the year before. In Canton, Ohio, the *Repository* had worked so effectively as to reduce the toll by three fourths. Special credit was given by the safety council to these newspapers:

Birmingham *News* and *Age-Herald*.
Columbus *Citizen*.
Dallas *News*.
San Diego *Union-Tribune*.
Gary, Indiana, *Post-Tribune*.
Syracuse *Herald*.
Tulsa *World*.

A Neglected Story

Youngstown *Vindicator*.
Washington *Post*.
Atlanta *Georgian*.
Kansas City *Star*.
Portland *Oregonian*.
Nashville *Banner*.
Fort Wayne *News-Sentinel*.
Rochester *Democrat and Chronicle*.
Providence *Bulletin*.

In New York the *Daily News*, a tabloid picture paper, made into a pamphlet a series of twenty-five cartoons by C. D. Batchelor, "Inviting the Undertaker," and in six months distributed 150,000 of them. Many were ordered in lots of thousands for school children. The pamphlet was sold at two cents a copy, to cover actual cost of production.

In addition to the papers cited by the safety council, mention should be made, even though the list cannot be complete, of certain others:

Dayton *Herald*.
Nashville *Banner*.
Kansas City *Kansan*.
Dallas *Journal*.
New York *Journal and American*.
Albany *Knickerbocker News*.
Tampa *Tribune*.
Atlanta *Journal*.
Akron *Times-Press*.
Pueblo *Star-Journal* and *Chieftain*.

In several States and cities, although the newspapers campaigned as vigorously there as elsewhere for safety, actual increases in the number of accidents and deaths were noted. Aside from the fatalities, the number injured, some maimed for life, often ran to a million through the nation. No civic or social cause called more loudly to be remedied, and to none did the daily press respond more ably, almost always with the earnest help of officials and organizations. This is not likely to be dismissed, within the memory of those now living, as "finished business." Newspapers must intensify their labors and improve their technique as they go along.

XIII

Civic and Social Betterment

VIRGINIA was first to establish, in 1773, a separate hospital for the insane. It was half a century before another State followed in her footsteps; then the Kentucky legislature appropriated funds for a similar institution, and it was opened in 1824 at Lexington. Even the older States on the seaboard sent patients there for treatment.

During the next century, in spite of the progressive spirit which had prompted its founding, there was little real improvement in Eastern State Hospital, as it came to be known. Barry Bingham, publisher of the Louisville *Courier-Journal*, found this out for himself. He did not assign a reporter to the job, although this newspaper offers a fine training ground, but made a personal tour of the three asylums in Kentucky, and wrote a lengthy article, in which he said:

> Other States entered the field of care for the insane, modern methods began to develop, and the Nation swept by in its progress. Kentucky, once the leader in this field of endeavor, fell back to the last rank. Now, wherever treatment for the mentally ailing is discussed, Kentucky is held up as the blackest example of a State whose institutions are a disgrace and a reproach to its citizens . . .
> Nothing brings home the horror of our hospital system like a personal visit, but most Kentuckians avoid the institutions and try not to think of their

existence. Friends and relatives of inmates hurry in for occasional visits and hurry out again, sick at heart from the sights they have seen.

However strong the sense of outrage in that first paragraph, however graphic the picture of a hospital scene and of patients "with the pitiful, helpless terror of woods creatures caught in a trap," the story was not hysterical but soundly reasoned, with a discussion of modern facilities elsewhere, an exculpation of the doctors and nurses, who seemed to be doing the best they could against insuperable odds, a warning that "political appointees" were not solely at fault, but that the people of the State must bear the brunt of the blame, and a sober discussion of possible remedies.

During January and April of 1937 the *Courier-Journal* printed a long series of illuminating articles on the care and cure of the demented elsewhere. From New York there was a story carrying the views of two outstanding administrators, from Boston an interview with a notable psychiatrist, another from the superintendent of the Missouri State Hospital at Farmington, another from the director of the Colorado Psychopathic Hospital at Denver, another from the administrator of the Massachusetts State Hospitals at Worcester, another from the superintendent of Iowa State Hospital at Mt. Pleasant, one from Baltimore, one from Iowa City. These were followed by interviews with Louisville psychiatrists and the president of the Kentucky Medical Association.

Strong editorial support accompanied the series of stories. On May 16 it was noted that members of the Mental Hospital Survey Committee had run across traces of the work done by an earlier board, in 1920–1924, "like evidences of a former civilization in an archeology find"; but "even the medical profession was rather

A Neglected Story

apathetic toward a change of policy." So long as there was no deliberate brutality, the public was satisfied. "But brutality can be committed by a policy as well as by an individual." And on the following day, under the heading, "Whatever It Costs Must Be Spent," there was an editorial about "the maintenance of the institutions on the early Eighteenth Century theory of custodial care alone," declaring that "slum tenements that Louisville is tearing down are not as insanitary or crowded as these institutions, nor half so dangerous." It dwelt upon the fire hazards, for one thing, and commented that "those responsible have been able to sleep in security they denied these helpless wards." The interest of the taxpayer had been ignored, too, for the State was carrying its own insurance. These excerpts will serve to illustrate the editorial method.

Within its orbit the *Courier-Journal* exercises strong influence. Among the newspapers which supported its crusade were the Bowling Green *News* and the *Times-Journal*, the Ashland *Independent*, the Union County *Advocate*, and the Middlesboro *News*. A. P. Bryan, state editor of the Lexington *Leader*, also visited the Eastern State Hospital for the Insane, not once but time and again, and took his camera along. He got in by saying he was visiting his brother, an attendant. One of his pictures showed a patient bound to his bed, although he was not violent but had a weakness for wandering about the ward occasionally. Bryan reported that he heard sounds of beatings but could not get a picture of one. As a result of his exposure five persons, including a former superintendent who resigned when he learned about the photographs, were indicted.

Subsequently a superintendent and seven attendants in Western State Hospital at Hopkinsville were indicted on charges of mistreating inmates.

Meanwhile, Governor A. B. (Happy) Chandler, one of those who had slept in a security denied to the patients, called a special session of the Legislature to act on a bill drawn to accord with the report of the survey committee. As summarized in the *Courier-Journal*, the measure included the following provisions:

> Removal of the institutional personnel from political interference.
> Procuring of qualified specialists in mental diseases for the State hospital staffs and protection of their tenure.
> Making possible eventual early treatment and cure of mental diseases.
> Council of the State Medical Association to nominate the director of the Division of Hospitals and Mental Hygiene.
> An assistant director and the superintendents of the institutions to be appointed on recommendation of the director.
> Specification of professional qualifications for technical members of the staffs.
> Removal from service only on written charges.

At the special session this bill was enacted and was accepted editorially by the *Courier-Journal* as "a sound piece of legislation." The newspaper had urged all along that an adequately trained personnel and modern treatment were more imperative than a new plant, and it urged now that the expense was "chargeable to the past, not the future." Delay, it argued, was "fatal extravagance." At a point where some might have dropped the campaign as a victory, it continued hammering to pull the bill into full operation. The result was a thorough renovation.

When newspapers learn of untoward conditions in State and local institutions, whether eleemosynary or

A Neglected Story

for discipline, they investigate as a rule at first hand. I have given space to the *Courier-Journal* crusade mainly because conditions were worse there than elsewhere, partly because the publisher himself took part in it, and partly because it serves to illustrate technique. Thus when 320 convicts died in a prison fire at Columbus in April, 1930, the Cleveland *Plain Dealer* was aroused to the situation in the Ohio penitentiaries and hospitals. It sent one of its ablest men to inspect each of them and entered upon what was described as "a good bludgeoning campaign." There, as in Kentucky, the fire hazards in overcrowded institutions, with no sprinkler systems or proper fire escapes and seldom with adequate extinguishers, were revealed; there, as in Kentucky, the remedy was sought in the improvement of methods and personnel rather than in a new physical plant for the penitentiary, hospitals for the insane, and schools for the blind and deaf. The rebuilding was left to a long-term program. As a result of a series of stories in 1930, many safety measures were taken by State officials, firetrap conditions were remedied, and the treatment was modernized. Owing to the overcrowding of the State buildings many demented persons were under care in private institutions, which billed the State for them; the *Plain Dealer* therefore investigated the private places along with the others and forced reforms.

Reports about the State hospital for the insane at Kankakee, Illinois, led to the voluntary commitment of an entirely sane reporter for the Chicago *Times*, a lively afternoon and Sunday tabloid paper. Another reporter, posing as a brother, gave him into custody, and at the end of a week assumed responsibility in order to get him out. His first story, "Seven Days in a Madhouse," told of the vile food and the crowding. The patients used a common drinking cup, and one was put into a tub of dirty water for fifteen hours because he was "violent." The circulation of the paper increased considerably but that was of minor importance in comparison with a drastic cleanup of the institution.

A year earlier, in 1934, the Chicago *Herald and Examiner* had exposed similar conditions in the Oak Forest Infirmary, the Cook County home for the aged. During a July heat wave thirty-nine of the residents died, and a reporter, who was sent to find out why, reported that the food was inadequate and improperly cooked, the inmates neglected, the medical attention poor. As a result of this the conditions were remedied. The Philadelphia *Record* revealed similar conditions, bordering on actual inhumanity, in the Byberry Hospital for the Insane, which caused investigations both by a grand jury and by a legislative committee, with consequent reform.

In North Carolina prisoners are maintained in State camps. The Charlotte *News* investigated and found that the feet of two prisoners had been frozen while in solitary confinement, so that it was necessary to amputate them. Another prisoner died in chains "in solitary." Publication of these facts led, for one thing, to a restoration of the whipping post, abolished ten years earlier, on the ground that at least it was the more humane. Only backward States, it is agreed, resort to the lash nowadays. Methods in the prison camps, however, were improved in other ways. In Ohio, which has prisons rather than the cheaper camps, the Toledo *News-Bee* demanded that the governor call a special session to

A Neglected Story

investigate the conditions in them; this was done and the conditions were remedied.

In Oakland, California, the *Tribune* set on foot a movement for a new county hospital, apart from the farm for the indigent, and over the opposition to a bond issue or a heavier tax levy succeeded, after a million and a half had been spent from taxes, in sponsoring and putting through a bond issue for an amount even larger. A model farm for the destitute and a new county hospital were the fruit of its campaign. The *Tribune* was successful also in procuring a new and better water supply for the city.

In Watsonville, California, the daily paper, morning and evening, is the *Register-Pajaronian*, a John P. Scripps paper. Pajaronia is a village adjacent to Watsonville, and in 1931 the jail there was a stone dungeon containing three cells, with no lights, no toilets, and little ventilation. Once a prisoner was locked within, it was considered superfluous to spend money on a guard. George Langley, a youthful runaway from Massachusetts, after escaping by the width of a continent, was imprisoned there. His cigarette set his cot afire, and it was an hour before passersby, who saw the smoke, could find anyone with a key to the place. Langley was alive when taken out, but he died soon of fright and burns.

The *Register-Pajaronian* tried to arouse the supervisors of Monterey county to some action, but was unsuccessful. By its editorials and its news stories, however, the paper attracted the attention of other larger dailies and so stirred the people of the State that money was voted to remodel the jail throughout.

Not always is a campaign for betterment of a State or local institution received with good grace by the readers.

Newspaper Crusaders

The taxpayer is sometimes more sensitive about his pocketbook than about the welfare of the State's charges. That it is difficult to arouse sympathy for prisoners, regarded as enemies of society, is not surprising; that the destitute or afflicted, usually through no fault of their own, should be subjected to callous indifference, is harder to explain. The newspaper that undertakes to improve conditions in prisons, hospitals, and poorhouses is subject at times to ill-natured derision, seldom to wholehearted approval. That this is so may be one reason why much work remains to be done in that field.

Wages, wherever paid, are a matter of valid public concern. More than once newspapers have served with distinction in revealing the hardships of the under-privileged and underpaid. Notable among such instances was a crusade undertaken on April 4, 1933, by the Cleveland *Plain Dealer*, of which B. P. Bole was president, Paul Bellamy editor, and N. R. Howard, predecessor of S. P. Barnett, managing editor. Two days after its first article, saying that workers in the city faced the lowest wage scales they had ever known, four shops employing women were notified by the sanitary police that they must provide decent working conditions; in a week three complied, and the fourth got an extension of time to move to better quarters, which it promptly did. This was an auspicious beginning, and the campaign continued auspiciously.

Thereafter articles and editorials were printed several times each week. The *Plain Dealer* declared that wages were "far below subsistence levels," and that "the worker is often as badly off as the workless in these distressing times." This was followed by an article showing that many workers for long hours got as little as $5 a week, and another saying that "one of the biggest factors in contributing to the low wages paid workers here is the large number of young people, boys and girls, employed in the various industries." Some children, starting in at $7 a week, were soon cut to $3.

Editorially, the newspaper demanded a State wage law "with teeth." A leading clergyman denounced the "private greed and public callousness upon which the sweatshop flourishes." The president of an oil company instructed department heads to buy no supplies from manufacturers who gave unreasonable pay. Presently a garment manufacturer installed a dressing room and lunch place; another moved from a basement to a floor where there was more light and air; a paper stock concern provided hot water at its washstands and installed a sanitary drinking fountain. William Green, president of the American Federation of Labor, in Cleveland to make a speech, gave the newspaper an interview condemning sweatshop employers "because the conditions under which these parasites thrive mean the exploitation of women and children." The *Plain Dealer* commented the next day on "The High Cost of Low Wages," and again demanded a minimum wage enactment. Such a bill had been introduced in the legislature by William R. Pringle.

The revelations prompted the chief prosecutor in the Cleveland police court to make an investigation, and he brought out testimony that women had fainted from overwork, that girls received fifty-five cents for thirteen hours' work and eighty-five cents for twenty-two hours' work. In that factory other employees worked long hours without lunch. Women were penalized for talking while at their machines in another shop. The president and secretary of a hat-manufacturing company were arrested on charges of violating the existent inadequate law.

The Ohio Chamber of Commerce urged that the Pringle bill be limited in operation to two years. This the *Plain Dealer* strongly opposed and reported in detail rallies throughout the State favoring the measure as it was. The campaign continued in the news columns and on the editorial page for some six months, and the bill became law substantially as it was written.

In Virginia the Richmond *Times-Dispatch* concentrated its campaign on better working conditions for women. Through its efforts a bill regulating hours was passed through one branch of the legislature but not the other; at the 1936 session success, by almost unanimous vote in each house, crowned the crusade. The law is by no means a model, for the Old Dominion, like other States south of the Mason and Dixon Line, balks at such measures; but it provides for a maximum forty-eight-hour week, with a stipulation against more than nine hours in one day. That it should be necessary to restrict employers anywhere to nine hours as a "short" day is a commentary on industrial conditions. The *Times-Dispatch*, a progressive paper and a leader, was the first to urge a county-manager form of government for Henrico County, adjoining Richmond, and won over a determined opposition by the "courthouse ring." At that time only six counties in the United States enjoyed this improved form of administration. The *Times-Dispatch* took the lead also in the movement for a new million-dollar State Library; two of its editorials in this cause were printed on the first page.

A Neglected Story

In Atlanta the *Georgian* specialized on better pay for city employes, school teachers, policemen, and firemen; the paper demanded editorially that women teachers, who did the same work as men, should get as much money, but that all should receive more; and when, after two defeats, it was victorious in a three-year campaign, it announced the result in an eight-column banner line. It had less difficulty getting better pay for policemen and firemen, whose lives, as it pointed out, were in constant jeopardy in the service of the public.

From the time when Hearst acquired the *Georgian* in 1912 it was active in behalf of better public schools, both in the city and the county. It campaigned for improved buildings and helped raise funds for Emory and Oglethorpe Universities and for Columbia Seminary. As a result of its initiative and cooperation Atlanta acquired an excellent public school system, with modern and sanitary buildings, properly equipped against fire. Wall maps, globes, and other educational equipment have been provided, with adequate playgrounds. The *Georgian* made the initial subscription to a fund to provide books and clothes for needy children. Among its other services to its public were campaigns for a better sewage system, a municipal golf course, and the paving of streets, some of them downtown, which were deep in mud on rainy days. It helped build a plaza above "Smoke Gulch," bisecting the business and shopping area, in which the railroads ran. It sponsored an ordinance for pasteurized milk, and when the mayor signed it, after a campaign which had gone on for years, it announced the news in a banner headline.

In Houston, Texas, Sue Barnett, a reporter for the *Press*, "disguised" herself and applied successfully for work in garment shops. She found that the average wage scales for girls were $3 and $4 a week, and wrote a series of articles about the conditions under which they worked, their food and health, the makeshifts of their lives. The state labor commissioner, as a consequence, investigated these "sweatshops" and cleaned them up.

Parent-teacher associations were born of the thrifty notion that valuable school property should not be permitted to stand idle so much of the time. Thus in Terre Haute John C. Schaffer's *Post* set afoot a movement to utilize them of an evening for gatherings of the faculties with the parents; the same thing was done in Atlanta and in scores of other places.

In some cities newspapers have recognized loan "sharks" as an anti-social force, and have crusaded to abate their extortions. In Portland the *Oregonian* printed a series of stories about victims who paid from $9.75 to $15 for the use of $30 for three months, and exposed jokers in the State law which made this possible. It closed its advertising columns to companies which charged more than three per cent a month, and caused the enactment of a new small-loans measure.

In Washington, D. C., the *Times* followed suit as late as 1939 by refusing to accept advertisements from usurers and by printing a series of stories about their avaricious practices. In San Francisco the *News*, much earlier, had forced the amendment of the city ordinance governing lenders, then had sponsored a new and better State law. In other cities and States similar reforms were effected.

In some cases these changes were abetted by a national philanthropic foundation, which formulated a model small-loans act and tried to get it adopted as a uniform

A Neglected Story

State measure. Its emissaries lobbied with varying success, and found that they could accomplish nothing without newspaper support, whereas in many instances newspapers singlehanded did better.

Gus Korach, a Slovak day laborer, became the central figure, "The Man Nobody Knows," in a crusade conducted by the Cleveland *Press*. Korach, who spoke poor English, managed to make Clayton Fritchey, a reporter for the *Press*, understand how and why he had invested the savings of thirty years' toil in a graveyard. He had been injured in the World War and thought his days were numbered, and he had a horror of the Potter's Field. Fritchey found that land bought for fifty thousand had been sold, mostly to persons in reduced or poor circumstances, for some five million. Throughout the United States, it was estimated, the annual turnover in graveyard graft amounted to thirty millions. In Ohio, and subsequently elsewhere, the racket was abolished and its ringleaders sent to prison.

After the Scripps-Howard group withdrew in 1938 from the Buffalo *Times*, the usefulness of Fred Charles, its chief editorial writer, was expanded by enabling him to do reporting as well as commenting. He was assigned to write a series of articles about the local traction company and its finances, another about cash relief for the unemployed, another about naturalizing citizens; he was nominated gratefully as "Public Servant No. 1." His work was confined to investigations and campaigns in the public interest.

Under the leadership of Lowry Martin, publisher of the Corsicana *Sun*, the Texas Good Roads Association, of which he was president, won the support of fifty daily newspapers and five times as many weeklies in a campaign to promote street and highway safety, and to oppose unsightly outdoor advertising, while emphasizing the scenic, recreational, and historic attractions of the State. Kentucky newspapers made possible, by their advocacy, the acquisition of 40,000 acres around Mammoth Cave, and its transformation into a national park. In the Dakotas the newspapers took the lead in reclaiming vast waste areas.

In Attleboro, Massachusetts, the *Daily Sun* devoted hundreds of columns between 1909 and 1914 to an exposition of the outgrown town government, and so promoted the adoption of a new and sound city charter. In 1934 it inaugurated a ten-year plan looking to a celebration in 1944, when the community would be 250 years old. To that end an exposition was held, and a committee of community leaders went to work. The *Daily Sun* made it a practice to give due credit when work was done for the city or money given to it, not with the purpose of buying money and services with publicity, as its publisher, C. C. Cain, explained, but to change public apathy into appreciation. This was so effective that before long it was a matter of comment when a sizable estate was settled which did not make some public bequest.

Intelligent community service of that sort is contagious. In 1922 the Minneapolis *Journal* began urging its readers to take stock of their community, and planned a week devoted to the city, its advantages, and its needs. Within twenty-four hours it had enlisted seventy-two organizations in its campaign; before the week began, December 3, 210 had pledged their support. Prizes of $25 to $250

A Neglected Story

were offered for the best essays on the history, status, and future of the town. During Minneapolis Week there were mass meetings and rallies, pageants, and exhibits of the city's products. It is a musical city and excellent symphony concerts were given free. Civic pride was awakened. A three-million-dollar auditorium was erected, a handsome new hotel was constructed, and the town grew vastly. A new public library, better paving and lighting, and an improved city charter were among the fruits of the movement.

Smaller towns followed suit. In Republican City, Nebraska, the *Ranger;* in Storm Lake, Iowa, the *Pilot-Tribune*, a weekly paper; and in Canova, South Dakota, the *Herald*, brought an awakening. In Quakertown, Pennsylvania, the *Free Press* printed eighty weekly editorials before it got an adequate sewerage system. The *Union-Star* of Schenectady formed a Civic Pride Committee and the *News-Index* in Evanston, Illinois, forced a city cleanup, as did Warren G. Harding's *Daily Star* in Marion. In Grand Rapids the *Press* promoted a campaign to beautify the town. Elsewhere, notably in Dallas, where the *News* took the lead, and in Springfield, Massachusetts, where the *Republican* took up the cause, city planning has been set afoot.

In Kansas City the *Star* campaigned five years to get a municipal auditorium and raised a fund to rebuild it when it burned. The Birmingham *News* and the Centralia, Illinois, *Sentinel*, have been among those which have stimulated community effort with loving cups in appreciation. Other dailies have seen to it that neglected street signs and house numbers were posted.

A ten-year improvement plan for Youngstown, Ohio, languished because of the 1929 depression, and was not revived until Federal funds became available to meet part of the expense. Under the urging of the *Vindicator*, a three-million-dollar plan to widen narrow streets and cut new traffic arteries, a million-dollar fund to build bridges, and a half-million-dollar fund for park improvements, were undertaken. Using red ink as well as black, the *Vindicator* told daily of the need for these improvements and of the progress of its campaign for bond issues, which required a vote of sixty-five per cent to be approved. While bond issues were failing in neighboring cities, the Youngstown improvement went over with a bang.

Scattering villages in the Hempstead area of Long Island were consolidated into a single community through the work of the *Nassau Daily Review-Star*, into which several weeklies and dailies were merged. One of its plans to arouse interest was an award for the most valuable service to the whole area; this went first to a surgeon who had plugged steadily for a hospital where the poor could receive treatment at the public expense, and who had been chiefly instrumental in putting through a bond issue for it at the depth of the depression. The newspaper gave a dinner in his honor, with a medallion and a citation.

Newspapers have exposed medical frauds and financial skulduggeries. The El Paso *Herald-Post* sent one man to the penitentiary for a bucket-shop swindle and three for a gold-mine bubble, while it caused the indictment of fourteen others. The Boston *Post* exposed Charles Ponzi, and a group of midwestern papers revealed the "Drake Estate" fraud, in which thousands had been victimized. Elmer S. Huckins of Milwaukee, whose scheme was similar to Ponzi's, in that he paid extravagant interest out

A Neglected Story

of new capital as it flowed in, was brought to terms by the *Journal* of that city.

In the role of amateur detectives, newspaper reporters have solved scores of crimes when the officials on duty seemed stymied, and have recovered more than one victim of kidnapers. They saved the life of a Negro from whom Pinkerton detectives had extorted a false confession while at work on the murder of a banker in Lexington, Kentucky, and two white youths were hanged for the crime. They solved the murder of a school teacher in Bedford, Indiana; in this case an innocent quarryman confessed to detectives of the same agency and was tried for his life but acquitted; the murderer, a well-to-do lawyer, was never brought to justice. The Cleveland *Press* caused the release of Frank Basey, unjustly imprisoned for robbery; the Buffalo *Times* procured a pardon for Edward Larkman, after he had been sentenced to imprisonment for life on account of a holdup in which he had taken no part.

A Negro sentenced to death for murder in the first degree was set free through the work of Julian Houseman, a reporter for the *News-Leader* of Richmond, Virginia. The man had been arrested in New York and extradited under mistaken identity for another Negro; he wrote to the newspaper, declaring his innocence, after he had been sentenced. Houseman obtained the evidence and made the affidavit on which a new trial was granted and the convicted man cleared.

Although certain phases and instances of social and civic activity on the part of the press are discussed elsewhere, the work in this field is so many-sided that it is impossible here to set down all that has been done. Providing clothes for the needy in winter, Christmas funds, funds for ice in summer, for fresh air, and for relief at all seasons, are by now almost a commonplace. In such campaigns the press cooperates with organized charitable and philanthropic groups.

Fire hazards have been reduced through newspaper effort, housing has been improved, and lecture courses promoted. Newspapers have encouraged the formation of poultry clubs for girls, pig clubs for boys, calf clubs for both of them. They have helped establish traveling libraries for the benefit of homes distant from book centers, and have labored almost everywhere for better educational facilities. They have evoked stimulating slogans. They have dealt with marketing problems and have aided rural producers in finding new markets. Their conspicuous display of weather forecasts and reports, which is a part of their community service, is taken quite as a matter of course by their readers, who seldom realize the value of the "ear" or other space in which the information is printed. Whether good or bad, the weather is a part of the newspaper's responsibility, just as is conduct affecting public welfare for good or ill. As an avenue of recognition and accolade, as an agency to safeguard the public against offenders and to bring offenders to justice, as a guardian, advocate, and counselor, the press serves constantly for betterment.

XIV

Janus in Chicago

CONSPICUOUS among useful crusades was one by which the Chicago *Daily News* lopped more than $1,000,000 off an extortionate schedule of receivership fees, and saved the money for investors who seemed unable to protect themselves. This was followed by slashing $500,000 from $721,000 fees in another case, and $235,000 in still another. More, the example was emulated successfully elsewhere, so that it became increasingly difficult for avaricious lawyers and financiers to batten on bankruptcies, like vultures on a corpse.

Although a "reform-by-exposé," in Sam Acheson's compact phrase, the Chicago campaign did not take the pattern of a political cleanup; it was directed against a group who were among the most devoted readers of the *Daily News*. Under the ownership of Victor F. Lawson this paper had worked for years for the establishment of postal savings banks, and its owner had come to be known as father of the system; it had been a leader in good causes, among others the establishment of a sanitarium for children of the poor. Lawson had suspended his Sunday issue because he thought it a desecration of the day.

Newspaper Crusaders

Yet despite the reputation of the *Daily News* for piety and civic progressiveness, it had engaged in a circulation fight with Hearst's *Evening American* in which two of its employees were killed just outside Chicago's City Hall, without legal redress. True, when the Chicago *Tribune*'s "Jake" Lingle was slain by gangsters, who suspected him of double-dealing, the *Daily News* apparently concluded that the time had come to speak its mind; On its first page, in an editorial two columns wide, it said:

> Some complaisant persons are wont to say that the gangsters merely kill one another, thus saving the public the cost of convicting them. That shallow view cannot be dismissed too summarily. It is a dangerous delusion. The murder of Alfred Lingle . . . is a plain notification that under the present police administration the gangsters regard themselves as free to run the city for their own vicious uses . . . The city of Chicago is the victim of a vicious administration system. That system must go.

Al Capone, however, and his henchmen continued for years "to run the city for their own vicious uses," and the Chicago press, preoccupied with its own internecine struggle, did not put an end to the administration which protected them. The newspaper conflict continued until after the death of Lawson in 1931, when Col. Frank Knox, former general manager of all the Hearst papers, acquired control of the *Daily News*. Gradually he built up for it a name as a conservative and painstaking repositary of current events, free of sensationalism or vulgarity, with a spineless and negligible editorial page. Thus, under the very nose of "the world's greatest newspaper," it was able to advertise:

> The Chicago *Daily News* has *greater* Home Coverage and reaches *more* Able-to-Buy families than any other daily newspaper in Chicago. Its penetration of home influence extends to every section of the city and suburbs. The fact that *as far back as the records go* this newspaper has carried *more*

A Neglected Story

Total Display and *more* Retail Advertising than any other Chicago newspaper—morning, evening or Sunday—is evidence of the results it produces for advertisers.

Boasting that it was "a newspaper to be read by every member of the family," the *Daily News* had an edge on the *Tribune*, which was not edited for adolescents.

At the core of Samuel Insull's utilities empire was a two-billion-dollar holding company, Middle West Utilities. It controlled fourteen systems supplying light, power, and heat, sometimes gas and ice, to five thousand towns in thirty States. When it was thrown into bankruptcy in 1932 its securities aggregated $1,250,000,000 and its floating indebtedness $600,000,000. The litigation thus begun continued nearly four years, with charges of mismanagement against officers of the company and of collusion in the appointment of receivers. Samuel Insull slipped away to Greece.

In a dispute between holders of $40,000,000 in "gold debentures" and bankers who had advanced funds amounting to $27,000,000 to the corporation there was expressed the first difficulty about disposition of what could be salvaged from the wreckage; when this had been straightened out, there was a reorganization. Sixteen months were spent in debating several plans submitted for a new setup. To be approved, such a plan under the Illinois law required the consent of two-thirds of each type of creditor, and there were purchasers of $220,000,000 in common and preferred stocks to be considered.

Not long before this the judge of a Federal District Court in San Francisco had been impeached on the charge that he had profited by the appointment of receivers and had manifested favoritism; in the Senate, although the vote was heavily adverse, the two-thirds necessary for conviction was not mustered, and the charge was dismissed. In the Federal court at Chicago, where the Middle West Utilities receivership proceedings dragged their weary length, no such suspicion arose. Judge James H. Wilkerson forecast, as the hearings grew more prolonged, that the company would "belong to the lawyers" unless an agreement were reached speedily; he saw to it that the lawyers did not get everything, nor even the half of what they demanded.

John A. Mirt, financial editor of the *Daily News*, had begun a series of articles dealing lucidly with the involved litigation. When finally a scheme of reorganization was accepted, it was hailed by the attorneys as a great victory; but Mirt observed that it made no provision whatever for the numerous holders of fewer than one hundred shares of stock, and a little later he warned that not even the others would enjoy the fruits of victory if the lawyers had their way. Already, he knew, bills for expenses and fees were being prepared; and he foretold "quite a formidable army, with many volunteer recruits in the last stages of the more than three and one-half years of litigation which ended in a questionable 'victory' for the stockholders." His sarcasm was directed repeatedly at the soldiery of counsel and "experts" in the Middle West Utilities case, as in this passage:

> Late hearings in the reorganization of the company showed these soldiers grouped three and four deep before Judge Wilkerson. Such patriotism one has seldom seen . . . there was always a volunteer to prolong the warfare. In the case of the World War, many of the objectors today are asking for a bonus. It establishes a precedent for those who "objected" in the Middle West war.
>
> The lawyer division of this bonus army may contain twenty or more regiments, but each regiment has its own ideas as to the worth of its patriotic services in the defense of Middle West stockholders. Each has his own ideas

regarding the peace terms and what constitutes liberal treatment of the vanquished. The League of Nations may have to be called into the picture.

Solidly behind the attorney contingent and serving as a protective force is the division made up of committees. That body is prepared to move forward, ready to give and take—mostly take. There are also several reserve forces.

Mirt had not set himself up as a seer, nor the seventh son of a seventh son. There was a solid background for his anticipatory wit, as was proved a week later when claims for fees and expenses of $1,604,095 were filed with Judge Wilkerson. Already, in prior proceedings, $400,000 in fees had been granted; now there was a demand for over a million and a half more; the expenses which, so it was asserted, had been incurred, amounted to less than $223,000.

Daniel G. Green, trustee of the property, had estimated its annual earnings at a million; the demands for fees and expenses, as Mirt observed, would devour "the prospective earnings of the Middle West Corporation for all of this year and most of 1937"; if the claim were met it would precipitate another receivership, he said, for the company had nothing like that sum, and added:

> Neither does it seem to make any difference to the askers that all they want is the prospective earnings of the company for the next two years . . . that five firms alone want the net profits of 1936. A month ago, when it became apparent that the "free army" was about to descend on the Federal court, Judge Wilkerson made it clear to those involved in the reorganization that he expected them to submit petitions for fees and expenses which were moderate and within the range of reason. It is hard to fathom what bills might have been submitted had this request not been made.

Supporting its financial writer editorially, the *Daily News* suggested that Judge Wilkerson "had been cast for the role of Horatius at the bridge." Mirt himself, wading diligently through the thick and tedious petitions, found that lawyers were charging for the time they spent in reading newspaper accounts of the proceedings. "Their time is most valuable," he reported; "a dollar or more a minute is a fair figure for their worth." When the attorneys telephoned him at his office, he urged that they talk fast, because he would hate to have the conversation cost Middle West stockholders too much money.

Neither the stockholders nor the note holders registered protest on their own account with the court. Their lawyers feared that if they said publicly, as they admitted privately, that fees demanded by others were exorbitant, the complaint might act as a boomerang. Mirt, commenting on the "laryngitis epidemic" which had smitten them, suggested that they had taken a cue from Shakespeare and thought that "the better part of valor is discretion." As for the reorganized corporation, a similar silence prevailed there.

> The situation is much the same as exists among attorneys [Mirt explained]. Represented on the board of the new corporation are several groups which are seeking fees in the case. Perhaps, being the outgrowth of a court decree, the new corporation must stand mute and depend on the court to obtain a full understanding without company assistance. It can be, therefore, that propriety rather than the personal interest of a director is responsible for this situation.

Some of the stockholders and creditors evidently read Mirt's columns, for they acted on advice which he gave, to write direct to the court. Then one of the attorneys for the note holders said he meant to object to some of the claims, whereupon another declared that the total asked was not unreasonable; he reminded his fellow at the bar that the government, in cases of fraud, sometimes paid informers as high as half of its recoveries.

A Neglected Story

Aroused finally by the furore, the Reconstruction Finance Corporation, which had taken 165,000 shares of the reorganized corporation, sent a lawyer into the court on the last day for entering objections to the fees, to ask for further time. Simultaneously a committee protested against paying nearly a quarter of a million dollars to six lawyers and an expert. After due study of the claims, the lawyer for the Federal agency presented a voluminous objection, listing five main points but pointing out also that some of the claimants were "pure volunteers," whose suggestions were wholly unacceptable, while others were "purely destructive."

Judge Wilkerson said from the bench that lawyers should collect at least part of their fees from their clients, and that there was a growing opinion that fees asked by counsel tended to become "grossly exorbitant." He even suggested that a "civic duty" might govern in certain cases. Certainly no such sense of duty—although the court did not say this—had actuated lawyers who had solicited security holders to enter the litigation, and had signed names to petitions in some cases without permission.

Citations showed that in other big receiverships, lawyers had charged as much as $11.09 an hour; in the Middle West case the fees ranged from $21 to $74 an hour; even budding junior partners were rated at $45 to $50 an hour.

Judge Wilkerson insisted that the client was the primary debtor for legal service, and that where a litigant had made an actual contribution to the reorganization he was entitled at least to as much compensation from the Middle West company as his lawyer. Without exception the attorneys who had figured in the case for a long while found this view most disquieting. Some of them insisted, in supplemental briefs, that the fees they had demanded were much less than they actually deserved.

In a thirty-page memorandum filed by one law firm there was the clear intimation that Judge Wilkerson's suggestion that "civic duty" should govern the claimants was downright communistic. The brief set forth that the whole notion of "equality, proper allocation of charges, reasonableness in the absolute sense, and so on" had been debated thoroughly at the seventeenth congress of the Communist Party in Moscow in 1934, and that these ideas had been abandoned as "unworkable." Joseph Stalin was quoted to confound the bench. This the *Daily News* reported with suitable comment.

Not in the least befuddled nor confounded, Judge Wilkerson, after due deliberation, slashed the fees to thirty per cent of the total. One claim by an expert witness of $71,797 was thrown out bodily, and $180,000 was cut off the fees of a single law firm. None was to be paid in full. In the *Daily News* of September 30, 1936, Mirt set down for his readers the points of law in Judge Wilkerson's opinion which might serve as blueprint for others who were fighting exorbitant fees in such cases, as follows:

> Obstructionists should not be paid for time wasted in pressing claims that are unreasonable and without merit.
>
> An applicant cannot claim more out of the general fund because he has assured his clients that he would not look to them for fees, but would look to the court for compensation.
>
> The court must try to draw the line between services and expenses incident to the reorganization and those which are strictly in the interest of an individual or group.
>
> Attorneys performing administrative matters, unless authorized by the court to act on behalf of the receivers, must look to their clients for compensation.

A Neglected Story

The court is not bound by any agreements as to amounts which the parties seeking such allowances may have made among themselves.

Hours of time spent, while an element to be considered, are not controlling, and sometimes of very little importance.

Items of expense incurred primarily for the benefit of a class of creditors or stockholders and contributing to the plan only indirectly or remotely cannot be allowed.

The value of the interest represented by an attorney is one of the elements which must be considered in fixing a fee.

Application of those sound principles, said the *Daily News* editorially, would make bankruptcies "unattractive to the lawyers who have been inclined, on slim pretext, to wedge themselves into such procedures. If their work is to entitle them to no claim upon the estate, obviously their intervention would be as profitless to themselves as to the public."

Among those to follow the trail blazed in Chicago were the *Evening News* in Newark, New Jersey, the *Evening American* in Boston, and the *News* in San Francisco, where a Federal judge had been impeached vainly on account of his attitude toward rapacious receivers.

Moreover, Attorney General Frank Murphy, addressing the annual lunch of the Associated Press in 1939, declared that there must be a thorough overhauling of the system by which the Federal courts had handled bankruptcies and receiverships, because it was bringing the judiciary into disrespect.

James Keeley, while managing editor of the Chicago *Tribune*, had been on the friendliest terms with Samuel Insull and an ally of his utilities exploits. Indeed, Insull and Lawson of the *Daily News* contributed to a million-dollar fund to finance Keeley when he left the *Tribune* to compete with it by purchasing the seedy *Inter-Ocean* and the *Record Herald*, which he merged unsuccessfully under the name of the *Herald*. Keeley had been a spectacular showman as managing editor of the *Tribune*, and was credited with devising its boastful title, "The World's Greatest Newspaper"; when its price was reduced he advertised: "The Greatest Show on Earth—1 cent." Observing the circulation, advertising, and influence of the *Daily News*, he decided to get out a morning paper of the afternoon type, with big headlines, snappy stories, and print easy to read. It was a vaudeville performance, and never the world's greatest newspaper from any standpoint.

Nevertheless, Keeley was the originator of crusades which came in time to exercise a wide national influence for good. On the evening of July 4, 1899, when he was beside a child gravely ill, the thunder of giant firecrackers outside disturbed her, and he telephoned his office to collect figures from thirty cities on fatalities and accidents that day. The figures showed that the celebration of a national holiday had cost more in suffering and life than the Spanish-American War. The next year the *Tribune*, demanding a "sane Fourth," presented a similar table of statistics, and thereafter other newspapers followed suit, until mortality and casualties were reduced by more than nine-tenths.

A campaign against public drinking cups was waged almost entirely with cartoons and editorials. An exposure of advertising doctors, who guaranteed to cure "social diseases" and always found evidence of them, even in thoroughly healthy reporters for the *Tribune*, resulted in driving the herd away.

So far as I can find the *Tribune* was first to campaign against the sale of firearms to the general public. It

A Neglected Story

showed that a single mail-order house had sold more than a thousand in one day, and commented editorially that Chicago, with half the population of London, had an average of ten times as many killings with guns. Its suggestion was that the government take over a monopoly of the manufacture and sale of such weapons, which was not done; but in Chicago and in other large cities ordinances were adopted finally requiring municipal permission for the purchase or ownership of revolvers.

In the effort to reduce automobile accidents and fatalities, the *Tribune* also was a leader. On January 1, 1924, it devoted ten columns to the victims of the motor during the year before; and during that year it had printed daily a "clock of death" cartoon, the hands on the dial pointing to statistics of fatalities not only from automobiles but from prohibition bootleg liquor and from firearms.

After Cincinnati had been put through the Scripps wash tub, Chicago succeeded to its unhappy title as the worst governed city in the United States. The *Tribune* railed more loudly than the *Daily News* against the partnership between the political machine, its rich supporters, and the racketeers, but did not succeed in disturbing the entente. Its revelations, indeed, caused strong resentment in some of its readers, who thought it was giving the city a black eye without accomplishing any improvement.

Chicago was known everywhere as the most racket-ridden city in this country, and its press appeared unable to cope with the condition. Federal prosecutors finally stepped in and, amid the mirth of a nation, convicted Al Capone, the town's chieftain in crime, of having impolitely evaded his income taxes. Capone had been on amiable terms with reporters for Chicago newspapers; this fact, which became widely known, besmirched the name of a craft noteworthy as a rule for its integrity.

Milton S. Mayer of the University of Chicago has described the city of "the world's greatest newspaper" as "the world's champion sinkhole." All but bankrupt, its teachers in a crippled school system were doubtful from month to month whether they would get their pay. Its streets were dirty and ill paved. The *Tribune's* platform, "Make Chicago the First City in the World," was a bitter jest on the lips of its readers. The call of the *Daily News* for a city-manager system inspired an essay contest on the subject in the public schools, and officials promptly put a stop to it. It was clear that Chicago officials did not want too much known about municipal administration and it appeared that Chicago newspapers could not combat that aim. The *Tribune* and the *Daily News* blanketed the city; there and in the suburbs not many literate persons could be found who did not read one or both of them; and although each of them had crusaded on occasion with conspicuously good effect they appeared incompetent, singly or together, to deal with the obvious and urgent evil afflicting a great metropolis.

XV

Phoenix in Toledo

SELDOM have newspapers manifested more clearly their capacity for constructive action than in Toledo. Here, at the heart of a vast area of mass production, when violent labor troubles were fomented by arrogant employers and had aroused adverse national attention, when banks had failed and big plants were moving away as from a plague, the daily press was the mainspring in establishing industrial peace, efficient self-government, confidence, and prosperity. Collapse was averted, possibly the flames of revolution. Through a complete overturn of public opinion, there and throughout this country, a city was reclaimed and restored.

Although the first bank failure occurred in 1931 and precipitated runs which closed two others, Toledo's troubles became critical during a strike called April 12, 1934, at the Auto-Lite plant. Executives there as elsewhere throughout the area, impatient with troublesome employees, thought that blackjacks, tear gas, and guns were the right means of dealing with them. The strike continued seven weeks, during which the National Guard was called out. Two lives were sacrificed, scores were injured, some maimed for life. Federal intermediaries brought a semblance of order, but captains of industry were dismayed, in some cases horrified, to see workers on every side scrambling to join labor unions.

There had been minor strikes before the bloody Auto-Lite battles and others were to follow; but the second major conflict came a year later, when three thousand employees walked out of the Chevrolet transmission plant, which supplied many assembly lines. As a consequence it was necessary to close a score of plants elsewhere, affecting thirty thousand workers. In Toledo pickets would not permit bookkeepers or telephone operators to enter the plant for fear they might be production workers. Edward F. McGrady, then First Assistant Secretary of Labor, was summoned, and at the end of three weeks peace was reestablished.

Unionization was going rapidly ahead, and there was a strike a month later of power-house employees, with the threat of a general walkout. In one large area the street lights were out and live wires dangled dangerously. By now the city's deplorable plight was being blazoned in newspapers elsewhere and was a common topic of discussion in clubs and smoking cars. Down the line went the word: "Get out of Toledo!" Auto-Lite set up a string of plants in Michigan, Illinois, and southern Ohio. At the behest of an important customer, one manufacturer built a million-dollar plant in another center.

The big news agencies did not maintain at that time bureaus in Toledo, but depended on part-time service by local newspaper men. The Associated Press, for example, sent out on June 5, 1935, a two-column story worth quoting in part, as an illustration of what people in other sections were reading about the situation:

A Neglected Story

A condition of virtual industrial paralysis fell on this city of more than 300,000 population today as union electrical workers went on strike, causing a serious shortage of power.

One after another huge factories shut down, unable to operate without electricity, and city officials predicted that before the day was done more than 30,000 industrial workers would be idle . . .

The police and fire alarm systems, nearly all radios, the drawbridges over the Maumee River, permitting the passage of lake freighters, and street cars and trackless trolleys are threatened.

Elevators in office buildings and even office work dependent on equipment operated by electricity, and electric sweepers and clocks are affected, and postal service is hampered because the machines used for cancelling and handling mail are operated by electricity.

Among the large plants threatened with closing are [here followed an imposing list] and a number of metal stamping plants which manufacture parts for automobiles.

The story quoted the general manager of the power plant as saying there was "no justification whatever" for the strike. From the newspaper standpoint, which puts a premium on violence, suspense, and all forms of emotional excitement, this was a good story, and the New York *Sun*, for one, thought it worth a two-column headline on its first page. The dire conditions described were not an actuality but were "threatened" or "virtual"; in a nation of headline readers this might escape notice.

By citing that instance I do not mean to imply that the Associated Press was more sensational than other agencies and correspondents, or that the *Sun* had a greater predilection for disaster than its fellows. I chose it because it constituted a fair example of what outside papers were using.

On a peremptory recall to Toledo, the Assistant Secretary of Labor, then flying from place to place as the ace mediator of industrial trouble, perceived that something drastic must be done. At seven o'clock of a Sunday morning he telephoned the editors of the daily papers for a conference: Grove Patterson of the *Blade,* Carlton K. Matson of the *News-Bee,* and Richard C. Patterson, general manager of the *Times.*

Every newspaper man feels entitled to sleep as late as he chooses on the Sabbath, but most newspaper men are inured to emergencies and know how to deal with them. They responded to the telephone message and discussed the situation over the breakfast table with Mr. McGrady.

Piecemeal settlement, the mediator told them, was a man-killing way of trying to cope with such a condition. He urged that there must be some more systematic and continuing method available. "You need a fireman when the house is burning," he said, "but a good sprinkler system might put out the fire before the firemen arrive." Crippled pay rolls, curtailed production, and hatred on both sides were costlier than a fire. Why not set up a permanent Industrial Peace Board, embracing representatives both of organized labor and organized manufacture, with an impartial chairman jointly chosen? Mr. McGrady had been turning that notion over in his head, and he perceived an opportunity to try it out where there was imperative need for some forward step, even if it were experimental.

> The newspaper men were in thorough accord with the peace plan, [Mr. McGrady said afterward] and they plunged right in to help put it over. Without them it could never have gained the wide acceptance it did. These men . . . did yeoman service in explaining the plan to the business and professional groups. They talked it from sunup to sundown to all who would listen, and their editorials punched the idea home.

Both sides were suspicious and uneasy at first, but the newspaper men, who had won their confidence, gradually allayed their apprehensions. An organization was formed

A Neglected Story

of business executives, really a publicity group, called Toledo Associates, which persuaded business men that both sides of disputes should be presented to the public. Joseph K. Close was at its head. It became a clearinghouse of realistic news about civic, political, and industrial events, with regular "releases" for the daily press there and elsewhere, special articles for magazines and Sunday supplements, background material in *Today in Toledo*, a serial story issued as a pamphlet every two months, and personal contacts with editors in other cities. Toledo newspaper men attended lunches and dinners in Cleveland and Detroit to give factual rather than rosy talks about the changing situation.

Only a stenographer and the director of the new peace board were paid. The others served as a matter of community obligation. Its first case, a cafeteria strike, was settled in forty-eight hours. Its next, when fifteen hundred employes of twenty-four cleaning and dyeing plants threatened to walk out, was adjusted before the men struck; so was the next, when four hundred employees of a textile firm planned to quit.

Eight impartial members were added to the board's representation of industry and labor; these included two judges, a rabbi, a priest, two lawyers, and two merchants, but it was seldom that the full organization found occasion to meet. A labor reporter on the *News-Bee* became the director after a few months, and the city council made the board a part of the municipal government. Money was appropriated for its expenses. The peace league was going along swimmingly.

Not all was beer and skittles. In a strike at the Federal Creosoting Company's plant there was a clash between the workers and the guards in which fifteen persons suffered minor gunshot wounds. The old atmosphere of mutual distrust had not yet been cleared. But the board called for an armistice until leaders on both sides could talk over their differences, the armed guards were withdrawn and the picketing was limited. Then there was an agreement satisfactory to both sides.

Mr. McGrady, who subsequently became vice president of the Radio Corporation of America in charge of industrial relations, called his scheme "the Toledo Plan," and it became nationally known under that name. In its first three years the Toledo Industrial Peace Board dealt with 182 disputes and failed outright in only seventeen. "The board hasn't won every skirmish," said a clergyman, "but it has won the battle."

Others heard of the victory. More than one hundred cities in this country and abroad made studies of it, and compared it with developments in Great Britain, where the Trade Disputes and Trades Union Act of 1927 had accomplished excellent results, chiefly by setting up boards, at the request alike of employers and workers.

As in many other cities, the administration of Toledo was wasteful and inefficient. The Toledo *Blade* took the lead in a movement for change to a city-manager system, and the Toledo Associates formed a sort of political machine, with district leaders held responsible for getting out the vote. Trained accountants were set to work on the city's books, and engineers began examining the water supply and the sanitation. A City Manager League, nonpartisan in character, was formed to root for the new plan.

Presently the Toledo Associates reported with pleasure that the community was not only reading news stories

A Neglected Story

in the daily papers about the campaign but was devouring editorials on so stodgy a subject as proportional representation. On January 1, 1936, a new government was installed, with John N. Edy as city manager and a unicameral council of nine.

Professional politicians, who had put up the best fight they could against the change, sought presently to oust Edy from office. A former mayor, who was serving in the city council, introduced a resolution to that end, but his attempt to get immediate action failed of a majority, and the matter went over a week. That was all the time needed by the *Blade* and the *Times* to defeat it, as it proved. Those papers egged on civic and fraternal organizations to adopt resolutions supporting the city manager and urging that he be continued in office. They got symposiums of opinion from leading citizens and displayed them prominently. So thoroughly did they arouse sentiment that the council chamber was overcrowded when the meeting was held to consider the resolution finally, and it got but one vote—that of the man who introduced it.

For five years the city had operated on a deficit, and it had defaulted on its bonds. To correct this, a budgetary system was put into effect which meant actual departmental control over expenditures, purchases by open bidding instead of from political favorites, and a reduction of the tax rate to the lowest point in seventeen years. While the rate was being lowered, the police and fire departments were newly equipped throughout and the collection of garbage was motorized. Pay cuts were restored to city employees. An intelligent welfare program was set afoot and an airport was financed. To modernize the sixty-six-year-old water system, the city approved a plan to cost more than nine millions, to pump water fifteen miles from Lake Erie through a seventy-eight-inch pipeline. Without increasing the water rates, the project was planned to pay for itself. The bonds were floated at a fraction less than three per cent, the lowest rate in the city's history, whereas five years earlier Toledo's credit had been extremely shaky.

Perhaps in recognition of a new order and a new day, the principal news agencies established bureaus in Toledo, and stories went out to the press here and abroad. They went to trade journals also, even to newspapers printed on transatlantic liners. The late Marlen Pew, writing "Shop Talk at Thirty" for *Editor and Publisher*, March 21, 1936, said every newspaper man should familiarize himself with what had been accomplished in Toledo, because the editors there had been leaders in "a crusade which now includes citizens of all classes, workers and managers, business and professional men, homemakers, all looking for relief from the intolerable and nonsensical view that capital and labor must fight their battle out in the street, devil take the hindmost."

The *News-Bee* did not take part in the fight defending the city manager because it had folded its wings. One of the oldest units in the Scripps-Howard chain, it took an active and admirable part in the campaign for industrial peace and the renovation of the city administration; then, having withstood a long depression and witnessed the rehabilitation of its city, it announced on August 2, 1938, on its first page:

> The *News-Bee*, for several years, has been published at a loss. So long as it appeared that there was a place in the Toledo field for the *News-Bee*, its owners have been willing to sustain these losses, and make further invest-

ments, on the chance that the *News-Bee* would, in time, become a reasonably profitable institution. This was done in the face of greatly increased production costs, due to mounting labor costs and rising newsprint prices.

The decision to retire from the field was based on the conviction, finally, that two afternoon newspapers cannot be published, with a fair profit for both, in Toledo. It was felt by the owners of the *News-Bee* to be sound business, as well as good journalism, to retire from a field which offered no hope of betterment—and to concentrate time and effort and investment on those properties within the Scripps-Howard concern which occupy more favorable fields for expansion and growth.

With expressions of regret and promises to take care of some of the three hundred employees thrown out of work, the paper declared its "friendliness and good wishes." Nearly one hundred of its employees were under Newspaper Guild contract and so received dismissal compensation.

To say that a city whose daily manufactured output ran past a million dollars, the eighth port of the United States and its third railroad center, could not support two afternoon papers invited an examination of the city, the ability of its population to buy newspapers, and the papers themselves.

The facts were these:

During the year when the *News-Bee* gave up the ghost, Toledo plants sold to General Motors alone $33,000,000 worth of glass, machinery, tools, dies, scales, furnaces, presses, stampings, gears, furniture, and paint-spraying equipment. The city's industries were vastly diversified, a condition tending to stability, for they embraced 301 out of 335 listed types. In terms of buying power, wages had increased seventeen per cent over the 1929 boom period, and products were being shipped to all parts of the world.

Prosperity and friendliness were the tone of the town. When the city celebrated the centenary of its incorporation in 1937, 2,500 persons attended a supper in a new million-dollar armory, and union leaders sat cheek by jowl with captains of industry whom they had hated and fought, men who had hated them and fought them with bullets and gas.

It is pertinent to inquire whether this friendly people could not or would not buy the *News-Bee*. Toledo is not an illiterate industrial slum center. It supports the University of Toledo, finances and operates it, and it has two thousand pupils. Its museum of art, richly stored, had an average of a thousand visitors daily in 1938. Of a Sunday afternoon its people throng its fine zoological gardens. Its music hall seats five thousand and gives entertainment nightly. This is a city of small houses, with few congested tenements. As a newspaper man of eighteen years' experience, I should say that it is the sort of city where a good newspaper should find an ample market.

What, then, of the *News-Bee?* This is a Scripps-Howard newspaper, and Gilson Gardner said in "Lusty Scripps," his biography of the founder of the chain, published in 1932, that it was "a property which, considering its limited field, has always been one of the best of the Scripps papers." It did not continue to be one of the best, but the fault lay, not with the local staff, but with headquarters direction.

When Toledo was well on its feet again the *News-Bee* was not doing so well as during the depression it had weathered. Its circulation had fallen off by nearly half from its peak; the Audit Bureau of Circulation, in its report of March 31, 1938, gave it 48,712 while its competitor, the *Blade*, had 130,059. The report on advertising showed large lineage losses in April, May, and June, as

A Neglected Story

compared with the year before. The obvious conclusion was that Toledo's people and advertisers did not think the *News-Bee* any longer as good a paper as the *Blade*.

Now, advertisers like to avoid two appropriations, in part overlapping, where one can be made to do the work. We may be sure the Toledo Associates did not lament the passing of the paper. Its death left the city with one morning and one afternoon daily under a single ownership, which is an unhealthful condition, if for no other reason than that the ownership tries to please everybody. This may have been "sound business," as the *News-Bee* asserted, but it was not "good journalism."

Other Scripps-Howard papers, like Hearst units, fell by the wayside then and later. In both cases these were confessions of failure.

XVI

Sins of Omission

F THE later Amendments to the Constitution would have failed without the support of the daily press, we may be sure that the proposed Amendment to put an end to child labor, pending since 1924, would have become a part of the organic law if the newspapers had been actively in its favor. The obvious but unconfessed reason for opposition or silence is that it might interfere with newsboys. There is good reason to doubt whether, in most cases, it would be so construed. As framed in a joint resolution of the Sixty-eighth Congress, it read:

> Section I: The Congress shall have the power to limit, regulate, and prohibit the labor of persons under eighteen years of age.
> Section II: The power of the several States is unimpaired by this article except that the operation of State laws shall be suspended to the extent necessary to give effect to legislation enacted by Congress.

There is no good reason to believe that Congress would forbid boys, working their way through school, to deliver papers before and after their classes. That the daylong crying of papers by juveniles on city streets might be regulated or prohibited is likely, and it is likely that this would benefit society; for it has been shown that a part of our criminal class is recruited from these youngsters.

A Neglected Story

That they get acquainted with gangsters and become toughs while peddling their wares appears to have no weight with the ANPA, whose members find them a cheap medium of distribution.

In States where laws have been enacted regulating the labor of children below the ages of twelve or fourteen, some newspapers have lent a hand to the legislation. In one noteworthy instance a daily took the initiative and forced the bill through. This was the Atlanta *Georgian*, whose editors noted with dismay in 1914 that although the State had laws amply protecting her forests, her game, and her fish, the lives of her children were being squandered. The newspaper sent Tarleton Collier, then a young reporter, to a near-by mill town.

If the series of articles written by that reporter, and the stinging editorials which accompanied them, were reprinted now as a pamphlet and broadcast, they might shame the bulk of our newspapers into a different attitude. Young Collier found a girl seven years old, weighing forty pounds, who had been working in a mill three months at thirty cents a week; he found a fifteen-year-old girl who had been working two years, and who was proud that she earned nearly seven dollars a week. He found a mother, twenty years old but looking forty, who had been discharged as "incompetent" because she could no longer keep up the production pace required. Haggard and worn, she expressed no resentment.

"I've been tired for years," she said.

With that first story the *Georgian* printed an editorial, "The Shame of Georgia," in which it said that the State permitted children to work eleven hours a day and that they did work eleven hours; that although the law stipulated that children as young as ten years must have certificates that their mothers were widowed or their fathers disabled, the ordinary of a district, to get his fee, would certify in the case of children of seven or more. It was shown subsequently that illiteracy in the mill villages ran as high as forty per cent, and that Negro children, who were not permitted to work beside whites, far surpassed the white children in education.

A bill prepared by the *Georgian* in cooperation with the National Child Labor Commission was put through the legislature in one of the bitterest fights ever known there. It provided, for the first time in Georgia's history, for compulsory education, at least twelve weeks annually. It would have failed, perhaps, without the earnest support of the State Federation of Women's Clubs and some forward-looking citizens of influence. The measure was by no means a model of its kind, but it liberated children from bondage and represented, in fact, a great crusading victory.

The *Georgian* has not supported the Federal amendment, holding that this is a matter for State regulation. Mr. Collier, however, continued to fight for social betterment in his column, "Behind the Headlines."

That the daily press is in good company in opposing the Child Labor Amendment cannot be denied. Twice the Supreme Court has vetoed acts of Congress: the first regulating child labor under the interstate commerce clause, the second under the taxing power conferred by the Constitution on Congress. Under the first of these, the Court held, "our system of government [might] be practically destroyed." The late Justice Oliver Wendell Holmes wrote a dissent, in which Justices McKenna,

A Neglected Story

Brandeis, and Clarke joined, and in which he pointed out that the Court thought it all right to regulate strong drink but not "the evil of premature and excessive child labor."

The Constitution, however, is distinctly a pro-slavery document; on this the notorious Dred Scott decision was based; on this the two decisions overruling the elected representatives of the public presumably were premised.

Efforts were made in the Philadelphia Convention of 1787 to introduce a clause prohibiting human slavery, but they were unsuccessful because many of the delegates, like George Washington, were slave owners, and because there were then many slaves north of what was to become the Mason and Dixon Line. New England skippers, moreover, profited highly from the traffic. Thus the best that could be accomplished was to prohibit the importation of slaves after twenty years; obviously this was not prohibition, since the slave stock on hand could be expected to multiply, and did.

Efforts by Congress to put an end to the worst phases of child labor began in 1906, when Senator Albert J. Beveridge, without the sanction of President Theodore Roosevelt, introduced a bill to prohibit it. "The evidence is before the Senate," he said, "of the slow murder of these children, not by tens or hundreds, but by the thousands." Senators Henry Cabot Lodge and John C. Spooner were in the vanguard of the opposition. A second bill introduced by Senator Beveridge was smothered in committee. If they had been sure of a backstop in the Supreme Court the opposition need not have besmirched their records. Child labor may justly be regarded as a form of human slavery, and doubtless a majority of the Court had a clear conscience, under the Constitution, in voiding each Congressional effort at abolition.

Ratification by thirty-six States is necessary to make the pending amendment effective. After fourteen years but twenty-eight had taken that step. It may be noted that Senator Lodge's State of Massachusetts is not on the honor roll, although our first legislative inquiry into child labor was undertaken there in 1825. It threw a light on the demands of industry as related to school attendance, and other States began passing laws setting a maximum on the hours of labor and a minimum on the hours of elementary education. Usually these left large loopholes. Thus New Hampshire, sister of Massachusetts, provided in 1847 that no child should work more than ten hours a day, unless with the written consent of the parent or guardian.

It is not on the ground of parental authority, however, that newspapers have been lukewarm toward the Child Labor Amendment, or have opposed it actively. They have been less concerned about the family than about their own interests. We cannot be sure that their inertia or outspoken opposition has not killed the amendment even now; for the Supreme Court handed down in 1921 a decision involving certain amendments which had failed, saying "that the ratification must be within some reasonable time after the proposal." What constitutes "some reasonable time" is within the sole purview of the august Court; it might decide that a decade was time aplenty.

Among those in favor of the Amendment have been the National Labor Party and the Newspaper Guild, the latter a union of reporters, columnists, and some editorial writers. The Guild has condemned newspapers roundly as exploiters of boy labor, in particular because of the attitude of the ANPA. So has the St. Louis *Star-Times*, which said editorially in its issue of October 5, 1938:

> The publishers' association fought against a high minimum age for child workers throughout the days of the NRA. They introduced all sorts of contentions to bolster up their position, including the false issue of the freedom of the press and the argument that newsboys were not employees but "little merchants," who bought their papers as independent contractors and resold them at a profit. Technically the latter argument had some validity, but essentially it was a sanctimonious excuse, not a justification for child laborers.
>
> It is a great pity, for the sake of the newspaper business, which is an important part of democracy, that the organized publishers delayed their decision to eliminate twelve-year-old newsboys until they were about to be coerced by law. The enlightened conscience of the country has long demanded that the labor of children for the profit of industry be halted. If the newspapers had been keenly aware of their obligations as spokesmen for the public good surely they would have been among the first rather than the last to establish a decent minimum age for child laborers.
>
> Perhaps this shortsightedness helps explain why the newspaper business is suffering so severely from the competition of new agencies for public information and education.

Warnings as candid as that have been exceptional and rare. As to the attitude of the daily press, by and large, we need only consult its official spokesmen. Thus Arthur Robb, editor of *Editor and Publisher*, admitted in his "Shop Talk at Thirty" on July 2, 1938: "And some of the counter lobbying by newspapers against the amendment, based upon theory rather than fact, has done the newspaper cause more harm than good." Even earlier *Newsdom*, another weekly organ of the trade, had confessed editorially on January 29, 1938: "Ironically, the country almost to a man is convinced that child labor, like Cato's Carthage, must be destroyed."

Newspaper Crusaders

If the public favored the amendment, why should the newspapers oppose it? *Newsdom*'s editorial was full of reasons. It would make children "virtual wards of the State," and it "would include any child who ran an errand for his mother or helped his overworked father milk the cow or mow the lawn"; it might even require that "a government barber shave him until he passed the statutory age limit." This paper was strongly in favor of the Wheeler-Johnson bill offered as a substitute for the amendment, and vowed that it had received "the greatest amount of publicity and consideration." Yet *Newsdom* confessed that its sponsors agreed that this measure was "merely a stopgap to minimize child labor."

Hope was expressed in some quarters that the new Federal wages and hours bill, prohibiting the shipment in interstate commerce of goods produced with child labor within thirty days of its movement, would prove helpful; but this could not affect migratory child workers or local newsboys; and, according to Homer Folks, chairman of the National Child Labor Committee, could not help more than one-fourth of all the children employed in non-agricultural occupations, than is in textile mills and other factories. The advantage to the manufacturer was that unorganized child labor was about as cheap in the North as Negro labor in the South.

That the press in twenty of our States had a shabby record in regard to so humane a measure as the Child Labor Amendment was not the only point in which it was remiss. It derided the early fight for equal suffrage, for example. Fairness demands that some of these points be set down, as offsetting the admirable record of crusades in other fields. In the Teapot Dome scandal the

A Neglected Story

newspapers, well enough informed in general, refused at first to take the initiative except in one instance, this for the purpose of blackmail. The real work was left to a Senate "smelling committee," derisively so named by the newspapers themselves; just as the real work was left to a committee in exposing the practice among captains of industry of hiring thugs, swearing them in as deputy sheriffs, and arming them with clubs, sawed-off shotguns, and poison gas to subdue upstart strikers. The newspapers were even better informed, that is more specifically informed, about feudal warfare in industry than about the Teapot Dome theft. They betrayed their attitude when they printed with docility, for example, misstatements about the Ludlow massacre, during the Colorado Coal and Iron strike, as broadcast by the late Ivy Lee, then press agent for the Rockefellers.

Again the daily press betrayed its constituency when it refused to demand that this country carry out its promise to free the Philippines, acquired in our most conspicuous imperialist adventure. To the newspapers as a whole, national honor was of less importance than the exploitation of the islands by industry and commerce. Their owners and editors calculated that they would thrive in proportion as business throve. The New York *World* was one of the few to urge that our obligation be fulfilled, but this was a newspaper which put honesty ahead of dividends.

For nearly three-quarters of a century the newspapers ignored a crusade which was under their very noses. Why did they not investigate the structure and the practices of the Pullman Palace Car Company? Is the answer that it has disbursed in dividends nearly half a billion dollars cash and a quarter of a billion in stock? Washington correspondents knew that somehow it managed to prevent nearly all railroads from using any but its sleeping cars, that it bought and scrapped scores of patents for more comfortable cars. They knew that its fee for sleeping quarters was higher than comfortable hotels impose for a single room and bath. They knew that when the company applied in 1938 to the Interstate Commerce Commission for even higher rates, it made a damaging statement regarding its rate structure. Yet they remained silent. More than that, the New York *World-Telegram* suppressed a letter dealing with this application and posing certain questions likely to prove embarrassing to the corporation. To print the letter would have been to admit that its Washington bureau either was incompetent or was silent under tacit or explicit pressure from the home office.

Definite proof of the newspaper bias, if needed, was given during the strike of Pullman workers in May, 1894. During the depression winter of 1893–1894, the company, while distributing dividends of $2,800,000, cut wages on an average one-fourth; but it did not reduce taxes or rentals on the company-owned houses in the "model" industrial village of Pullman outside Chicago. It was this situation that provoked the strike. George M. Pullman, president of the corporation, the son of a mechanic and mover of barns, refused flatly to arbitrate the request for better wages.

Eugene V. Debs had resigned as secretary of the Brotherhood of Locomotive Firemen to organize a "vertical" union of all railroad workers. Founded in the autumn of 1892, it boasted within a year a membership of 150,000 in 463 locals. It had come through a successful

A Neglected Story

strike against the Great Northern Railroad. When the Pullman workers struck, some twenty-four railroads, employing more than 200,000 workers, formed a defensive combination in the General Managers' Association, with headquarters in Chicago.

Debs, an able executive, peaceful in temper, took every means to avoid violence after the affiliated unions had declared a boycott against handling the antiquated Pullman cars. It is a matter now of documentary proof that when violence did occur it was subsidized by the employers. It is unnecessary here to describe the progress of that strike, one of the most famous in our history; it is enough to say that Grover Cleveland, acting on the advice of Richard S. Olney, his Attorney General and one of the founders of the General Managers' Association, sent Federal troops into Chicago. Neither Governor John P. Altgeld nor the mayor of the city had asked for help, so that the act was illegal.

Debs declared that the combination of railroads had gone "into partnership with Pullman in his devilish work of starving his employees to death." The daily press retorted with cries about "the tyranny of Debs" and "mob control." Governor Altgeld, who protested vigorously against the invasion by the Federal army, was branded by the newspapers an "Anarchist," Debs a "dipsomaniac."

The Governor telegraphed President Cleveland that the presence of the troops was unnecessary and unjustifiable. "I will say that the State of Illinois is not only able to take care of itself, but stands ready to furnish the Federal government any assistance it may need elsewhere. Our military force is ample." He added that the autocrat of all the Russias could not lay claim to greater power than Cleveland had usurped.

The President replied that this was "a rather dreary discussion of constitutional principles" and that "all in authority" must protect "life and property." Altgeld's messages were greeted generally by the press with epithets, the President's with applause.

It is true that the *Eight-Hour Herald*, an obscure paper then being published in Chicago, did venture to take the side of the strikers. It spoke in an editorial of "the insane policy of exaggeration and misrepresentation" adopted by other dailies; and said at another time that the press was "inflaming the passions of the people and doing its level best to arouse class prejudices. From the first these papers have used every effort to magnify the difficulty, and to prevent attempts to arbitration, conciliation, or peaceful settlement." These charges were warranted.

Before the turn of the century the Pullman Company became an undisputed monopoly by taking over the Wagner Palace Car Company, a merger arranged by J. P. Morgan and Company. The Wagner firm had enjoyed but a negligible fraction of American railway mileage. The monopoly, under the spur of the loss of business to motor vehicles, modernized some of its rolling stock during the third decade of this century. On a few crack trains it was possible at long last to sleep in some degree of sanitation and comfort; but on most of its "palace" cars the passengers who could stand the gaff of its extortionate rates suffered the same inconveniences and discomforts as their grandfathers.

In regard to patent medicines, the daily press has been even more vulnerable. Ferdinand Lundberg says, in

A Neglected Story

"America's 60 Families": "In 1934 the press, virtually unaided, smashed the proposed Tugwell Pure Food and Drug Act, which provided for more honest advertising. The opposition was openly organized by the various publishers' associations from the ANPA down through regional bodies." It is not accurate to say that the newspapers killed the measure "virtually unaided," for they had help from powerful lobbies for the manufacturers of nostrums and for certain medical associations. But it is true that with newspaper support, even half-hearted, this bill would have become law, and the similar bill finally enacted would have been much more nearly adequate.

My attention was first attracted to this matter in 1928. Like many others I supposed that the Pure Food and Drug Act of 1906, enacted as the result of a crusade, not by newspapers but by *Collier's* under the editorship of Norman Hapgood, had some teeth in it, and that dangerous decoctions could not be sold to a gullible public. If patent medicines were advertised, I thought, it must be in rural papers, which were hard put to it for survival. On a trip to Buffalo, New York, I examined the *Evening News* of November 13, 1928, and was astonished to find in its pages twenty-seven advertisements of patent medicines. Not all of these were dangerous, but almost without exception they were quack preparations.

Now, the owner of the Buffalo *Evening News* was Edward H. Butler, a millionaire under no compulsion to resort to this disreputable revenue. He had inherited the paper from his father; he was then president of the ANPA and vice president of the Associated Press. He was a bank director, a leading light in educational institutions and of the Presbyterian church in Buffalo. Perhaps his patent medicine advertising paid the dues of the eight clubs of which he was a member.

In the *Evening News* I found nine advertisements of cold "cures," not all so designated. I found a medicine for heart attacks, and another which warned of "the danger signals of high blood pressure." I found a bath salt of which the manufacture gave the comforting assurance, "you can reduce two to four pounds in a night." Most of the decoctions pretending to reduce weight drastically and suddenly have been pronounced extremely hazardous. There were advertisements of medicines for asthma and rheumatism, "medical cigarettes," laxatives and purgatives, an ointment for blood trouble and pimples, others for fever, malaria, kidney trouble, two for fretful babies. Mothers for the most part know better than to dope their children.

Thereupon I made inquiry about the patent medicine advertisements in the daily press of this country during the first six months of 1928. It was a disheartening quest. More than one hundred medicines were being advertised in the larger newspapers, which, like the Buffalo *Evening News*, were independent of such a livelihood. I examined with dismay newspapers published in Atlanta, Jacksonville, Albany, Boston, Indianapolis, Kansas City, New York, Philadelphia, San Antonio, San Francisco, St. Louis, Syracuse, Cleveland, Brooklyn, and Nashville. In larger towns, I learned, the daily press carried 12,200 medical accounts, of which 478 were "proprietary" (I could not find a druggist who knew the difference between a "proprietary" and a "patent" medicine) and of which at least five were assuredly harmful.

In a survey published by the *New Republic* of October 29, 1930, Hart, Kingsbury, and Rowe found only eight

A Neglected Story

newspapers in this country which were free from advertisements of fraudulent and unsavory drugs and potions. These were listed as the *Christian Science Monitor*, a church publication but an admirably newsy journal; the *United States Daily*, not a commercial enterprise; the Milwaukee *Leader*, a Socialist publication; the New York *Evening Post* (this was before J. David Stern acquired the property; since then it has printed such advertisements); the Boston *Transcript*, the Minneapolis *Journal*, and the New York *Times*.

As for the New York *Times*, it may have been "clean," as designated, at the period when the survey was made, but I have noted patent or proprietary medical advertisements in its pages casually in 1928 and for the ten years following. In 1929 the manufacturer of a remedy boasted that he had received "many mail orders" from a full-page rotogravure advertisement in this paper. During the next year I noted, among others, the advertised warning, "Don't cough your energy away," (there were four other remedies for colds in that issue) and a "pure food antidote for stoutness"; the promise of "effective and quick relief" for asthma or hay fever, and the ballyhoo of a cigarette which would give "blessed, quick relief from distress" in the case of hay-fever sufferers. Since I know at first hand that this newspaper is extremely scrupulous about the character of its advertising, I believe that none of these remedies was harmful; and the men who made the *New Republic* survey may well have had in mind only deleterious drugs.

William Allen White of the Emporia *Gazette*, in a letter to *Editor and Publisher*, challenged another newspaper man, who had questioned his fear of future advertiser influence, to "write a bristling, convincing editorial about the danger of misbranding foods, of allowing patent medicines to be sold as cures, and of the unrestricted sales and advertising of fake drugs and phoney foods." Mr. White was willing to bet that the Doubting Thomas would "get a letter from some agency that will reveal exactly what I mean"; and he continued:

> I am not afraid of consolidating newspapers, I am not afraid of a one-newspaper town. What I am afraid of is that advertising agencies who are also political and public relations advisers to big groups of advertisers like steel, oil, copper, automobiles, and the like, may see the tremendous advantage they have by cutting down or cutting out advertisements from liberal papers.

It should be said that *Editor and Publisher* has never expressed tolerance toward the attitude of the daily press in regard to pure food and drugs. On August 24, 1929, it warned its readers against agencies advertising Lydia Pinkham's decoction; and on August 9, 1930, it printed an editorial, "Wanted: Pure Drugs," in which it told of a senatorial subcommittee's findings that "drug manufacturers have sacrificed integrity for profit," and that extract of ergot, a preparation used in obstetrics; ether, a potential cause of death during or after surgical operations; and digitalis, a drug used in heart troubles, were sold in adulterated or substandard form by some of the most famous pharmaceutical houses. "The subject of health and its preservation," said this organ and monitor of the industry, "is one for thoughtful and diligent treatment by newspapers."

When this was printed patent and proprietary medicines constituted more individual advertising accounts in the daily press than any other classification, although by no means a major part of the revenue. Nowadays this country spends $20,000,000 a year on laxatives alone, most of which do more harm than good, according to

A Neglected Story

competent medical opinion; many of which are unmistakably injurious and nearly all habit-forming. This is still a subject "for thoughtful and diligent treatment by the newspapers."

The campaign for a competent Federal food, drugs, and cosmetics law, which resulted in a measure in 1938, began in June, 1933. Reviewing the stages in this legislation, *Public Opinion*, a quarterly published by Princeton University, said that certain professional groups and "a very limited number of consumers" realized the need for better protection, and added: "The public press usually passed over such criticism and touched lightly, if at all, on such unpleasant incidents as the casualties resulting from the use of inadequately regulated proprietary products." This was in its July issue, 1937. "Every effort was made," (by commercial and manufacturing interests) the quarterly continued, "to enlist the press in arousing consumer as well as commercial prejudice against the bill. Newspapers and trade publications, with only rare exceptions, were strongly opposed to new legislation unless designed to weaken the existing law. A surprising amount of false and misleading information about the situation flooded the country."

National organizations, especially of women, were actively in favor of a better bill, and the magazine presented an imposing list of them. The American Federation of Labor joined the fight. The subject, however, was of a technical nature, and for a long time it was easy to befuddle the public, already misinformed by its newspapers. Bulletins of the Departments of Agriculture and of Commerce, giving official and significant facts about low-grade foods, drugs, and cosmetics constantly being advertised, were ignored by the daily press.

When finally an act with teeth in it was passed, its worst fang, from the newspaper standpoint, had been drawn; this would have regulated advertising, and it was necessary to enact a supplementary measure to that end. The first of these gave the United States Government control over foods, drugs, and—for the first time—cosmetics. (Some women using dyes for their eyelashes had been blinded, and others had been poisoned by lipsticks and skin treatments.) It provided that no new drug could be advertised without a permit for its sale.

Radio, under the supervision of the Federal Communications Commission, continued in many instances to broadcast ballyhoo of dubious decoctions to a larger audience than the daily press could reach. Some of the big chains, to be sure, manifested a sense of public responsibility by rebuking 128 advertisers of patent medicines whose claims over the air were more preposterous than others. Of the paid or "sponsored" time on the radio, toilet goods, cosmetics, and patent medicines took about one-fifth in August, 1938.

Not all newspaper publishers have been venal. James King of William—note the name—founded the *Daily Evening Bulletin* in San Francisco on October 5, 1855; and George Henry Payne records in his "History of Journalism in the United States" that "from the beginning he refused to accept low medical advertisements." Edward W. Scripps, after he founded the Cleveland *Penny Press*, warned Robert F. Paine, its editor: "I want you to clean the questionable and dirty medical ads out of my papers. Clean 'em out, no matter who yells, understand?" In 1926 "Bob" Paine returned for a short time to his editorial desk, and the *Press* printed a story about him, quoting that injunction. Back to back with this was a full-

A Neglected Story

page advertisement of a notorious medical quack, Dr. William Oakley Coffee of Davenport, Iowa. Samuel Hopkins Adams, exposing him in *Collier's*, had called him "an Eminent Thief and Pre-eminent Liar." Newspapers continued to print his full-page advertisements, in spite of this and of protests by the American Medical Association. After the death of E. W. Scripps, the Scripps-Howard chain of papers repudiated his stand toward "dirty medical ads," as they disavowed others of his policies in the public interest.

The proprietor of an herb "laboratory," who advertised by radio and otherwise that his products were effective remedies for twenty-eight diseases, ran afoul of the Federal Trade Commission in 1936, and makers of fake aspirin have been indicted and prosecuted. Armour and Company, meat packers, have been fined for misbranding butter.

The food and drugs act passed in June, 1938, was immensely superior to the measure enacted a generation earlier, as may be judged by the fact that newspapers, including the New York *Herald Tribune*, gave space to the wail of a manufacturer that it was "the swansong of rugged individualism" and would kill many of his brethren. The weakness of that law was that it did not regulate advertising, which was left subject to the Federal Trade Commission; the Commission took no action except on complaint after the advertising had been printed, and often too late to be of effect. The bill had another weakness in that poisonous hair dyes could be sold still, if properly identified. The first weakness was remedied by the passage of the Wheeler-Lea Act to govern false advertising claims. R. E. Freer of the Commission noted that the ballyhoo of proprietary products had been "in large measure responsible for consumer and Congressional demands for stricter regulation," and warned that the Commission had power at last to require "absolute honesty" from advertisers, in particular of "food, drugs, devices, and cosmetics."

One of the uglier chapters in the history of this country's newspapers was written by that Commission when it investigated the "million-dollar lobby" of the so-called "power trust," which had carried on a "systematic campaign of misinformation, or propaganda . . . of lies and falsehoods," as Franklin D. Roosevelt subsequently described it. Senators and governors, school superintendents and teachers, many conspicuous men and women, writers and the radio were enlisted in that shameful campaign; even textbooks were doctored. But nowhere did the public suffer so great disadvantage as from the complaisance of the daily press.

Fifty-two volumes of testimony and documentary evidence were published by the Commission, naming thousands of newspapers, but the hearings either were ignored or minimized in most of the press, save the Hearst chain. It was shown that public utilities owned some newspapers and subsidized others. Elisha Hanson, who appeared as attorney for the International Paper Company, one of the offenders, stepped from that post into a place as chief counsel for the ANPA. Influential members of the association owned stock in the paper corporation. H. M. Aylesworth, who was then managing director of the National Electric Lighting Association, became an executive with the Scripps-Howard newspapers, as they became more conservative.

A Neglected Story

Four-fifths of the American press printed utility propaganda without revealing its source, the Commission showed. Among the honorable exceptions were the Raleigh *News and Observer* and the St. Louis *Post-Dispatch*. There was testimony that the New York *Times* could not be bribed; but its sympathies were revealed by J. S. S. Richardson, an agent of the National Electric Lighting Association, who testified that he prepared the material for an article in the newspaper on power development, and that another article was printed in the Sunday magazine of the *Times*, edited by Lester Markel, which had been written by Dr. Frank Bohn, known to be in the employ of the NELA.

Nor did that powerful lobby neglect schools of journalism. "Embryo editors" were considered worth "educating." Samuel E. Boney, a former newspaper man, lectured to budding journalists. He boasted also that he got the Associated Press to carry one of his propaganda stories throughout the country, and was "pop-eyed" when he saw it in one newspaper under a seven-column banner headline.

Not even that humiliating exposure cured the daily press of its weakness for the "power trust"; this was shown by its attacks, sometimes mendacious, against the Tennessee Valley Authority.

In the British Museum there is an Egyptian writing board, four thousand years old, which says: "The poor man hath no strength to save himself from that which is stronger than he." From quack medicines and utility rapacities the poor man is now being saved, to some extent at least, by the Federal Trade Commission, not the newspapers.

XVII

Cerberus of the Cash Box

THOSE who frown upon movements to reform or even to improve State institutions welcome with applause efforts on the part of newspapers to reduce taxes and introduce efficiency into governmental expenditures. In such cases not voters but the men they put into office are the chief obstacle. When the press undertakes to bring about lower utility rates, such as charges for gas and electricity, it encounters the solid and sometimes sly opposition of vested interests backed, on occasion, by unscrupulous legislators and officials. Nevertheless crusades looking to lower exactions in both fields have saved many millions of dollars for the American public.

While New Jersey's lawmakers were deliberating at Trenton on the 1938 budget, the press of the State, almost with one voice, raised an outcry against it as excessive. The publication of the increases proposed gave pause to the legislators, who appointed a special committee to look into the departmental demands. This committee offered a bill which was six millions below the total department heads were asking, and more than two millions less than the amount of the measure then under consideration. In addition, the supplemental highway

A Neglected Story

appropriation was reduced by nearly a million and a half. As a fact, the assemblymen and senators were so impressed by the furore they had aroused that they began "devising ways and means," according to the Newark *Evening News*, "to kill off prospective raids on the treasury in the form of special appropriation bills." Late reports, it announced, indicated that the situation and the cash were well in hand. "New Jersey is indebted," said an assemblyman who had served on the special committee, "to the newspapers of the State for the fight they have made for economy." On a flat basis the taxpayers were nearly three millions richer in the mass than if the bill first proposed had been passed without protest. Eventual savings promised to be much larger

In Ohio, newspapers sniped here and there at the administration of Governor Martin L. Davey. The size of the State's budget was a matter of common gossip and complaint. The *Plain Dealer*, suspecting that the principal waste was in the highway department, set a reporter to work on the records at Columbus. After three months he emerged with material for a series of seventeen stories, showing connivance among contractors, exorbitant prices for road materials, favoritism to certain supply houses, the building of roads for political considerations rather than as an outcome of sound planning, and the maintenance on the highway pay rolls of a force which served virtually as a secret police for the governor.

While the *Plain Dealer* series was appearing, other newspapers took up the cudgels, and the governor, to still the clamor, appointed engineers from four colleges as a board of inquiry. The board corroborated most of what had been published and disclosed also "shakedowns" of contractors and others who did business with the State, dishonest practices in the liquor enforcement department, and the payment for certain sorts of coal of twice its worth. Thus there was a general audit of the State's departments and a drastic reorganization, with substantial tax reductions.

Among the States which have worked reforms in their assessments and expenses none is so celebrated as Nebraska. The Omaha *World-Herald*, published mornings, evenings, and Sundays, began fighting in 1932 for a balanced budget and a pay-as-we-go policy, and was supported by other papers, such as the Beatrice *Sun*. It happened that the complaints centered finally around a single sturdy and sensible figure, Frank G. Arnold of Fullerton, a town of 1,600. His farm holdings in Nance County were considerable, and he became head of a committee of taxpayers. Discontented with mere vocal objections, which were ineffective there and elsewhere, he employed an auditor to go over the county books, in order to find out just what was collected and how it was spent. The survey revealed, for one thing, surprising inconsistencies in prices paid. The committee report "packed popular appeal," as Arnold put it, and was widely published. The result was the formation of the Nebraska Federation of County Taxpayers' Leagues, of which he became president.

County warrants at that time were worth not much more than the paper on which they were printed, and the State was in a bad way for funds and for credit. Other counties made their surveys, and when these were compared singular discrepancies were discovered, such as that one might pay $700 for an item which cost another but $52.50, one $1,103.20 for ballots which cost another

A Neglected Story

$45. Comparison of such figures in the Nebraska press embarrassed the politicians and outraged most of their constituents. Some taxpayers, to be sure, said gloomily that this sort of adverse publicity would ruin the State, and others were honestly fearful that to curtail tax levies might impair legitimate and necessary services. But in time the league won a consolidated support.

During the ten years preceding 1939, Nebraska saved, it was estimated, nearly $140,000,000 in general tax levies, while paying off $38,000,000 of county, city, town, and district bond issues. It was on a budget system because officials were required to pay spot cash on delivery, and shopped around for bargains, whether the outgo was in pennies or in thousands of dollars. In six years of that time other States had increased their aggregate indebtedness by more than $500,000,000 and were saddled in all with $2,500,000,000 of long-term issues. Nebraska had no bonded indebtedness. She had no sales tax, no cigarette tax, no service or luxury tax, no income tax. Through all the lean years after 1932 her only new levy was on liquor. The State spent $5,000,000 a year on a social security program, it had an old-age fund, it maintained an excellent public school system, and owned a $10,000,000 State capitol free of encumbrance.

At the University of Denver a fellowship was established to train men in the Nebraska method of making the tax dollar do a dollar's worth of work. In the United States there are nearly four thousand taxpayer organizations, but not many of them have profited by their neighbor's example. They operate locally and are ineffective partly for that reason; some of them are being tied together into State federations. "What Nebraska is accomplishing," says the *Times-Advertiser* of Trenton, New Jersey, "can be accomplished by any other State whose citizens are sufficiently interested to keep tabs on the costs of government." And the *Chronicle* of Houston, Texas, reminds its readers that "only militant, nonpartisan organizations of taxpayers can succeed in obtaining tax relief." The *Times* of New Orleans, in an editorial on "Driblets and Dabs," observed that the "rise in governmental costs is traceable to a shower of small items."

Prof. T. S. Adams of Yale University has emphasized that sporadic organization and scattering discussion cannot bring control of public expenditures. "To achieve the desired aim," he says, "it is probable that the taxpayers of every State will find it necessary to organize permanent associations guided by leaders of broad views, and assisted by experts who give their entire time to the work of reducing costs and increasing efficiency." Such leagues can be assured of generous newspaper support; without it, as the Nebraska leaders are emphatic in saying, they cannot get far.

In at least one instance a newspaper campaigned for a year on behalf of higher rather than lower taxes. This was the *Reporter and Republican* in Pottsville, Pennsylvania, capital of Schuylkill County. Under this county is about one-half the State's supply of anthracite coal; Joseph H. Zerbey, publisher and editor of the morning and afternoon newspaper, held that the immensely rich mineowners should pay levies high enough to give the county and townships good schools and roads. They were assessed at fifty-three millions; he thought a billion a modest estimate of the property's value.

A Neglected Story

John J. Leary, Jr., has told in *Editor and Publisher* about that crusade. Schuylkill County was one of the poorest in the State, and in one mining village the school teachers, some of whom had not been paid for fifteen months, struck for their wages. Schools built above opulent coal mines were closed for lack of money to buy fuel. Zerbey hammered away in news and editorials on the imperative need for a new board of county commissioners who would make just assessments, and finally won the fight. The new board employed experts from outside the county to make a valuation; and although the amount set did not approach the true value, it produced five times as much revenue as the county had been receiving.

Dr. Walter S. Landis, vice-president of the American Cyanamid Company, has commented in a national radio broadcast on the fact that if a new chemical is to be produced he wants a skilled technician; that if a bridge is to be planned and constructed or a new motor car designed, we are exacting in our demands for experience and understanding; but that we make no such stipulations regarding those who are to impose our taxes.

> They pass no test for fitness or ability, [he said] show no credentials. A glad hand will produce more votes than a super-intellect . . . You, my tax-paying listeners, are responsible for this situation. Blame no one else for the hodge podge of words, ideas and laws that come from legislative chambers. Because of your apathy and your gullibility they flow interminably in a torrent of platitudes, a deluge of nonsense, bunk and abuse. It is from such sources that much of our tax legislation springs.
>
> It is immaterial upon whom or what taxes are levied, we all pay them in the end . . . Do no delude yourself by thinking you are not a taxpayer. . . . Every citizen wants to bear his fair share of the cost of government. Every citizen wants the best government he can afford. But the times demand that taxes shall be just, equitable, and in proportion to benefit. They demand also that revenue be wisely and economically expended. They demand par-

ticularly the election of well informed, better trained, more widely experienced legislators; the placing in office of men and women educated in the fundamentals of taxation and cognizant of sound principles.

Newspapers have done good work in bringing to terms ignorant and wasteful legislators, but have adapted to their purposes too seldom the theme of Dr. Landis, that those who lay the taxes should have a competent knowledge of an intricate subject.

Many persons were profoundly shocked at the corruption of the daily press and other avenues of information by the public utilities, as divulged in voluminous testimony before the Federal Trade Commission. Not every one was shocked. The *Public Opinion Quarterly* of July, 1937, published at Princeton University, found space to let a contributor praise these corporations, which had bought many newspapers outright and had found ways to win others over to the publication of misleading material. As an example, the article said:

> The finest job of public relations ever done was that by which the public utilities rallied millions of people to buy their securities and fight their battles. Ultimately a few leaders—out of excessive ambition, greed, and finally fright—stultified the whole effort, but this robbed the development of none of its importance as an outstanding exception to the rule that public opinion seldom makes business conditions.

It is true enough that misguided public opinion did make good business conditions for the public utilities, and a satisfactory market for their securities, until the methods employed to warp and mislead opinion were exposed. Before the corporations began their campaign of corruption and afterward, there were many journals which fought ably and courageously for better service and lower rates.

A Neglected Story

Back in 1915, for example, the *Evening World* urged the New York Telephone Company, then the biggest and richest of its group and the cornerstone of the Bell system, to make friends, not enemies. The newspaper demanded a reduction in the rate for individual calls from ten to five cents, and this was accomplished, at a saving to the people of the city of five millions annually. Additional toll charges between the boroughs were abolished, too. The corporation heeded the advice.

The San Francisco *Examiner* won lower telephone rates in a 1936 campaign. The Detroit *Free Press* forced the Michigan Bell Telephone Company to reduce its rates within the State to interstate levels. The Michigan Public Utilities Commission issued the order to this effect on June 29, 1938, after the newspaper had shown that the company was discriminating against telephone users there. This, to be sure, was part of a nine-month campaign under the title "War on Waste: Save the People's Money." Clifford A. Prevost wrote a series of illuminating articles on the fiscal affairs of Detroit, Wayne County, and the whole state, in the course of which he brought to light, for one thing, a malodorous deal in sanitation bonds. Two county auditors involved in the deal were defeated for reelection and the tax commissioner of Wayne County was ousted. The crusade as a whole compelled economies estimated by the *Free Press* as totaling more than forty-eight millions.

The Southern Bell Company bestowed favors on the press in its area to win its support or to silence criticism. It gave free telephone service to the North Carolina Press Association for several years; it adopted the old trick of giving advertising to papers which began calling for better service and lower rates; and it made a point of personal contact with editors and publishers as part of its policy of "friendly public relations." Evelyn Harris, chief of its publicity bureau and a former newspaper man, gave this testimony before the Federal Trade Commission.

An illustration of the methods likely to be used on both sides when a fight is made on high electric rates was afforded by Dr. Ernest Gruening's crusade against the Central Maine Power Company when he was editor of the Portland *News*. The power company was an Insull subsidiary. The *News* analyzed its structure in 1928 and showed that above the producer there were four layers of holding, investment, and finance corporations, to all of which the consumer paid tribute. The electric rates were high enough, in other words, not only to pay a legitimate profit to the company supplying the current, but also interest on seven bond issues, dividends on three preferred stocks, two at six per cent and one at seven per cent, and a dividend on common as high as nineteen per cent. Residents of Portland, the largest city in the State, became aware for the first time how they were being milked.

That the facts had not become known was due to the fact that the other Portland papers were under the domination of Guy P. Gannett, who was interested financially in Central Maine preferred stock and closely allied with Samuel Insull's personal representative in the State. The Gannett papers, the *Press* and the *Herald*, were "power trust" organs. When the *News* began its campaign the leading Portland merchants, including the big department stores, withdrew their advertising from its columns. *Editor and Publisher* spoke of this as "the ugliest

A Neglected Story

situation we have noted on the newspaper map of the United States in a long time."

In Maine, a State law forbade corporations to export current generated there. It was known as the Fernald Law and was accepted without question until the Maine company was sold in 1925 to the Insull interests. Under their influence a bill to permit the sale of hydroelectric power outside the State was enacted in 1927 by a slender margin but was vetoed by the governor. This was before the *News* took up the cudgels. The next governor signed a similar measure, in spite of the vigorous opposition of the *News*, and Dr. Gruening began a fight to annul it under the initiative and referendum. The Insull propaganda machine showered the State with pamphlets and posters and was confident of victory. Nevertheless the *News* won the battle.

In Massachusetts, the Worcester *Post* won a drive to reduce electric rates, and in Minnesota the St. Paul *Dispatch* and the *Pioneer-Press*, which are jointly owned, did likewise.

Fights for reductions in gas rates have been more numerous. The Chicago *Herald and Examiner* began a campaign there in 1933 which continued intermittently for years. The Peoples Gas, Light, and Coke Company persisted in raising its rates, after reductions or stabilizations had been won, and even procured a court injunction against interference with a raise. It put into effect on February 4, 1938, an increase which amounted to thirty cents a month for its average customer. Spurred by the Hearst papers, the Illinois Commerce Commission carried to the Appellate Court the injunction which the monopoly had obtained, and got a reversal. Its effort to invalidate the 1938 increase was made to the State's

Newspaper Crusaders

Supreme Court, where it was won on February 21, 1939. About three million dollars which had been impounded by the commission, when it was collected under the higher rate, was then on hand to be returned to 800,000 domestic consumers.

Similar campaigns have been waged by the Kansas City *Star*, the Buffalo *Times*, the Akron *Times-Press*, and the Columbia *Missourian*.

Streetcars are disappearing from our cities, but the fares have been the occasion of newspaper fights now and then. The Portland *Oregonian* and the Rochester *Times-Union* have led such campaigns. When the family automobile and the bus reduced the streetcar to obsolescence, the daily press faced a new front. The Sacramento *Union*, for example, waged a two-year battle for lower automobile tolls on the Carquinez bridge, on the main east-and-west highway between San Francisco, Reno, and Salt Lake City. The charge was sixty cents for each car and ten cents per passenger. On February 9, 1938, a State commission reduced these by one-fourth for cars and one-half for passengers. Dissatisfied, George J. Lilley, editor and general manager of the *Union*, sought further reductions.

On another salient, the Chicago *Herald and Examiner* undertook to find out whether motorists were getting all the fuel they paid for. Owners said they sometimes got short measure, but this was merely a suspicion. The newspaper told a reporter to see whether the suspicion was justified. He took with him two deputy city sealers, and they bought gasoline at random from seventy-three filling stations. Their machine had a removable tank, which they drained into a standard measuring can after each purchase. Half the filling stations, they found, were

A Neglected Story

half a gallon short on a five-gallon purchase. Sixteen of the proprietors were prosecuted. It was estimated that Chicago motorists had been paying half a million a year for gas they had not got.

As a watchdog over the public's purse, the daily press has been faithful at times when its own purse was depleted thereby. Its record is by no means so bad as one might suppose if one were acquainted only with the results of Washington investigations. The fat prosperity of the Gannett papers in Portland, in contrast with the boycotted *News*, tells the story of the temptations they have resisted when they have put up these fights. When a newspaper crusades against a public utility it demonstrates unmistakably that it has the courage of its convictions.

XVIII

Castor and Pollux

WHETHER news or editorials prove the more effective in crusading is open to debate. Almost always they do teamwork, and it is difficult to estimate their relative pulling power. Among newspaper men there is a widespread cynicism, which I believe to be unjustified, regarding editorial influence. My inquiries indicate that forthright opinion, criticism, and argument have been undervalued.

Yet Oliver K. Bovard, whose work as city editor and managing editor of the St. Louis *Post-Dispatch* engaged my admiration, once comforted a reporter who complained of lack of editorial-page support, during a crusade against the traction monopoly there, by saying that only five per cent of the paper's readers followed the editorials, and only one per cent understood them. As a fact that page was a model of hard-hitting clarity, and I doubt whether any of the noteworthy campaigns carried on by this militant daily could have succeeded without its help. But Mr. Bovard was low in his mind in somewhat the same fashion that the business office was always despondent about mere writers.

The skepticism which Mr. Bovard voiced has found expression on the editorial page elsewhere. Thus the

A Neglected Story

New York *Daily News* of March 25, 1938, speaking its mind about campaigning for and against the Administration, said:

> We read the New York *Herald Tribune* editorials with great interest—with more interest, indeed, than we read a lot of pro-New Deal writings, because the *Herald Tribune's* editorials stir our emotions. We doubt that the *Herald Tribune's* editorials from year to year convert one pro-New Dealer into an anti-New Dealer. But they do satisfy the feelings of *Herald Tribune* readers who hate Roosevelt and all his works.
>
> We also read our own editorials with considerable interest; and we likewise doubt that they ever convert an anti-New Dealer into a pro-New Dealer. But they seem to satisfy the feelings of quite a lot of people who like Roosevelt and most of what he does and says.

Conceding that newspaper readers "humanly tend to read opinions they like and ignore opinions they don't like," the *News* suggested that its own columns were read mainly by those in favor of the New Deal, while its contemporary's outgivings "must be pretty generally confined to ardent anti-New Dealers."

In reply to this it may be said that if the two had taken opposing sides on an issue directly and acutely affecting the social and economic welfare of their readers, rather than on a strictly partisan matter, both of them might have enjoyed a wider audience. An illustration is at hand in the experience of Chattanooga newspapers when the community undertook to buy an electric plant and reduce rates. This involved, to be sure, the Tennessee Valley Authority, a New Deal project; but it was a matter which touched the pocketbooks of all residents there and affected the whole standard of living.

Chattanooga, finding itself unable in 1935 to purchase at a reasonable figure the property of the Tennessee Electric Power Company, serving that area, held an election to authorize an $8,000,000 bond issue to build its own plant. In opposition, a Citizens' Taxpayers Association was created, which spent more than $23,000, some of it to distribute whiskey on election day, some to buy vacant lots in the name of nonresidents, to enable them to vote, some in the distribution of misleading circulars and pamphlets. Nevertheless the proposal carried by two to one.

The local electric monopoly supplied, it was subsequently learned, $20,000 of the money spent by the "citizens' association"; nor did the opposition cease with the first defeat. Technical objections were raised, such as questions whether the city enterprise could string wires on the streets used by the old system, whether the bonds should be general obligations or strictly for revenue, and it was here that the daily press took its most effective part.

From the first the Chattanooga *Times* was a bitter antagonist of public ownership. This newspaper, acquired by Adolph S. Ochs before he bought the New York *Times*, and still the property of the family, with Julius Ochs Adler as president and publisher and Adolph Shelby Ochs as general manager, veered to neutral in August, 1935, when Julian Harris was taken over from the Atlanta *Constitution* to be its executive editor. Harris could not swing it into the camp with the Chattanooga *News*, of which George Fort Milton was president and editor and which had consistently fought the power monopoly; but at least he changed its position to a tepid middle course.

Bereft thus of a champion, the Tennessee Electric Power Company got behind the *Free Press*, a semiweekly paper put out as an advertisement by a local grocery chain. This was converted into a daily, with an attorney for the power monopoly as one of its chief owners,

A Neglected Story

with Roy McDonald as president, W. G. Foster as editor, and Everett Allen as business manager. A young lawyer who had been active in arguing the technical questions raised to befuddle the voters said that half the money he spent was supplied by McDonald of the *Free Press;* and a Congressional committee investigating the TVA learned also that while a local department store was spending 54.9 cents an inch with this paper, the electric corporation, using somewhat more space, was paying $1.26. The power people withdrew advertising from Mr. Milton's *News,* obviously as discipline on account of its crusade for better electric rates.

Undeterred by financial losses, the *News* continued the fight and won handily. There was a reduction of forty per cent in electric rates, estimated to save consumers more than one million dollars during the first year and to effect still higher economies as time went on.

Now, I am credibly assured that not only officials of the Tennessee Electric Company but those employees who worked and voted against the municipal project scanned the *News* as well as the *Free Press;* and that those in the majority, who favored it, were as eager to see what the *Free Press* was up to as they were to arm themselves with arguments from the *News.*

On disputed matters, public opinion usually divides into three sections, and all three were accurately represented in Chattanooga: the pro, the con, and the neutral. The groups favoring and opposing the utility plan were so loudly vocal as to give the impression that there were but two. If this had been so, the *Times,* although alone in the morning field, would have lost heavily in its following, and this did not happen. In part the intermediates embraced, as usual, some who did not know what they believed, some who leaned to one side or the other but objected to certain phases of the program. Often the final verdict is written by the neutral group, when its members are won over; but in Chattanooga this sector and its organ, the *Times*, were negligible.

In the Chattanooga instance, at any rate, the editorial page vindicated itself. It is true that the *News* ran an eight-column banner headline and devoted half its first page to the findings of the Congressional committee in one hearing at least, and was not niggardly with news space or display at other times; but the main battle was fought in editorials. A single instance, however well it may illustrate reader-interest when the reader's real interests are involved, is not likely to mollify journalistic misgivings in other times and places. Heywood Broun, discussing in the *Nation* the decline and fall of the editorial empire, has said:

> The way has been cleared for the syndicated columnist by the abdication of American editors . . . At least it is my opinion that Westbrook Pegler and General Johnson, either singly or together, carry far more weight with the reader than the official Scripps-Howard editorials ever obtained.

As a columnist contributing to the Scripps-Howard chain concurrently with Pegler and Gen. Hugh S. Johnson, Broun had firsthand opportunities to observe the decline of those papers in editorial power, and to know about the mail he and his fellows got, as indicating their weight with the reader. Terry Ramsaye, editor of the *Motion Picture Herald*, once applied to Broun a descriptive phrase which fits as well all others of the breed: "a crooner of the Corona"; he might have said "a Rudy of the Remington." It happened that Broun's outgiving was published while the American Society of Editors was in session, and at that meeting a resolution was presented which ran as follows: "This society sees in the increasing use in the press of syndicated columns of opinion and interpretation—for which individual newspapers assume no responsibility—a threat to the independent thought of the newspaper public."

My own objection to that resolution is that the columnist constitutes no greater threat to independent thought than the syndicated editorials in chain newspapers, and that the papers printing syndicated material do assume enough responsibility to kill contributions which their publishers or editors do not like. Many times outspoken columnists have looked in vain for their fulminations. Supporting the resolution, however, Tom Wallace of the Louisville *Times* observed that this country had entered "an era of department store journalism," in which "over advertised columnists" were being inflicted on readers. The opponents of the proposal voted it down on the ground partly that syndications enabled small papers to print the work of writers they could not afford to hire individually, and partly on the ground that the move, if approved, would smack of censorship. The society thus refused to go on record, save by its negative vote, in the matter of syndicated comment and opinion.

A pleasant theory persists, despite the editorial misgivings, that syndicated columnists offer "interpretative" comments on current events. Walter Lippmann, one of them, undertook to show that this was impossible, as regarded the New Deal; noting that Administration officials nursed grievances against the daily press, he set up a plea in confession and avoidance, in a column worth quoting somewhat at length, by saying that neither he nor anybody else could understand the plans of these officials.

Newspaper Crusaders

> They will find, I believe, [he commented] that they neglected almost entirely to educate public opinion, or even Congress, about the real meaning of the [reorganization] bill. The propaganda flourished in a vacuum of general ignorance . . . While this was happening we were supposed to understand and interpret fairly a thirty-thousand-word bill regulating agriculture, a most complicated dispute about capital gains and undistributed profits taxes, the impending reversal on gold, bank reserves, the budget balancing, the wages and hours bill, and the problem of the railroads. What is more, nobody could have understood them all because it would have taken the undivided attention of any newspaper man to understand any one of them adequately.
>
> If any New Deal official doubts that this is a main cause of the difficulty, let him ask himself how many New Deal measures he could explain. . . . But newspaper editors are supposed to explain them all, and to distinguish infallibly between propaganda and truth.

Aside from the fact that any truth emanating from Washington in those days would have been stigmatized straightway by the opposition as propaganda, Lippmann's remedy, that the Administration meet the situation by educating the public, embodied an element of high comedy, implying, as it did, that politicians could do what editors were incompetent to accomplish.

It must not be supposed that all observers were as despondent about the editorial page as the *Daily News*, Broun, Lippmann, and others who might be cited. *Editor and Publisher*, for example, devoted nearly two pages to an account of the campaign by which the newspapers of New York persuaded delegates to the State Constitutional Convention to submit the new document in sections, instead of as a whole, so that the voters might exercise discretion as to its various clauses. Editorially, it said:

> Critics who have been zealously asserting that the editorial influence of daily newspapers is waning should take time out from their labors to study

A Neglected Story

what happened in New York State last week. For here occurred one of the most convincing cases of recent record where editorial pressure, quickly and energetically applied, brought an about-face in the attitude of a public body on a question of the widest public interest.

In that instance the newspapers of a State, espousing a more democratic method of dealing with a vital public issue, vindicated the editorial page as emphatically as the Chattanooga *News* had proved its power. The generalization that nobody reads editorials "is largely cynical nonsense," in the opinion of W. W. Waymack, an editor of the Des Moines *Register and Tribune*, and winner of a Pulitzer prize in 1937. Declaring that the editorial page was re-educating the public, he said:

> Of course, only a minority reads serious discussion. I believe that serious times greatly increase that minority. We have had such times since 1929. . . . Obviously, the multitude does not go to these pages to find out how votes should be cast. Nineteen thirty-six was not necessary to tell intelligent editors that. But these pages do, in my judgment, influence gradually the thinking of the more intelligent minority, which in time will influence decisions. And I certainly do not mean by "intelligent minority" any élite based on wealth or even formal education.

Mr. Waymack's observations were distinctly sensible, and merit further attention. Extreme bias, he said, might decrease the value of an editorial page "about to zero," which was reminiscent of the comment by the *Daily News* on the *Herald Tribune*.

> Our typical newspapers [Mr. Waymack continued] are not class publications any longer; they go to all strata . . .
>
> Unquestionably the American press has its problems and its defects. The shift of the press into fewer units, each representing a relatively huge capital concentration, is a shift which obviously imposes sharper obligations on those who manage the press for private profit. Power does carry obligation. And control over any of the major agencies of public information is power. With this, among other future problems, recognized, I want merely to add that the American press is not only the best in the world but that it is better today, in terms of honest performance and social value, than it has ever been.

Mr. Waymack's confidence that more persons read serious editorial discussions after the debacle of 1929 was sound psychologically. During carefree prosperity the reader's attention is likely to run to materialism.

> Why should anyone have been interested in editorials in the gay twenties? [J. David Stern has asked.] The people of the entire country wanted just what the people of my own Philadelphia desired: conservative and pleasant comment, a big splurge on the Fourth of July, Pippa Passes optimism, and, above all—no rocking the boat. Added to the enervating effect of general prosperity was newspaper prosperity and the consequent disappearance of editor-ownership. Newspapers became button-moldy machines for making money. Publishers were too engrossed in making profits to be prophets . . .
> Depression found the American editor disposing of most subjects by a trip to the encyclopedia and a few classical allusions. But a chaste comparison of the stock market collapse to the loss of the wings of Icarus did not satisfy the lambs that were sheared . . . Every big bank that smashed created thousands of editorial readers . . . The renaissance of the editorial page has been real and definite. For the first time in our generation it has become possible to sell a paper because of its editorials, not in spite of them.

When Mr. Stern wrote that article for the *Literary Digest* he was owner and editor not only of the Philadelphia *Record* but of the New York *Post*, and in the latter paper he—or one of his editorial writers—admitted that editorial opinion must color a newspaper's presentation of news. This was in reply to a letter from E. K. Merat, graduate student of the Advanced School of Education at Columbia University, asking whether the *Post* permitted its editorial policy to affect its news policy. In an editorial which took the form of an open letter to the professor, the paper said:

> We're surprised at you. We don't know who has been handing you this line about "the theory of American journalism that news is separate from opinion," but we'll bet it wasn't a working newspaper man. Not a good one, anyway.

A Neglected Story

Come off it. The theory that the news columns of a paper are solely reserved for the facts and the editorial columns held sacred for opinion is one of the hoariest pieces of bunk ever peddled to a class in journalism . . .

A certain proposed constitutional amendment comes up at Albany. The *Post* headlines: "Child Labor Amendment Is Up for Vote." The *Herald Tribune* headlines: "Youth-Control Amendment Is Up for Vote." Both papers are reporting the news. Or are they?

We're not talking about deliberate distortion, mind you. That's something else, and American newspapers have been cleaning themselves of it for years. They are more honest right now than they have ever been. Such stuff as the *Journal's* constant reference to the Spanish "Reds" when they mean the Government forces is becoming rare. We're talking about the honest judgment that an editor has to make to get up an edition.

There are, also, numerous borderline cases where editorialization goes on under the guise of smug "fact." If Senator Gloober introduces a bill to tax shoelaces and a newspaper happens to be friendly with the shoelace people, it can, strictly as "background," write a news story about Senator Gloober and his odd hobby of standing on his head while reciting "Casey Jones." That doesn't help poor Gloober—yet there isn't a word of untruth in it. Is this editorializing or is it strict news presentation?

The [New York] *Times* is a great paper. We think the *Times* could make any issue fairly important by putting it under a four-column head on Page I often enough. The *Times*, a newspaper of record, tries not to editorialize. But it doesn't pick its headlines out of a paper bag, either.

The President called a special session of Congress last November 15. The purposes: To pass a wages-and-hours bill and a crop-control bill. But on November 9 the *Times*, in a top story, Page I, brought in the need for revising the capital-gains tax. On November 10, top story, Page I, on general conditions, again the same capital-gains tax was mentioned as likely to be revised. On November 11, top story, Page I, the same tax was attacked in an account of an economists' dinner. On November 12, top story, Page I, Senator Harrison attacked this tax. On November 13, top story, Page I, Representative O'Connor attacked this tax. On November 14, top story, Page I—a "dope story"—it was said that there existed "a strong sentiment among arriving members of Congress" for this kind of tax revision.

On November 15, top story, Page I, the *Times* headlined: "Congress Convenes Today With Its Course Uncertain; Revolt on Taxes Possible." Then followed much matter about revision of these same taxes. The capital-gains tax was pictured as a burning issue. Yet it affects not five per cent of the population; the other ninety-five per cent couldn't even define it. One might have thought from the *Times* that on every street corner citizens were discussing this tax. We assure you they weren't. Yet capital gains became an issue of the session . . .

We think it's good for newspaper readers to know the facts of life. We do the best we can to print both sides of everything. But we're only human. So, thank God, are our competitors.

Seldom do newspapers speak so frankly about others; rare and refreshing is such candor about themselves! *Newsdom*, commenting at length on the editorial, said:

> Virtually every newspaper in existence for any length of time has been attacked because its standards of news did not concur with those of some of its readers; because it put in a small head in a comparatively obscure part of the paper a story which readers believed should have been given widespread, front page prominence.
>
> These newspapers in many cases have been accused of "distortion" and "suppression," due no doubt to the public ignorance that there is no such thing as completely objective news.

Dr. Raymond Pearl's report on "Tobacco Smoking and Longevity," for example, was not treated as "completely objective news." George Seldes, author of "Freedom of the Press" and an able critic of modern journalism, told me over a lunch table that he had learned of this report from LaFollette's weekly *Progressive*, and that the New York newspapers had ignored it completely. As cigarette manufacturers are big advertisers, and as the report, on the authority of years of research by the distinguished biologist of Johns Hopkins University, declared that tobacco had done more than alcohol to impair efficiency and shorten human life, this seemed a credible statement. But when I looked into the matter I found that the New York *Sun* alone had failed to mention the report, and I was disposed to make allowance in that case, because any item may get left out in the hurry of making up an afternoon newspaper. The others had

A Neglected Story

printed the news under "a small head in a comparatively obscure part of the paper."

Newsdom, whose phrase I have just quoted, said in the same editorial that "in the selection of news stories, individual editors must accept those for prominence which they believe to be most significant to their subscribers." None can doubt the significance of Dr. Pearl's findings to newspaper readers, most of whom smoke tobacco, but the report was not selected for prominent display, so far as I have been able to find, in other than the LaFollette paper. Dr. Pearl wrote me, however, that it had not been ignored.

> The idea that the newspapers are suppressing this story [he said] strikes me as slightly comic. I only wish the gentlemen who are circulating that rumor would pay for the clippings that have come in about the matter. To the best of my knowledge and belief there cannot be to exceed seven newspapers in the United States that have not carried the story, in one form or another.

Doubtless millions of newspaper readers missed altogether the mention of Dr. Pearl's report, which could hardly have failed to startle and interest them, had they seen it. Many instances such as this might be cited to show that the daily press does not give the public what it wants, so that the public is skeptical of what it reads in the news columns or experiences an actual distaste. In time even the appetite for scandal and crime must become vitiated, and there is evidence that the appetite for more substantial fare sometimes goes unsatisfied. Dr. Belmont Mercer Farley of Teachers College at Columbia found that this was so when he made a survey of news about schools.

Dr. Farley questioned persons of varied social and industrial status in thirteen cities representing a wide range of geography and occupation, and received more than five thousand replies as to what kinds of school news was preferred in thirteen categories, ranging from pupils' progress, methods of instruction, and health, to extracurricular activities. Against these answers he checked the school news actually printed in each community. He discovered that extracurricular activities, ranked last in interest by his correspondents, took forty-seven per cent of the space given to school news; and that less than one-fourth of his clippings dealt with the subjects in the preferred six classifications of news, whereas the hindmost six items took more than three-fourths.

If the public has a tendency to distrust the news columns, or to feel that the news it wants most to see gets inadequate treatment, the news sections are likely to be less influential during crusades. A sampling of news influence during a crusade took place in St. Louis, when a contractor and certain former city officials, charged with obtaining money under false pretenses on a city contract, asked for a change of venue on the ground that they could not get justice in St. Louis, owing to prejudice aroused by the *Post-Dispatch*, the paper which had exposed them.

The *Post-Dispatch* had reported that the city had been overcharged in a contract for installing lighting equipment. An engineering firm which made a survey reported that the city had paid $157,064 more than was due the contractor. On the application for trial elsewhere, veniremen were summoned to tell the court what impressions they had got from the newspaper and whether they were capable of giving a fair trial if selected as jurors. Of the first group of forty-two, all said they believed one or more of the defendants guilty, on the basis of what they

A Neglected Story

had read or heard. The vice president of a plow-manufacturing company said there was a general impression that "something was wrong, somebody was guilty." A second block of veniremen was called from other courts, and the testimony elicited had the air of a cross section of the public.

Of thirty-five men so examined, only eight believed actively from the newspaper accounts that the contractor was guilty or that the city had been defrauded. Three said they read only the sports pages, one that he believed the series of articles to be inspired by politics, two that they wouldn't believe anything they read in a newspaper, and of these two one was the vice president of a lumber company: "I don't form an opinion of a man's character or guilt from a newspaper article," he affirmed stoutly. Three made a practice of reading headlines only and had formed no opinion from them. A disheartening number took no interest in such matters, and a still larger number, after reading all the news stories, had formed no opinion. One or two had formed opinions not from reading the series of stories but from gossip about them.

Such a showing must have taken Oliver K. Bovard somewhat aback, after his statement that only the news counted in crusades. He was still managing editor of the *Post-Dispatch.* He resigned subsequently, owing to differences of opinion with the younger Joseph Pulitzer, its chief owner.

During my own service of more than six years with that newspaper, I came to a confident belief that the strong editorial page had more pulling power than the news columns in our frequent campaigns. It was a well-written page, and the statement that only five per cent of the paper's audience read it was a negative exaggeration; it had the attention of nearly all literate readers, certainly of the more influential groups.

That was, I hasten to reassert, a matter of opinion. The relative influence of the editorial page and the news columns in campaigns must depend in part upon the newspaper involved and still must remain largely a matter of guesswork.

XIX

On Varied Salients

IN THE western part of North Carolina privation and actual hunger had fallen upon the farming population when the Asheville *Citizen-Times* undertook a campaign to promote the cultivation of foodstuffs for local consumption and to create markets for them. Although there were ups and downs, the outcome was a marked economic improvement in that part of the State and the profitable spread of the movement over a wide area.

After years of severe competition the morning *Citizen* and the afternoon *Times* found that rivalry had depleted their resources until both were on the verge of bankruptcy. To save their necks they combined in 1931, and the general manager of the merger suggested that Bruce Webb, son of the *Citizen's* publisher, make a minute survey of that area.

Almost at once it was apparent that the eastern counties of the State had been recovering in much better fashion, after the crash of 1929, than those in the western section, which had become impoverished, in fact, long before the depression. This was due mainly to greedy and shortsighted lumbering operations. As soon as the first railroad pushed into that region, in the early eighties, huge band mills began devouring hundreds of thousands of acres of timber, until only the mountainside forests, in what is now Great Smoky Mountains, a national reserve, were left standing, and they were too far from railheads to be exploited successfully. By 1931 most of the lumber operators had closed down or gone into bankruptcy. Some twelve counties, which had been cut over thoroughly and which depended on Asheville for their food, clothes, machinery, and repairs, were unable longer to trade there.

Analysis of *Times-Citizen* circulation showed that the loss of $30,000 annual gross income from those counties simmered down to the inability of former readers to buy the paper. If those fellows could be put back on their feet they could subscribe and could buy advertised commodities. For years the North Carolina Extension Department, intelligently directed, had been preaching to deaf ears the doctrine that one reason for the State's adverse trade balance was the purchase of imported foods. The newspaper, therefore, did not originate the idea but seized upon it in a dire emergency, hoping thus to recoup its circulation and advertising revenue. "It started out as a cold-blooded proposition," Bruce Webb has told me; and it was inspired in part by the success of Frederick E. Murphy of the Minneapolis *Tribune* in persuading northwestern farmers to diversify their crops instead of growing wheat solely.

Webb "combed the coves," as he expressed it, and persuaded some 1,400 persons, including farm leaders, to attend the first meeting in Asheville. "When it was over," he said, "we realized we had a ring-tailed cootie tied to us . . . We had to go on . . . And I had hold of the hot iron and couldn't turn loose." A retired Presbyterian clergyman, James G. K. McLure, Jr., had organized and was at the head of a Farmers' Federation, which lent a hand. The *Times-Citizen* organized a committee in each county and arranged monthly meetings of the chairmen in Asheville. It "publicized loudly and to the heavens" everything the groups did. Men and women traveled from twenty-five to one hundred miles in all sorts of weather to attend the Asheville meetings, and at the first anniversary there was as much enthusiasm as if it were a religious revival.

Pedigreed bulls were bought and distributed by the newspaper, and farmers were encouraged to get others. Pig clubs were started. An effort was made to teach each farm family to produce enough food to supply its own balanced diet. Women's clubs were urged to demand products from western North Carolina in the food markets, but a difficulty was encountered there because vegetables sent in by trained growers were cleaner and more attractively packaged. In localities where farms and gardens had been put on a good basis, neighbors were found who had not profited by the campaign; it was necessary to stimulate their envy, their competitive impulse.

Inspired by what was being done at Asheville, Hugh MacRae of Wilmington organized the Southeastern Council, to spread through the South what was being done in one corner of North Carolina. He encountered, as the *Citizen-Times* had, a conservative opposition to change, which proved a hindrance. Another obstacle was the governmental plan to restrict production, which Administration papers did not like to oppose even though what their readers needed most was more production of the actual necessaries of life. What had started out as "a cold-blooded proposition" broke Webb's health in 1933, and thereafter he could work only at brief intervals; but an active and energetic crusading spirit had been aroused, and others carried on. The work extended through eighteen counties to their advantage.

A campaign even more novel than that waged by the *Citizen-Times* and more quickly fruitful, but within a small area, was the bright idea of William J. Duchaine, managing editor of the *Daily Press* in Escanaba, Michigan. The little city's main sources of livelihood, mining and lumbering, were in a decline. Duchaine, who had tried vainly to popularize the spot as a tourist resort—*Newsdom* described him as "Escanaba's publicity agent without portfolio"—hit suddenly upon smelt as a means to that end. The fish had been introduced into Michigan lake waters by the State Game Commission in 1912, after an unsuccessful attempt six years earlier; during late March and early April it swarms up the rivers at night to spawn, while the water is still crusted, as a rule, with ice.

Duchaine, a member of the Kiwanis Club and a sportsman of parts, got the club and other local sportsmen to help him stage an "Escanaba Smelt Jubilee" in the spring of 1935. The fish were offered to other Kiwanis clubs through the Midwest free if they would pay the express; in the first jubilee eight tons were thus disposed of, for the clubs organized dinners and devoted the profits to their funds for underprivileged children. The word spread around, and tourists began visiting Escanaba to watch the populace dip the silvery fish from near-by streams, lighted with picturesque bonfires on the banks; men and women, boys and girls, used long-handled nets or, if they lacked the usual equipment, kitchen strainers, burlap

A Neglected Story

bags, wash tubs, bird cages, and butterfly nets. At the fourth jubilee there were 20,000 tourist visitors, 5,000 more than the city boasted in population.

After the first year a trifling charge was put on the fish, and a $50,000 industry was generated. Active, able-bodied men were known to dip as much as a ton of smelt in a night, but a good average was a third of that weight, which meant, at the prices prevailing in 1938, $10 in the pocket of the dipper.

Duchaine, remarkably fertile in ideas, introduced the fourth jubilee with an original musical comedy, "Smeltania," with its smelt king and its smelt queen; a new dance step was introduced called "the Smelt Run," which proved to be a cross between the Big Apple and the Shag. There was even an official jamboree smelt song.

Once the smelt jubilee was an established success, Duchaine campaigned to make a national park out of Isle Royale, in Lake Superior near by, and finally got an allotment from Washington. Then he inveigled the State into buying the Tahquamenon Falls area as a park. He staged the lost art of logrolling for the lumberjacks thereabout, and conducted a contest which got national publicity through newspapers, radio, and newsreels. He organized a "Deer Hunters' Shindig" in the fall months, and attracted other tourists. Thanks to an ingenious and public-spirited newspaper executive, the city found itself on its feet once more.

Newspapers elsewhere have conducted crusades, not for greater production and new markets, as in Asheville, or for publicity and prosperity, as in Escanaba, but for better milk and, when the price seemed too high, for cheaper milk. In Denver the *Rocky Mountain News* exposed the release from a storehouse of $3,000 worth of rotten canned eggs, so that the governor discharged the food and drug commissioner. The press, ever on guard for the public's pocketbook, is not unmindful of its stomach.

Disregarding the risk of presenting a mere medley, I am noting here certain diverse crusades, in order to give a final impression of the field's scope and variety. Fancy, for example, taking an anti-noise campaign seriously enough to curtail extra editions! That is what John Stewart Bryan, president and publisher of the *News-Leader*, did in Richmond, Virginia. For the first time in many years there was a gubernatorial election in 1937 without an extra from the presses of this newspaper. The early vote was broadcast by radio in what the paper called "armchair returns," but with a special caution to avoid making a nuisance of the loud speaker.

In Manchester, New Hampshire, the principal industry was the Amoskeag Manufacturing Company, owning the largest single cotton mill in the world. Situated on a bank of the Merrimack River, at the heart of the thriving city, it employed five thousand workers. At the beginning of 1936 the plant was unable to reopen, and the District Federal Court in Boston appointed a referee in receivership. Citizens of Manchester had a disheartening vision of higher taxes, shrinking trade, and general misery.

In that emergency the *Union* and the *Leader*, morning and evening papers under a common ownership, stepped into the breach to get the exact fiscal facts about the manufacturing company, and began printing them without big headlines or excited editorials. Edmund F. Jewell, assistant publisher of the papers, received word from the

A Neglected Story

Chamber of Commerce that unless he stopped publication of these stories, he would be boycotted.

"You will either retract your threat to boycott me or I will publish your letter," he replied, "and show you up as selfish merchants trying to milk the town of its last drop."

The stories were continued and the threat was not executed. The referee sent from Boston formed a committee of citizens, with Arthur E. Moreau, former mayor, at its head. Moreau and Jewell offered to raise $3,500,000 to enable the plant, which had a bonded indebtness of eleven millions, to reopen; but the referee, threatening to liquidate, demanded at least five millions. Within half an hour of publication of that fact in the *Union* and the *Leader*, half a million was available and within a month the entire sum had been pledged.

A new concern, Amoskeag Industries, was incorporated with Moreau as its president; workers were reinstated in the brick tenements erected by the cotton corporation; and a part of the factory was put into operation. Moreover, sixteen new industries, employing two thousand men and women, were attracted to Manchester. More than two-thirds of the indebtedness assumed by the committee and its friends was paid off within a year, and thousands of willing workers had been saved from the humiliation of the relief rolls.

Pennsylvania's first conviction of men for inflicting the "third degree" on a prisoner was procured through the efforts of the *North Penn Reporter* in Lansdale, with the assistance at times of two weekly papers, the Ambler *Gazette* and the Collegeville *Independent*. In that case an entire political setup, including a part of the judiciary, was finally defeated.

William G. Campbell, a Negro, was arrested by Brooks Cassidy, township police chief, on suspicion that he had tried to bomb another Negro's home. The prisoner was shifted from one place to another, then taken to an attic in Jeffersonville for "questioning." He said subsequently that he was beaten with a blackjack, then strung to a rafter with his own overalls while a State trooper paraded in a sheet in an effort to frighten him into a confession by this ghostly visitation. He was innocent and did not confess. When arraigned he was released on his own recognizance and went to a physician to have his injuries treated.

The physician sent the Negro to an associate justice. The judge heard his story and turned him over to the district attorney, who shrugged his shoulders and did nothing. Walter L. Sanborn, publisher of the *North Penn Reporter*, heard what was going on and made inquiries. He was warned that this was "dangerous" stuff, and that there would be libel suits if he printed the facts; nevertheless, on June 12, 1931, he gave an account of the brutalities to which the prisoner had been subjected. This he followed with another story, asking why the Bar Association took no action, and with an editorial demanding an investigation. E. S. Moser, editor of the weekly *Independent*, chimed in with stories and editorials. The Negro was rearrested but this time was able, owing to the publicity his case had received, to give bail. The State attorney general appointed a special deputy after warrants had been issued for the police chief, assistant district attorney, and a county detective.

These men were tried before President Judge J. Ambler Williams sitting on a bench which, with one exception, was hostile to the prosecution. The Montgomery Bar Association was stirred by the situation, and its members volunteered their services to protect the Negro and his attorney. In a new trial, before another court, the judges who had sat in the first took the stand as character witnesses for the accused officials, a spectacle described by Sanborn of the *Reporter* as without parallel in the history of the State. The jury, on May 12, 1934, returned a verdict of acquittal.

That verdict, the *Reporter* declared, was a gross miscarriage of justice. The course taken by the judicial character witnesses to help procure the miscarriage was denounced. Declining flatly and openly to apologize for its conduct, the newspaper continued its fight, in which the weekly Ambler *Gazette* had joined. Together the three papers mustered a circulation of but five thousand, but their voices were heard above the voices of the judges and the political ring, who declared that this was "a political conspiracy"; and in the end Judge Williams was sentenced to prison with the three county officials, for periods ranging from six months to three years.

In Nashville the daily newspapers united in a three-year campaign to rid the city and county of a system by which justices of the peace were dependent on fees for their livelihood. They charged that this was the cause of frequent injustice and that the poor, unable to employ competent counsel, were the most often victimized. In cartoons and news stories, beginning in the summer of 1934, they portrayed the situation and were supported in their stand by the Nashville bar and by the Library Association; but the political leaders who found the system useful, and the justices who found it profitable, successfully resisted the change until 1937, when the legislature supplanted the old courts with courts of general sessions, over which salaried judges presided.

Libraries and schools have been the subject of newspaper attention as often as courts. In New Orleans, the *Tribune* ran stories intermittently for four months in order to show that the city librarian was incompetent, ignorant of books, and wasteful; he was removed, and the salary for the post was reduced from $7,500 annually to $4,000. In Clearwater, Florida, the schools were closed for lack of funds, and a committee failed to raise enough by popular subscription to keep them open. The *Sun* proposed that children whose parents were able to pay should be put on a tuition basis, and that the others should be financed by what Victor H. Morgan, editor of the paper, dubbed the "Adopt-a-Child" method. It was necessary to "adopt" 730 pupils, but measures were taken to prevent them and their more favored fellows from knowing which ones were on a cash footing and which owed their schooling to public generosity. In Lynn, Massachusetts, through a six-month exposure by the *Telegram-News*, the principal and two teachers of a school were disciplined for cruelties to pupils. The newspaper printed the entire transcript of the testimony.

Harry B. Haines, publisher and editor of the *News* in Paterson, New Jersey, learned that the fuel allotted by the town to the poor was of bad quality. The newspaper printed a series of articles disclosing that the coal was mostly stone and slate, that it gave about one-third less heat than another brand chosen at random, and that the city was paying a price which would have bought a coal of good grade. As a consequence of the campaign, contracts for nearly nine thousand dollars' worth of the poor fuel were canceled.

John R. Rathom, then editor of the Providence *Journal*, made a hobby of radio during his spare time, and as a part of the sport began decoding stock quotations and funeral directions which were transmitted in 1917 from powerful transatlantic stations. The result was his famous exposure of German espionage and sabotage in this country. He died in 1923, full of honors.

No such acclaim accrued to Rives Matthews, although he began a campaign which newspapers usually favor strongly, against billboard advertising. During the absence on vacation of the editor and publisher of the *News* at Hastings-on-Hudson, his assistant began attacking the unsightly advertisements thereabout, and suggested that the name of the place be changed to "Hastings-on-Billboard." He even threatened to picket the eyesores. The publisher, returning hastily on the call of his friends, found that they were indignant at the slurs on their well-meant posters and discharged his subordinate. Matthews, a graduate of Princeton and the Sorbonne, was puzzled but philosophic. He expected to get another job pretty soon, writing anything but billboard copy. "Only God can make a view"; he said; "only man can mar it."

There remains one of the oddest, most obvious, and most fully justified campaigns of all, which appeared to make no more than a dent in the consciousness of the men to whom it was directed; and those men were newspaper editors and publishers, who should be more susceptible than most, or at any rate more ready to vindicate a sound crusade.

Elzey Roberts, publisher of the St. Louis *Star-Times*, on a day when that newspaper, subscribing to several syndicates, printed eleven comic strips for children, only one of which had a humorous twist, wrote an editorial suggesting that this feature was being "overemphasized to the detriment of American youth." He listed the other "funnies"—wide of the mark, that name!—as picturing a fist fight, domestic quarrel, torture, death, murder, arson, despair, deception, fright, theft.

> Certainly no editor in his right mind [said the editorial] would have selected such subjects to run in ten out of eleven comics in one day. . . . Should the editor drop a comic strip permanently when it overemphasizes the horror of the crime angle? And if so, how should he answer the complaints of the readers who want to continue it?

The newspaper asked for comment from its readers, and got a plenty. One letter said the comic strips dealt with "murders, tortures, and stuff we absolutely refuse to let the kids see in the movies." Another suggested that the police "raid the newspapers which no longer have any respect for decency." Another said he preferred the obituaries.

However wry the face with which other publishers may have received that outgiving, *Newsdom*, a lively and outspoken as well as open-minded weekly organ of the business, hailed it as "a pioneering step of unusual significance." It said that newspaper comics were "leading to more public resentment than perhaps even editors surmise," and that "such resentment has in it the makings of public demands for censorship of the press." George Henry Payne of the Federal Communications Commission, it reminded publishers, had threatened regulation of the radio unless it mitigated the horrors of the "children's hour" and cleaned its own house. *Newsdom* continued:

Undoubtedly the comic strip continuity is more effective in building circulation than the gag cartoons which have new situations every day. The ghastliness in comic strips results from this necessity of creating continuity. It is comparatively easy to get a reader to buy a newspaper if he is palpitatingly curious to find out how the scantily clad heroine manages to get out of the way of a fortieth-century mysterious death-dealing machine which threatens to blow her lovely, futuristic form into gory little bits . . . It is much harder to build sustained interest around less pulsating matters.

Some sort of action must be taken both by the syndicates and by the newspapers "if the matter becomes much more acute," *Newsdom* thought; but newspapers continued to harp upon the "funnies" in their promotional advertising. A piece of this promotional copy, from the syndicate maintained by the Chicago *Tribune* and New York *Daily News*, was sent to *Newsdom;* in it Dick Tracy, sleuth, undertook to explain the comic aspect of crime. "He sounds," said *Newsdom*, "like the circulation-mad editor of a cheap, sensational, mob-appealing tabloid." This strip, it declared, was "a source of valuable information for every criminal and potential criminal." That it was popular the commentator did not deny, "as popular with the mob as the New York *Daily News*, the nation's most vulgar shopping guide." The sleuth was a pioneer in the field and a symbol of characters which had made the comic pages "a blood-and-thunder harum-scarum pattern of trash."

In a symposium, published April 22, 1939, on the newspaper of 2000 A.D., gathered by *Editor and Publisher*, Walter M. Harrison, the discerning editor of the *Oklahoman* and the *Times* in Oklahoma City, forecast flatly the death of the comic strip. George Olds, managing editor of the *News* and the *Leader* in Springfield, Missouri, thought that before the turn of the next century the strips would have ceased to be thrillers, and would teach history and grammar, mathematics and science, with some "clean, exciting fiction." Other editors thought they must go ultimately into the discard.

Whether that could happen within sixty years appeared doubtful when one examined the enthusiastic promotion material and advertisements devoted to the comics. In an earlier issue of *Editor and Publisher*, for example, I had found an advertisement by the *Tribune-News* syndicate, quoting a letter from Robert Choate, managing editor of a daily paper in that hub of culture, Boston, saying: "The *Herald-Traveler* leads all other New England newspapers in advertising, year after year, because of the consistent reader appeal of such features as The Gumps."

The advertisement listed thirty-two features carried by the *Herald-Traveler* for its presumably erudite audience, ranging from short stories and a daily serial through beauty, love, and deportment to a horoscope. If the comic strips increase advertising as well as circulation, what prospect is there that the daily press will be emancipated from them?

Whether or not Elzey Roberts of the St. Louis *Star-Times* and the editors of *Newsdom* have fired a shot into the vitals of the comic strip, it is undeniable that more than nine-tenths of the crusades undertaken by newspapers bear fruit. The fruit may be long in ripening, and often is, but it is worth nursing. Almost always a well-grounded campaign is an irresistible sledge hammer in the hands of editors and publishers.

A Neglected Story

Aside from the intangible returns in the manifestation of power, the accomplishment of worth-while ends and the sense of a public responsibility acquitted, all campaigns, even those actuated solely by aspiration for a better social structure, can be audited in the cash register. Harry B. Haines, editor and publisher of the Paterson *Evening News*, made such an examination in 1930 and concluded that crusading did not pay. He recalled with relish that he had once averted a three-million-dollar realty deal by certain city commissioners, that he had put a stop to the practice of requiring city firemen to pay for their jobs by mortgaging their homes, and that he had performed other services for the community, but he thought it hurt instead of helping his business.

> Crusading is a rich man's game, [he told John W. Perry of *Editor and Publisher*] especially in a city the size of Paterson. You lose advertising, you lose circulation, you even lose prestige. People begin thinking you have a personal ax to grind. Even when you have thwarted the plans of scheming politicians and saved the city or county millions of dollars, what happens? Nobody gives a damn!

Although another editor once expressed precisely that viewpoint to me, it is clear that this mood of disillusion is all but unknown to the newspaper men of the United States. No, they have carried on more than once in spite of severe monetary loss and actual personal peril. Neither salesmanship nor exhibitionism, neither partisanship nor malice, can explain all they have done. No economic audit gives a satisfactory explanation.

For crusading is a normal, sometimes a routine, activity of the newspaper. Whether it consists in a special emphasis and editorial treatment of run-of-the-mine news or the creation of news, whether it involves meeting issues as they arise or making issues, it is a primary function.

Newspaper crusaders themselves would be the first to disavow any pretension to the glory of a Galahad. They might even disclaim comparison with Hercules in slaying the Lernaean hydra; yet not all the "twelve labors" of this legendary hero measure up in scope and courage to their achievements.

Bibliography

ACHESON, SAM: "35,000 Days in Texas: A History of The Dallas News and Its Forebears."
ANDREWS, CHARLES M.: "The Colonial Period of American History."
BEARD, CHARLES A. and MARY R.: "The Rise of American Civilization."
BEARD, MIRIAM: "A History of the Business Man."
BELL, JAMES R.: "A Study of Typical Crusades Undertaken by Chicago Newspapers, 1833–1930."
BENT, SILAS: "Ballyhoo: The Voice of the Press"; "Strange Bedfellows."
BLEYER, WILLARD GROSVENOR (editor): "The Profession of Journalism."
BOWERS, CLAUDE G.: "The Tragic Era: The Revolution after Lincoln."
BRITT, GEORGE: "Forty Years—Forty Millions: The Career of Frank A. Munsey."
CHAFEE, ZACHARIAH, JR.: "Freedom of Speech."
CHAMBERS, WALTER: "Samuel Seabury: A Challenge."
COCHRAN, NEGLEY D.: "E. W. Scripps."
CRAWFORD, NELSON ANTRIM: "The Ethics of Journalism."
EGGLESTON, GEORGE CARY: "Recollections of a Varied Life."
FURNAS, C. C.: "The Next Hundred Years: The Unfinished Business of Science."
GARDNER, GILSON: "Lusty Scripps."
HEATON, JOHN L.: "The Story of a Page: Thirty Years of Public Service and Public Discussion in the Editorial Columns of The New York World."
HOWE, M. A. DEWOLFE: "John Jay Chapman and His Letters."
HUDSON, FREDERICK: "History of Journalism."
IRWIN, WILL: "Propaganda in the News."
LEE, ALFRED MCCLUNG: "The Newspaper in America."
LIPPMANN, WALTER: "Liberty and the News"; "Public Opinion."
LUNDBERG, FERDINAND: "America's 60 Families."
LYNCH, DENNIS TILDEN: "Boss Tweed."

Newspaper Crusaders

MILLIS, WALTER: "The Road to War."
MYERS, GUSTAVUS: "The History of Tammany Hall."
NEVINS, ALLAN: "The Evening Post: A Century of Journalism."
OLDER, FREMONT: "My Own Story."
PARRINGTON, VERNON LOUIS: "Main Currents in American Thought."
PAYNE, GEORGE HENRY: "History of Journalism."
PRESTON, JOHN HYDE: "Revolution, 1776."
RADDER, NORMAN J.: "Newspapers in Community Service."
RAUSHENBUSH, HILMAR S.: "High Power Propaganda."
RIEGEL, O. W.: "Mobilizing for Chaos: The Story of the New Propaganda."
ROSEWATER, VICTOR: "History of Cooperative Newsgathering in the United States."
SALMON, LUCY MAYNARD: "The Newspaper and Authority."
SEASONGOOD, MURRAY: "Local Government in the United States: A Challenge and an Opportunity."
SCHLINK, FREDERICK JOHN, and ARTHUR KALLET: "100,000,000 Guinea Pigs."
SCHMALHAUSEN, SAMUEL D. (editor): "Behold America."
SEITZ, DON C.: "Joseph Pulitzer: His Life and Letters."
SELDES, GEORGE: "Freedom of the Press."
THOMAS, ISAIAH: "History of Printing."
WERNER, M. R.: "Tammany Hall."
WINKLER, JOHN K.: "W. R. Hearst."
WOODWARD, HELEN: "It's an Art."
ZABRISKIE, FRANCIS NICOLL: "Horace Greeley, the Editor."

Index

A

Abolition, 128, 130, 132, 135
Abolition Intelligencer, 126
Acheson, Sam, 141, 211
Adams, Abijah, 117
Adams, Henry, 90
Adams, John, 88, 91, 94, 100, 101, 115–117, 121, 134, 135
Adams, Samuel, 81, 83, 84, 86, 87, 91, 101
Adams, Samuel Hopkins, 251
Adams, T. S., 258
Adams, Thomas, 117
Adams, Thomas W., 141
Advertising, 9, 74, 83, 247–251
  billboard, 291
  patent medicine, 13, 245–250
  radio, 250
African Observer, 126
Albany, 163, 246
  Argus, 121, 129, 130
  Evening Journal, 129, 130
  Knickerbocker News, 191
  Patriot, 129
  Times-Union, 189
Albany Regency, 121
Alexander, James Waddell, 26, 27
Alien and Sedition Acts, 115, 118
Altgeld, John P., 243, 244

American Antiquarian Society, 88, 89
American Federation of Labor, 201, 249
American General Gazette, 94
American Newspaper Guild, 78
American Newspaper Publishers Association (ANPA), 41, 235, 239, 245, 252
American Protective Association, 148
America's Sixty Families, 11, 12, 147, 244, 245
American Society of Newspaper Editors, 4, 5, 270, 271
Anderson, Judge A. B., 69, 71
Antilynching laws, 149–154, 152–154
Anti-noise crusade, 286
Antislavery movement (*see* Slavery)
Archbold, John D., 53, 54
Arizona *Republic*, 8
Armistice, false report, 75, 76
Armour and Company, 251
Arnold, Frank G., 256
Asheville *Citizen-Times*, 281–284
Associated Press, 219, 224, 225, 245
Astor, John Jacob, 158, 159
Atlanta, Georgia, 139, 140, 146, 246
  Constitution, 181

299

A

Atlanta, *Georgian*, 191, 203, 235, 236
   Journal, 181, 182, 191
Atlantic City, 178, 179
   Evening Union, 179
   Morning Press, 179
Atlantic Monthly, 13–15
Attleboro *Daily Sun*, 206
Augusta, Georgia, 132
   Chronicle, 180
   Herald, 180
Aurora, 106, 116
Austin, Benjamin, Jr., 106
Auto-Lite strike, 223-224
Automobiles, 264
   accidents, 185, 221
Aylesworth, Merlin H., 77

B

Bache, Benjamin Franklin, 106, 107, 116–117
Bacon's Rebellion, 91
Baily, Dr. Gamaliel, 129
Ballot-stuffing, 35–38
Baltimore *American*, 170
   Anti-Democrat, 107
   Evening Sun, 14
   Federal Republican, 121, 122
   News-Post, 170
   Sun, 169, 170
Baltimore Crime Commission, 169
Barnett, Sue, 203, 204
Beard, Charles A. and Mary, 43, 44, 91, 98, 120, 124
Beatrice, Nebraska, *Sun*, 256
Bediner, Robert, 79
Bennett, James Gordon, 44, 45, 104, 109, 133, 134
Bennington *Free Press*, 126
Berkeley, Governor William, 91
Beveridge, Albert J., 237
Bill of Rights, 4, 99, 102, 103, 119

Billboard advertising, 291
Billings, Warren K., 168, 169
Bingham, Barry, 193, 194
Birney, James Gillespie, 128
Black, Frank, 25
Black, Hugo L., 144–145
Blake, James G., 176
Bliven, Bruce, 11
Block, Paul, 145
Boney, Samuel E., 253
Borah, Senator William E., 145
Bossert, Walter E., 148
Boston, 81–89, 94, 104, 144, 172, 194, 246
   antislavery movement, 125, 127, 136
   Centinel, 102, 104, 106
   Chronicle, 95, 106
   Courier, 132
   Courant, 89
   Evening American, 219
   Evening Post, 95
   Gazette, 83, 84, 88, 94, **116**
   Herald-Traveler, 294
   Independent Advertiser, 84
   Independent Chronicle, 105, **117**
   News-Letter, 83
   Post, 208
   Transcript, 247
Boston Massacre, 83, 86, 87
Boston Tea Party, 83, 86–88
Bovard, Oliver K., 40, 41, 266, **279**
Bowers, Claude G., 142–144
Bradford, William, 93
Bradford's *Gazette*, 96
Brandeis, Louis D., 79, 237
Bridgeport *Post-Telegram*, 173
British Guiana, 20
Brooker, William, 83
Broun, Heywood, 79, 270, **272**
Bryan, A. P., 195
Bryan, John Stewart, 286

A Neglected Story

Bryan, William Jennings, 26, 48, 49, 52–53
Bryant, William Cullen, 157
Buffalo *Evening News*, 245, 246
  Times, 205, 209
Burke, Aedanus, 108, 109
Butler, Ben, 144

C

Calhoun, John C., 120, 131, 132
Callender, James Thompson, 117
California, 44, 57, 148, 199
Calles, 58
Camden *Courier and Post*, 187
Campbell, John, 83
Canton, Ohio, *Repository*, 190
Capone, Al, 212, 221, 222
Carlisle, John G., 23–25
Carnegie Phipps & Co., 29
Carney, Leo E. J., 172
Carpetbaggers, 142, 143
Carranza, 57, 58
Carroll, Charles, of Carrollton, 94
Cash, J. B. Jr., kidnaping, 151, 152
Cedar Rapids *Gazette*, 181
Centinel, Boston, 102, 104, 106
Century Magazine, 75
Chambers, Walter, 50
Chandler, Governor A. B. (Happy), 196
Chapman, John Jay, 16–18, 149, 150, 154
Charles, Fred, 205
Charles II, 91
Charleston, South Carolina, 132
  Courier, 133
  Gazette and Country Journal, 94
  Mercury, 133
  News, 198
Chase, Judge Samuel, 117–119

Chattanooga, electric rates, 267–270
  Free Press, 268
  News, 268–270
  Times, 268–270
Chevrolet strike, 224
Chicago, 53, 170, 173, 211–222, 263–265
  American, 47
  Daily News, 11, 211–222
  Evening American, 212
  Examiner, 47
  Herald, 219, 220
  Herald and Examiner, 198, 263, 264
  Times, 7, 197, 198
  Tribune, 165, 212, 213, 219–222, 293, 294
Chicago, University of, 222
Child labor amendment, 13, 234–249, 275
Choate, Joseph H., 162
Choate, Robert, 294
Christian Science Monitor, 247
Cincinnati, 61–68, 183, 221
  Commercial, 62
  Enquirer, 62
  Gazette, 132
  Post, 60–67, 69, 71, 80, 128
  Times-Star, 62
Cincinnatus Association, 65, 66
Citizens Committee on Control of Crime, 170
City manager plan, 66, 68, 182, 183, 222
City Manager League, 228
Civic betterment, 206–208
Civil War, 32, 45, 113
Clay, Henry, 120, 129
Clearwater, Florida, *Sun*, 290
Cleveland, Grover, 20, 21, 23, 243, 244

Cleveland, 170, 246
  Penny Press, 250
  Plain Dealer, 182, 188, 189, 197, 200–202, 255, 256
  Press, 60, 205, 209
Clogston, George W., 69–71
Coatesville, Pennsylvania, 16–18, 149, 150
Cochran, Negley D., 63, 67, 73
Cockran, Bourke, 162
Coleman, William, 113, 119
Collier, Tarleton, 235, 236
Collier's, 245, 251
Colonial crusaders, 81–98
Columbia College (King's College), 94, 103
  Graduate School of Journalism, 7, 11
Columbus, Georgia, *Enquirer-Sun*, 141
Columbus, Ohio, 53, 197
  Citizen, 182, 190
Comic strips, 292–294
Commonweal, 12
Communist Party, 218
Congress, 47, 57, 97, 106, 109–110, 116, 120–121, 149, 234
  and slavery, 135
  taxing power, 236
Connecticut, 104, 110, 112, 147, 174
Connolly, "Slippery Dick," 159, 162
Constitution, 19, 57, 100–106, 109, 236–238
  amendments, 4, 99, 102, 103, 105–113, 146
  and slavery, 127, 136
Constitutional Convention, 1787, 100–102, 109
Constitutional Courant, 86
Continental Congress, 95, 103, 134
Cook, Sir Robert Head, 23
Coolidge, Calvin, 166

Cooper, Peter, 158, 159
Cooper, Dr. Thomas, 117
Copeland, Senator Royal S., 145
Copeland pure food and drugs bill, 41
Corsicana, Texas, *Sun*, 205, 206
Cosby, Governor, 96
County-manager plan, 202
Covington, Virginia, 153
Cox, George B., 62–65
Crime, 84, 169–182, 208, 209
Croker, Richard, 161–163
Cromwell, Oliver, 126
Cross, Prof. Harold L., 7
Cross, Governor Wilbur, 174
Crusades, 13
  definition of, 4
  by newspapers, 3–19
Cummings, Attorney General Homer S., 177

D

Dailey, Frank G., 71
Daily Mirror, 59
Daily News (*see* New York *Daily News*)
Dale, George R., 140
Dallas, Texas, 72
  Journal, 191
  News, 141, 190, 207
Dana, Judge, 117, 119
Davey, Governor Martin L., 255
Davis, John W., 147
Dawes, Charles Gates, 166
Dayton, Ohio, 182, 191
Debs, Eugene V., 242, 243
Declaration of Independence, 89, 116
Delaware, 90, 104, 124
Democratic party, 31, 34, 35, 45, 49, 52, 53, 68, 117, 119, 121, 134, 147, 156, 162

302

Denver, 181
 Rocky Mountain News, 285, 286
Denver, University of, 257
Depew, Chauncey M., 25
Des Moines Register and Tribune, 273
Detroit Free Press, 186, 261
 News, 60, 186
 Times, 186
Dewey, Thomas E., 79, 164
Diaz, Porfirio, 58
Dickinson, John, 105
Dillinger, John, 177
District of Columbia, 104
Dorsey, S. W., 34
Dred Scott decision, 237
Dreiser, Theodore, 14
Duane, William, 116, 117
Duchaine, William J., 284, 285
Duer, William Alexander, 103
Dunlap, John, 89
Dwight, Theodore, 113
Dwight, William, 181

E

East India Company, 87
Edes and Gill, 116
Editor and Publisher, 7–9, 16, 230, 239, 247–249, 262, 272, 295
 symposium, 293–294
Editorial page, 266–280
Edward VII, 22
Edwardsville Spectator, 126
Edy, John N., 229
Eggleston, George Cary, 23
El Paso Herald-Post, 208
Electoral College, 111, 112
Electric rates, 262, 263, 267–270
Elmira, New York, Star-Gazette, 182
Embree, Elihu, 125
Emerson, Ralph Waldo, 137

Emporia Gazette, 247, 248
England (see Great Britain)
Equitable Life Assurance Society, 26, 28
Espionage, 291
Escanaba, Michigan, Daily Press, 284, 285
Evans, Hiram W, 138, 148
Evanston, Illinois, 170, 188, 207
Evansville Press, 68
Evening Post (see New York Evening Post)
Ewald, Henry P., 179, 180
Exeter, New Hampshire, 87

F

"Fabius," 105
Fairbanks, Crawford, 68–70
Farley, Dr. Belmont Mercer, 277, 278
Fauquier, Governor, 94
Federal Bureau of Investigation, 179
Federal Communications Commission, 250, 292
Federal Trade Commission, 46, 252, 253, 260, 262
"Federalist, The," 102, 103, 105–107
Federalist party, 90, 99, 100, 105, 106, 107, 112, 113, 115–119, 122, 125, 138
Fenno, John, 99
Fillmore, Millard, 129
Fleet, Thomas, 95
Florida, 30, 31, 120, 138, 148, 151, 152, 182
Folks, Homer, 240
Force bill, 1871, 146
Forrest, Gen. N. B., 143
Fort William and Mary, 86, 87
France, 21, 56

Frank, Leo. M., 147
Frankel, Frank, 176
Franklin, Benjamin, 81, 84–86, 94, 96, 101
    antislavery campaign, 127
Franklin, James, 81, 84, 85
Franklin, John, 85
Freedom of the press, 3–9, 16, 95, 96, 99, 102, 116, 128, 164, 183, 239, 276
Freer, R. E., 251, 252
Freneau, Philip, 99, 100, 107, 108
Frick, Henry Clay, 30
Fusion movement, New York, 79

G

Gambling, 33, 39, 60, 174, 175, 177, 179, 180
Gallup Institute of Public Opinion, 151
Gannett, Guy P., 262, 264
Gardner, Gilson, 61, 66, 232
Garrison, William Lloyd, 125, 128
Gas rates, 31, 263, 264
Gazette of the United States, 107
General Motors, 231
Genêt, Citizen, 107, 108
Genius of Universal Emancipation, 125
George III, 19
George V, 22
Georgia, 53, 85, 104, 141, 152
German espionage, 291
Gladstone, William E., 22
Goethe, 7
Gold, Charles, 176
Gold standard, 52
Gould, George J., 25
Gould, Jay, 158
Grand Rapids *Press*, 182
Grant, Hugh, 162
Graves, John Temple, 53

Graveyard graft, 205
Great Britain, 20–22, 55, 56, 83–91, 95, 96, 101, 107, 108, 120, 228
Greeley, Horace, 32, 134, 143, 144, 157
Green, Daniel G., 215
Green, William, 201
Greenleaf, Thomas, 105
    "Brutus," 105
    Journal and Daily Patriotic Register, 105
Gruening, Dr. Ernest, 262, 263
Gutenberg, 88

H

Hackensack, New Jersey, 8
Haden, Judge Benjamin, 153
Hague, Frank, 12
Haines, Harry B., 290, 295
Hall, A. Oakley, 156
Hamilton, Alexander, 99–103, 107–109
Hamilton, Andrew, 96, 97
Hammond, Charles, 128
Hancock, John, 86, 87, 89, 102
Hanna, Mark, 48, 54, 110
Hanson, Alexander, 121, 122
Harding, Warren D., 147, 148, 172
Harlan County, Kentucky, 146
Harper, J. C., 63, 67–69, 71
Harriman, E. H., 25–27
Harris, Evelyn, 262
Harris, Julian, 141
Harris, Kitty, 178
Harrison, Walter M., 293
Hartford Convention, 112–114
Hastings-on-Hudson, *News*, 291
Hawkes, William F., 175
Hearst, George, 48
Hearst, William Randolph, 26, 43–54, 58, 60, 145, 212

Hearst papers, 59, 77, 112, 170, 203, 233, 252, 263
Heaton, John L., 21
"Hell Fire Club," 84
Heney, Francis J., 167
Hepbron, James Merritt, 169, 170
Henry, Patrick, 93, 94, 101
Higgins, Governor Francis W., 27, 28
Hisgen, Thomas L., 53
Hitler, Adolf, 58
Hoffman, John T., 156
Holmes, Justice Oliver Wendell, 236
Holyoke, *Transcript-Telegram*, 181
Homestead, Pennsylvania, 29
Hoover, Herbert, 45, 46
Hoover Reconstruction Finance Corporation, 166
Hornblow, Arthur, Jr., 75, 76
Houseman, Julian, 209
Houston, Texas, 72
   Chronicle, 258
   Press, 141, 203, 204
Howard, Roy W., 73, 75, 76, 78–80
Howe, M. A. De Wolfe, 17, 18
Hudson, Frederick, 104, 155
Hughes, Charles Evans, 27, 28, 50–52
Hurd, Carlos F., 35
Hyde, James Hazen, 26–28
Hynicka, Rudolph Kelker, 64–65

I

Illinois, 170, 197, 243, 263, 264
   Intelligencer, 126
   Philanthropist, 128
Income tax, 110, 221
Indentured servants, 124
Independence League, 50, 53
Indiana, 34, 138, 147
Indianapolis, 34, 35, 68, 69, 71, 148, 246

Indianapolis, *News*, 186
   Star, 186
   Times, 140, 141
Insane, 193, 194, 197
Insull, Samuel, 213, 219, 262
Insurance, 26–28
International Harvester, 25
International News Service, 56, 57
Interstate commerce, 236, 242
Ithaca *Chronicle*, 129

J

James, William, 64
Japan, 55–58
Jay, John, 95, 102, 103, 107, 113, 119
Jefferson, Thomas, 99–103, 105–108, 115, 118, 119, 121, 127, 134
Jerome, William Travers, 163
Jersey City, 12
Jewell, Edmund F., 286, 287
Johnson, Gen. Hugh S., 270
Jones, George, 157–160
Jones, Richard Lloyd, 10
Journalism, early American, 98
   first history of, 88
   schools of, 253
Justices of the peace, fees, 289, 290

K

Kahn, Howard, 177, 178
Kansas, 170
Kansas City, 34, 35, 170, 246
   Journal-Post, 182
   Kansan, 191
   Post-Dispatch, 34
   Star, 38, 191, 207
   World, 72

Keeley, James, 219, 220
Kelly, "Honest John," 160–162
Kendall, Amos, 132
Kentucky, 104, 126, 134, 170, 193–197, 206
Kentucky and Virginia Resolutions, 114, 118
Kidnaping, 41, 126, 151, 177, 178, 209
King, James, of William, 250
Kirby, Rollin, 80
Know-Nothings, 148
Knox, Col. Frank, 212
Knoxville *News*, 68
Ku Klux Klan, 138–154

L

La Guardia, Fiorello, 79
Labor, 29, 63, 64, 77, 134, 223, 240
LaFollette, *Progressive*, 276, 277
"Lame duck" amendment, 111
Landis, Dr. Walter S., 259, 260
Lawson, Thomas W., 53
Lawson, Victor F., 211, 212, 219
Leary, John J., Jr., 259
Lee, Alfred McClung, 93
Lee, Gen. Henry, 122
Lee, Ivy, 241
Lee, James Melvin, 107
Lee, Robert E., 143
Lexington, Kentucky, *Leader*, 195
Liberal Republican Party, 32
Liberator, The, 125, 126, 128
Liberty Party, 128
Libraries, 290
Lincoln, Abraham, 56, 111
Lingle, "Jake," 212
Lippmann, Walter, 172, 271
Liverpool, 133, 135
"Loan sharks," 204, 205

Lodge, Henry Cabot, 45, 147, 237, 238
London, 82, 92, 94
London Coffee House, 81, 84
London *Daily News*, 23
Long Island, New York, 208 *Chronicle*, 176
Longstreet, Augustus Baldwin, 132, 133
Lorimer, William, 165
Los Angeles, 170, 188
Lotteries, 74, 179, 181
Louisville *Courier-Journal*, 133, 134, 183, 193–197, 272
Times, 272
Lovejoy, Elijah, 130
Low, Seth, 163
Lowell, James Russell, 111, 136
Ludlow massacre, 241
Lundberg, Ferdinand, 11, 12, 147, 244, 245
Lundy, Benjamin, 125, 128
Lynching, 12, 141, 147, 149–152
Lynn, Massachusetts, *Telegram-News*, 290

M

McAdoo, William G., 147
Machine system, 183, 184
McClellan, George B., 49
McGrady, Edward F., 224–228
Mackay, C. H., 25
McKinley, William, 50, 51, 54
McKinley [tariff] Act, 29
McLean, J. and A., 103
McLean, John R., 62
McLure, James G. K., Jr., 283
McLevy, Jasper, 174
MacRae, Hugh, 283
McRae, Milton, 61, 67, 72
Madison, James, 101–103, 112, 118, 121, 127

Manchester, New Hampshire, *Union and Leader*, 286, 287
Manumission Journal, 125
Marcy, William L., 121
Marshall, Chief Justice John, 8
Martin, Lowry, 205
Maryland, 104
  Gazette, 94
Massachusetts, 79, 81, 82, 101, 104, 112, 117, 118, 127, 170, 238, 263, 290
Massachusetts Spy, 85, 86, 88, 89, 105
Mather, Cotton, 82–84
Matthews, Rives, 291
Mayer, Milton S., 222
Meeman, Edward J., 69
Mein, John, 95
Mellon, Andrew, 48
Memphis, Tennessee, 72, 170
  Commercial Appeal, 141, 189, 190
  Press-Scimitar, 190
Mencken, Henry L., 13–16, 160
Merat, E. K., 274
Mercantilist theory, 92
Mexico, 57, 58, 120
Miami *Daily News*, 179
Milk crusades, 285
Millis, Walter, "Road to War," 55, 56
Milwaukee *Journal*, 208, 209
  Leader, 247
Minerva, 125
Minneapolis *Journal*, 206, 207, 247
  Star, 187
  Tribune, 187, 282
Mirt, John A., 214–216, 218
Mississippi, 104
Missouri, 32, 33, 42, 170
Mobile *Press-Register*, 179, 180
Monroe Doctrine, 20–22
Mooney, Tom, 167–169
Moreau, Arthur E., 287

Morgan, J. P., 28
Morgan (J. P.) and Company, 23–25, 56, 147, 244
Morris, Gouverneur, 96
"Muck-raking," 15
Muncie, Indiana, *Post-Democrat*, 140
Municipal Ownership League, 48–50
Murphy, Charles F., 49–52, 161, 163
Murphy, Attorney General Frank, 219
Murphy, Frederick E., 282
Mutiny Act, 97
Myers, Gustavus, 163

N

Napoleon, 84, 120
Nashville, Tennessee, 72, 143, 246, 289, 290
  Banner, 7, 191
Nassau (Long Island) *Daily Review-Star*, 208
Nation, The, 79, 270
National Child Labor Commission, 236
National Era, 129
National Gazette, 99, 100, 107
National Labor Relations Board, 59, 78
National Labor Party, 238
National Philanthropist, 125
National Safety Council, 190, 191
Nazi camp at Yaphank, 146, 149
New Bedford, Massachusetts, *Standard-Times* and *Mercury*, 171, 173
New Deal, 78, 267, 271, 272
New England, 83, 86, 120, 124, 126, 237
New England Courant, 84, 85
New Hampshire, 87, 104, 112, 238

New Jersey, 90, 104, 110, 170, 254, 255
New Orleans *Item*, 189
  Liberalist, 126
  Times, 258
  Times-Picayune, 182, 189
  Tribune, 290
New Republic, 10, 11, 145
  patent medicine survey, 246, 247
New York City, 27, 31, 34, 48, 49, 68, 74, 79, 87, 89, 90, 94, 130, 131, 144, 155, 170, 246
  Courier and Enquirer, 131, 133
  Daily Advertiser, 103, 113
  Daily News, 78, 191, 267, 272, 273, 293, 294
  Evening Post, 99, 107, 113, 119, 131, 132, 134, 156, 157, 161, 247
  Evening World, 261
  Freedom's Journal, 126
  Gazette and Post-boy, 94
  Gazetteer (Royal Gazetteer), 94, 96
  Globe, 75
  Herald, 104, 109, 135
  Herald Tribune, 138, 139, 251, 267, 273, 275
  Independent Journal, 103
  Journal, 275
  Journal and American, 47, 178, 191
  Journal of America, 130, 131
  Mercury, 102
  Morning Journal, 48–50, 59
  Post, 8, 274, 275
  Sun, 21, 225, 276
  Times, 21, 22, 156–159, 247, 268, 275, 276
  Tribune, 134, 143, 157
  Weekly Journal, 96
  World, 15, 20–32, 51, 73, 76, 139, 140, 146, 147, 241, 261
  World-Telegram, 68, 73–79

New York Life Insurance Company, 27
New York State, 146, 170
  and Constitution, 104, 105, 272, 273
  and Hartford Convention, 113
  savings-bank insurance, 79
  slavery conflict, 124, 127
New York Telephone Company, 261
Nebraska, tax reforms, 170, 256–258
Negroes, 110, 124, 127, 134, 138, 141–144, 147–150, 152, 209, 236, 240, 288, 289
  children, 236, 240
  New York riots, 131
Nevins, Allan, 134, 161
Newark *Evening News*, 182, 219, 255
Newcastle, New Hampshire, 86, 87
Newport *Mercury*, 94
Newsboys, 140, 234, 235, 238, 239
Newsdom, 8, 239, 240, 276, 277, 284, 292–294
Newspaper Guild, 58, 231, 238, 239
Newspapers, Colonial, 19, 97
  as crusaders, 3–19
  cited by National Safety Council, 190, 191
Nixon, Lewis, 163
North Carolina, 198, 281–283
North Dakota, 30, 206
North Penn Reporter, Lansdale, Pennsylvania, 287–289
Northwestern University, Medill School, 12
  Traffic Safety Institute, 188
Nullification, 113, 114, 118, 132
Numbers game, 174, 175

O

Oakland, California, *Tribune*, 189, 199
O'Brien, James, 157

Ochs, Adolph S., 268
Oglethorpe, James, 126
Ohio, 54, 110, 197–199, 255, 256
Ohio State Journal, 54
Oklahoma, 147
Oklahoma City *Oklahoman* and *Times*, 293
Older, Fremont, 166–168
Olds, George, 293, 294
"Orleans, Territory of," 104
Oxman, Frank, 168

P

Page, Walter Hines, 56
Paine, Robert F., 72, 250
Paine, Tom, 97, 101
Parent-teacher associations, 204
Parker, Alton B., 52, 53
Parrington, Vernon Louis, 136
Partisanship, 183
Parton, Lemuel, 167, 168
Patent medicines, 13, 245–250
Paterson, New Jersey, *News*, 290, 291, 295
Payne, George Henry, 106, 107, 292
Pearl, Dr. Raymond, 276, 277
Pegler, Westbrook, 79, 270
Pendergast, T. J., 34, 35, 38, 39
Penny Post, 60
Penny Press, 60, 61
Penrose, Boies, 54, 147
Pennsylvania, 104, 110, 124, 127, 170, 287–289
  Evening Post, 89
  Gazette, 86, 94, 127
  Journal, 93, 97
  Packet, 89
Pepper, Claude, 151, 152
Perkins, George W., 25, 27, 28
Peters, F. Romer, 69, 70
Pew, Marlen, 230

Philadelphia, 87, 109, 136, 170, 237, 246
  Aurora, 106, 116
  Bulletin, 187
  Courier-Post, 186
  Daily News, 187
  Evening Ledger, 174, 175
  General Advertiser (Aurora), 106, 107
  Inquirer, 187
  Ledger, 187
  Record, 175, 176, 187, 274
Philanthropist, The, 125, 128
Philippines, 13, 241
Phillips, Wendell, 136, 144
Phoenix *Gazette*, 8
Picketing, 153, 224
Pilgrims, 81, 124
Pinkerton detectives, 29, 30, 60
Pittsburgh *Post-Gazette*, 145
Political corruption, 165–184
Polk, James K., 129
Ponzi, Charles, 208
Portland, Maine, *News*, 262, 263, 265
  Oregonian, 191, 204, 264
  Press and *Herald*, 262, 265
Portsmouth *Mercury*, 95
Postal savings banks, 211
Pottsville, Pennsylvania, *Reporter and Republican*, 258
Pound, Arthur, 15
"Power trust," "million dollar lobby," 252
Pratt, Julius W., 120
Prentice, George D., 133, 134
Press, 98, 116, 185
  freedom of, 3–9, 16, 95, 96, 99, 102, 116, 128, 164, 183, 239, 276
  (*See also* Newspapers)
Preston, John Hyde, "Revolution, 1776," 86, 87

Prevost, Clifford A., 261
Pringle, William R., 201, 202
Printing, 88, 91, 116
    press, 88, 93, 95, 105, 107
Prisons, 196–200
Providence, Rhode Island, 127
    Bulletin, 191
    Investigator, 126
    Journal, 291
    Phoenix, 106
Public utilities (*see* Utilities)
Publick Occurrences, 81, 82
Public Opinion Quarterly, Princeton, 86, 249, 260
Pueblo, Colorado, 72, 191
Pulitzer, Joseph, 12, 20, 23–28, 32–34, 40, 41, 45, 46, 48, 67, 73
Pulitzer, Joseph, Jr., 40, 42, 270
Puliter, Ralph, 15, 16, 22
Pulitzer prizes, 10, 74, 140, 141, 145, 154, 181
Pulitzer School of Journalism, 7, 11
Pullman Company, 13
    strike, 241–244
Purcell, William A., 171–173
Pure food and drugs, 244–253

Q

Quakers, 124, 125

R

Racketeering, 47, 63, 79, 164, 177, 182, 221
Radio, 187, 250, 252, 291–293
Raleigh *News and Observer*, 253
Ramsaye, Terry, 270
Randolph, Edward, 92
Rathom, John R , 291
Raymond, Henry J., 156
Receivership fees, 11, 211–219
Reconstruction, 109, 110, 142
"Red scares," 58, 80, 108

Redman, Eli, 70, 71
Referendum, war, 57
Republican Party, 32, 34, 45, 52, 53, 63, 67, 68, 144, 148, 156, 162, 165
Revere, Paul, 87
Revolution, American, 19, 88, 91,
    "of 1800," 118
Rhett, Robert Barnwell, 133
Rhode Island, 101, 104, 112, 127
Richmond *Enquirer*, 113
    Examiner, 117
    News-Leader, 209, 286
    Times-Dispatch, 149–153, 183, 202
Riegel, O. W., 56
Rivington, James, 94, 95
Robb, Arthur, 239
Roberts, Donn M., 68, 70, 71
Roberts, Elzey, 292–294
Robertson, Harrison, 183
Rochester *Democrat and Chronicle*, 191
    Times-Union, 264
Rockefeller family, 53, 54, 241
Rogers, H. H., 53
Rolfe, John, 124
Roosevelt, Franklin D., 45, 78, 79, 145
Roosevelt, Theodore, 25, 27, 28, 44, 50, 51, 237
Root, Elihu, 51, 160
Rosebery, Lord, 22
Rosewater, Victor, 57
Ruef, Abraham, 165–168
Russell, Ezekiel, 95
Russell, Major Benjamin, 102, 104, 106
Ryan, Thomas Fortune, 28, 52, 163

S

Safety campaigns, 185–192
Saginaw, Michigan, 182, 183

St. Louis, 32, 35–37, 39, 42, 72, 246
  Chronicle, 67
  Post-Dispatch, 9, 32–41, 67, 253, 266, 278, 279
  Star-Times, 239, 292, **294**
St. Paul, 187
  Daily News, 177
  Dispatch, 263
  Pioneer Press, 263
San Francisco, 47, **167–169**, 173, 181, 213, 246
  Bulletin, 166, 167
  Call, 166
  Call-Bulletin, 188
  Daily Evening Bulletin, 250
  Examiner, 48, 261
  News, 188, 204, 219
Sanborn, Walter L., 288, 289
Schaffer, John C., 204
Schoenstein, Paul, 47
Schools, 91, 203, 204, 290
Scripps, Edward Wyllis, 12, 60–76, 77, 80, 232, 250
Scripps, Ellen, 60, 61
Scripps, James, 60, 61
Scripps, John P., 199
Scripps, Robert P., 73
Scripps, R. W., 72
Scripps chain, 68, 72
Scripps-Howard chain, 59, 73–80, 205, 221, 230–233, 252, 270
Seabury, Samuel, 48, 49, 51, 52
Sears, Isaac, 95
Seasongood, Murray, 66
Secession, 113, 114, 134
Sedition Act, 99, 116–118, **121**, 144
Seldes, George, 55, 276
Senate, United States, 108, 109, 140, 145, 151, 165, 167
Senators, Archbold letters, 53, 54
  direct election, 110
Seward, William H., 129, 156

Sherrill, Colonel C. O., 67
Simmons, William Joseph, 139, 140, 146, 147
Skinner, Chads O., 188
Slavery, 19, 45, 113, 124–128, 237
  newspapers and, 124–137
Slot machines, 181
"Smelt Jubilee, Escabana," 284, 285
Smith, Alfred E., 147
South Carolina, 104, 132, 133, 136
  Gazette, 94
Southern Pacific Railroad, 58, 59, 166
Spain, war with, 45, 55
Sprigle, Raymond, 10, 11, 145
Springfield, Massachusetts, *Republican*, 207
Springfield, Missouri, *News* and *Leader*, 181, 294
Spy, Massachusetts, 85, 86, 88, 89, 105
Stahlman, James G., 7
Stalin, Joseph, 218
Stamp Act, 81, 83, 90, 93
Standard Oil, 25, 52–54
Stark, Governor Lloyd C., 39
State Rights Centinel, 132
Steffens, Lincoln, 63, 65
Stephenson, D. C., 140
Stern, J. David, 8, 9, 274
Stowe, Harriet Beecher, 129, 130
Street cars, 264
Strikes, 29, 30, 78, 152–154, 223–227, 241, 242
Sunbury and Northumberland Gazette, 117
Supreme Court (*see* United States Supreme Court)
Sweatshops, 201–204

311

T

Tabert, Martin, 30, 31
Taft, Charles P., 62
Taft, William Howard, 53, 62
Taggart, Thomas, 68
Tammany Hall, 14, 31, 48–51, 62, 155–164
Tappan, Arthur and Lewis, 130, 131
Tariff, 29, 106, 132
Taxes, 7, 8, 18, 29, 49, 66, 67, 80, 83, 91, 93, 94, 106, 141, 179
   capital-gains, 275, 276
   definition of, 8
   fight to reduce, 254–260
   tea (*see* Tea)
   Toledo plan, 229
Tea, 83, 86–88, 179
Teapot Dome scandal, 41, 172, 240, 241
Telephone rates, 261, 262
Tennessee, 104, 141, 143, 146, 267–269
Tennessee Valley Authority, 267
Terre Haute *Post*, 63, 68, 71, 204
Texas, 141, 211
"Third degree," 287
Thomas, Isaiah, 85, 88, 89, 103, 105
Thomason, S. E., 7
Thompson, Dorothy, 145, 146
Tilden, Samuel J., 111, 158
Tobacco, 179, 276, 277
Toledo, 223–232
   Blade, 226, 228, 229
   Industrial Peace Board (Toledo Plan), 226
   News-Bee, 198–199, 226, 227, 230–233
   Times, 226, 229
Toledo Associates, 227, 228, 233
Tories, 90, 94–96, 115
Towne, Benjamin, 89
Traffic safety, 185–192
Trenton *Times-Advertiser*, 258
Turrou, L. G., 8
Tweed, William M., 14, 155–161, 165

U

Union Leagues, 142
Union Pacific railroad, 26
Unions, labor, 63, 78, 225, 232, 243
United States, 20–23, 27, 249
United States Daily, 247
United States Gazette, 99
United States Supreme Court, 8, 117, 118, 144, 168, 236–238
Utica, New York, *Press* and *Observer-Dispatch*, 180, 181
Utilities, 31, 48, 49, 166–168, 213, 214, 267–270
   propaganda, 252, 253
   rates, fight for lower, 254–256, 260, 265, 278, 279

V

Van Buren, Martin, 121
Van Hamm, C. M., 26
Venezuela, 20–23
Vermont, 104, 112
Vincennes *Commercial*, 141
Virginia, 90–93, 104, 118, 124, 126, 193, 202
   antilynching law, 152–154
   antislavery movement, 124, 126
   Gazette, 97
"Virginia-Centinel Papers," 97
Von Moltke, 164

W

Waechter, James A., 36, 37
Wagner Act, 41, 78

Wagner-Van Nuys bill, 149–152
Wages, 30, 200–204
   and hours bill, 240
Wakefield, Alanson B., 33
Wallace, Tom, 271
War of 1812, 112, 119
Ward, General Artemas, 89
Warren, General Joseph, 88
Washington, George, 89, 100, 105, 107, 108, 125, 127, 134, 237
Washington, D. C., 115, 170
   Post, 191
   Times, 204
   United States Telegraph, 131
Waterbury *American*, 174
   Republican, 174
Watson, James E., 147, 148
Watson, Tom, 147
Watsonville, California, *Register-Pajaronian*, 199
Watterson, Henry, 134
Waymack, W. W., 273, 274
Webb, Bruce, 281–284
Webster, Daniel, 97, 136, 137
Webster, Noah, 102, 125
Wechsler, James, 79
Weed, Thurlow, 129, 130, 156
Wellman, Walter, 60, 63
Werner, M. R., 156
Wheeler-Lea Act, 251
Whigs, 90, 95, 96, 115, 128

Whiskey Rebellion, 108
White, William Allen, 6, 7, 247, 248
Whittier, John G., 135
Wiegand, Karl von, 7
Wilkerson, Judge James H., 214–219
Williams, Judge J. Ambler, 288, 289
Williams, Roger, 126, 127
Willis, Raymond E., 146, 148
Wilson, Admiral Henry B., 76
Wilson, S. Davis, 175
Wilson, Woodrow, 55, 56, 168
Winkler, John K., 44
Wise, John Dana, 183
Wolseley, R. E., 12
Woman suffrage, 111
Women's clubs, 236, 283
Worcester, Massachusetts, 88, 89
   Evening Post, 190, 263
Works Progress Administration, 87
World War, 52, 54, 57, 75
Wormser, Richard, 77

Y

Yaphank, 146, 149
Youngstown, Ohio, *Vindicator*, 191, 207, 208

Z

Zenger, John Peter, 96, 97
Zerbey, Joseph H., 258, 259